Hazel Underhill
Christmas 1990

An Adventure on the Old Silk Road

By the same author:
Into Thin Air
Backpacking in Chile and Argentina (*with Hilary Bradt*)

An Adventure on the Old Silk Road

FROM VENICE TO THE YELLOW SEA

John Pilkington

CENTURY
London Sydney Auckland Johannesburg

First published in 1989 by Century Hutchinson Ltd,
Brookmount House, 62–65 Chandos Place, Covent Garden,
London WC2N 4NW

Century Hutchinson Australia Pty Ltd, 89–91 Albion Street,
Surry Hills, Sydney, New South Wales 2010, Australia

Century Hutchinson New Zealand Limited, PO Box 40–086,
Glenfield, Auckland 10, New Zealand

Century Hutchinson South Africa (Pty) Ltd, PO Box 337,
Bergvlei, 2012 South Africa

Photoset in Linotron Palatino by Deltatype Ltd, Ellesmere Port

Printed and bound in Great Britain by
Anchor Press Ltd, Tiptree, Essex

British Library Cataloguing in Publication Data

Pilkington, John
    An adventure on the old Silk Road: from
    Venice to the Yellow Sea
    1. Asia. Description & travel
    I. Title
    915'.04'428

ISBN 0–7126–2560–7

Contents

Maps

Acknowledgements

It is one of those fondly held myths that solo travellers are loners. Mustering inner resources, plunging from one adventure to the next, they seem blessed with a natural self-sufficiency. But if such explorers exist, I'm not among them. I return from even the briefest of journeys thrilled and humbled by the generosity of both strangers and friends.

On this trip, much of what I carried in my rucksack – not to mention the rucksack itself – was provided by others. For basic equipment I am indebted to Vango (Scotland) and to Berghaus Ltd. My thanks, too, to David Plumb for help with film, and to Arran Poyser for a vital water filter. Margaret Percy, having persuaded the BBC to lend me some sound recording equipment, rose to the even greater challenge of teaching me how to use it. Hampshire's Marwell Zoo showed me how to handle Bactrian camels 'in case you should be unlucky enough to meet one'. I did, and was grateful for the training.

In Tehran, Nick Oundjian spent several hours at the Ministry of Foreign Affairs, arguing the case for my Iranian visa. In Pakistan, Jill and Mark Dunham provided support from their base in Karachi; while John Hague (then Second Secretary at the British Embassy in Islamabad) willingly acted as expedition postman.

Back in London, my progress along the Silk Road was being closely followed. Anthony Lambert, my editor, provided dogged support, having already authorized a handsome advance to the charity Intermediate Technology. They, in turn, backed the trip with the infectious enthusiasm that has become their hallmark.

Like a growing number of people, I had been following Intermediate Technology's efforts to help Third World people work themselves out of poverty. By developing simple tools which can be made and maintained locally (rather than complicated ones needing know-how and spare parts) the charity is taking the opposite approach to traditional 'aid': it is making people less dependent on charities. From fuel-saving woodstoves in Nepal to wind-driven water pumps in Kenya, it is finding practical solutions to problems which concern us all. The bigger charities, and even one or two governments, now acknowledge the value of Intermediate Technology's ideas – although our donations are a drop in an ocean of need.

Many other people lent helping hands to the journey and to the book. Some of their contributions are mentioned in the text; others, I must leave to your imagination. I would particularly like to thank Ronald Latham and Penguin Books Ltd for permission to quote extracts from *Marco Polo: The Travels*.

Every good expedition has a Base Camp, and mine in North London was manned with quiet efficiency by Liz Berryman, to whom this book is dedicated.

1
A Meeting on a Hill

The Kirghiz turns his collar against the wind, and studies the distant approaching figure. From his craggy vantage point he can see that the man is younger and taller than himself, and alone. The stranger is walking briskly up the sunny valley, heading north towards the Buramsal Pass. What is his purpose?

Even in this remote western tip of China's Xinjiang Region, the Kirghiz is accustomed to strangers. Chinese soldiers, bitter and sullen, have been patrolling the area since he was a child. More recently, surveyors have come, talking about connections with the new motor road to Kashgar – a welcome proposition which has not so far materialized. Then there have been the dark-skinned people from the south, crammed into lorries on that same motor road, and telling of a land called the Punjab where it is warm enough to go naked all the year round. And his father speaks of even more exotic visitors in centuries gone by: merchants from the far west, beyond the stone tower at Khokand, who carried bronze jewellery, ceramics and mirrors in their caravans, and returned with cargoes of a curious material they called silk.

But this newcomer, still half a mile distant in the wide valley, nevertheless holds the tribesman's gaze. His keen eyes focus on the man's unusual apparel – a bright green cotton shirt; a jacket duller in colour but ample in proportions; a woollen hat; a full rucksack well hung with straps and buckles; and, most fascinating of all, thick leather boots.

The figure continues up the valley, and the Kirghiz creeps down the hillside to intercept him.

It is a week since I left Tashkurghan. The track, distinct in places but almost indiscernible in others, has climbed steadily for the last eight miles. The pass for which it is heading is marked on my sixty-year-old map as 'Buramsāl-dawan, 14,940 feet'. Although the map is labelled 'Survey of India', it is many days since I stood on soil which has ever been part of India. In those far-off days of Empire, surveyors were less inhibited by frontiers than they would be now. But they were no less painstaking: time and again since reaching China, I have been grateful for the thoroughness with which they applied their dumpy levels to this unforgiving terrain.

I am anxious to cross the pass and find water, so my head is down and my thoughts elsewhere when the Kirghiz hails me. I look up with a start; I was not expecting to meet other people today, least of all so close to the pass. He stands squarely on the path, a thickset figure in a vast greatcoat, arms akimbo, blocking my way.

I approach smiling but with some trepidation. It is only a few decades since caravans on this route used to vanish without trace, victims of Kirghiz and Tajik brigands armed with Russian or British rifles procured from previous raids. But this shepherd seems unarmed, and the face beneath the fur hat returns my smile. I relax a little, and greet him with the words he is most likely to recognize: '*Salaam alaikum!*'

The Kirghiz breaks into a broad grin. '*Salaam!*' he replies, extending a horny hand. We look each other up and down, each curious: I to inspect his hand-made felt moccasins and leather cummerbund, and he to know the feel of Goretex and the contents of my Berghaus rucksack. After a few speechless seconds we laugh spontaneously and sit down on a pile of rocks.

Using grunts and signs, we tell each other a little about ourselves. I describe Britain as a country beyond the farthest western foothills of these Pamir Mountains. The Kirghiz, in turn, indicates that his family are camped in a grazing ground a few miles beyond the pass. Gradually, I realize that he is inviting me to eat and sleep with them. Delighted and relieved, I put away my map and we set off across the hillside, continuing our unorthodox but engrossing conversation as we walk. The possibility occurs to me that my new acquaintance, in forty years among the mountains, may never before have set eyes on a European.

2
Departure

GOVERNMENT OF PAKISTAN HANDOUT

Subject: Khunjerab Pass opens for Foreigners

The Khunjerab Pass will be opened to the foreign nationals,
wishing to travel by road between China and Pakistan, from
1st May, 1986.

The foreign nationals wishing to travel through the pass
will be required to obtain valid visas. This would apply even
to nationals of the countries which have exemption agree-
ments with Pakistan or China.

It may be added here that the 500 miles Karakoram
Highway snakes through the rugged mountain ranges of
Himalayas, Hindukush, Karakorams and Pamirs touching
the Chinese territory at Khunjerab at 16,000 feet (approx.
4795.06 metres) above sea level. The Highway has reopened
the path which was trekked by Chinese pilgrim FaHsien in
fourth century, Albaroney in 11th century and Marcopolo in
the 13th century.

MUNEERUDDIN
Deputy Chief (Operations)
Tourism Division
Government of Pakistan
5.1.86

I must be dreaming. The news is scarcely credible. I look again at
the unexpected handout which has been included, almost as an
afterthought, in the Pakistan Embassy's reply to my inquiry
about trekking. It is undoubtedly genuine, and goes on to
describe in detail the intended arrangements for passport, visa,

customs and health controls. A map shows the familiar route of the Karakoram Highway extended tantalizingly to the Chinese caravanserai of Tashkurghan. I settle down to scrutinize the flimsy pages, and slowly there unfolds the beginnings of an idea. . . .

Beyond the Karakoram, in the land that was once called Tartary, atlases show a great desert. Vaster than the Gobi, more remote than the Sahara, scorched by the summer sun and wracked by winter blizzards, this nightmare region offers travellers the choice of being baked alive or frozen to death. Not surprisingly, no one has ever had a good word to say for it. The explorer Sven Hedin called it the worst and most dangerous desert in the world. Sir Aurel Stein thought those of Arabia tame by comparison. Other descriptions vary from 'a land of death' to 'the very abomination of desolation'. Sandstorms, hurricanes and wailing demons are among the terrors reported by those who have survived a crossing of this 'Taklamakan Desert' – which means, in the local Uyghur language, 'Go in, and you won't come out'.

Why should anyone want to leave the comforts of civilization to pit their wits against such appalling conditions? If you had put this question to central Asia's explorers through the ages, some would certainly have pointed to its precious minerals, such as asbestos and jade. Others might have cited its archaeological riches. Yet others would have spoken vaguely of the artistic splendours of Cathay. But whatever their particular lodestar, these adventurers would have concurred on the prime attraction of the land they called Tartary, wondering no doubt why you even needed to ask. For was not Tartary simply another name for Seres – the fabled land of silk?

The Romans thought silk grew on trees. As demand for it burgeoned among the middle classes of successive European empires, Chinese cultivators managed to conceal its true origins, and a lucrative trade developed through the Taklamakan oases. The Chinese caravans returned from Europe with glass, ivory, coral, amber and gold.

The so-called Silk Road was not one road but several: braided and interwoven like plaited hair. After leaving China by the 'Jade Gate', one route followed the northern oases round the Taklamakan, another those to the south. After meeting again at

Kashgar, one of its branches continued west through the Tien-Shan ranges towards Samarkand; another struck off south-west to Balkh in what is now Afghanistan. From Yarkand a substantial proportion of the trade went south, the caravans climbing to over 16,000 feet in the Pamirs and Karakoram before dropping down to the Punjab plain, southern Persia, and the *dhow* ports of the Arabian Sea.

Eric Shipton, the mountaineer and one-time British Consul at Kashgar, wrote in 1948: 'I am still amazed at the great good fortune that gave me the chance to know something of Sinkiang, and, having watched the recent turn of events, I shudder to think of the narrow margin by which I got that chance. For the Iron Curtain has already clanged down behind me, and it may be many decades before a Western traveller is free to travel there again.'

I read once more the handout, written nearly forty years after Shipton's prophecy. Of FaHsien and Albaroney I know nothing; but Marco Polo caught my attention at an early age when, by a quirk of chance, his thirteenth-century travels were given as the subject for a school essay. My childhood imagination was captivated, and the lure of Polo's adventures grew with the years. As a merchant's son, Polo was of course motivated initially by the prospect of trade rather than the spirit of adventure which fired later explorers. But during his seventeen years as an envoy for Kublai Khan, as he became familiar with more and more of what we now call China, his writing reveals a growing appreciation of travel for its own sake. Uniquely among the narrow-minded denizens of medieval Europe, Polo understood the call of faraway places, and the fascination of living and working among people whose ways of life were different from his own.

For years my admiration for Polo, and my interest in the forbidden places about which he wrote, have lain dormant. Now, for the first time in four decades, Westerners will once more be able to retrace the road he made famous. How much will have changed since Polo's journeys? And how much will still be as he described? The idea begins to take shape. . . .

If it hadn't been for another quirk of fate, Polo's celebrated book, *Divisament dou Monde*, might never have been written. In 1292, returning to Venice wild-eyed and unkempt after twenty-six years of Asian travelling, he regaled his fellow-citizens with tales of civilizations beyond the known horizon – only to be roundly debunked. Fashionable Venetians, afraid of seeming naïve, made a show of dismissing the extravagant claims of this merchant turned vagabond, and nicknamed him *Il Milione* – 'Mister Million'. In spite of the wealth he had accumulated through skilful trading on his travels, Polo became less and less inclined to talk about the wonders of the East.

Then came war. Venice's supremacy in the Adriatic was challenged by the growing power of Genoa, and the fleets of the two city-states clashed time and again. Polo was appointed captain of one of the Venetian warships, and in 1296, at the Battle of Curzola, the Genoese took him captive. His next three years were spent in gaol, and to relieve the tedium he began recounting his stories again. One of his fellow prisoners, a man from Pisa called Rustichello, had been a professional writer and storyteller before being captured, and he offered to write down Polo's tales. The work was finished in 1298, and became a bestseller among Italy's literati. Sadly, history does not record the reaction of the smug disbelievers in Polo's own city, but by the time he was released in 1299 he had become the talk of Venice. The vagrant was fashionable once more.

Although now a celebrity, Polo was still obstinately referred to as *Il Milione*, and this gives a clue to the narrow outlook of medieval society, for *Divisament dou Monde* was regarded by most as a work of fiction. Partly this was due to the romantic embellishments of Rustichello, which make the book read like a fairy tale. But mainly it was because so much of what Polo described was quite beyond the comprehension of the medieval mind. People who used banknotes rather than coins, and who kept warm by burning black rocks, were simply beyond belief. Even when a sample of Polo's 'wonder cloth' (asbestos) was brought to Rome, his countrymen continued to regard him with affectionate derision, and the nickname stuck for life. When, on his deathbed, the old man was asked if he would come clean and admit that his claims had been a little exaggerated, he replied: 'I haven't told the half of it.'

A few weeks after the unexpected news from the Pakistan Embassy, another chance incident reminds me of the old Venetian. Near the floodlit turmoil of London's Smithfield

Market, I am due to meet some fellow travellers in a pub. Arriving early, I pass the time by ambling through the Barbican, and find myself suddenly in Spitalfields – the decaying quarter behind Liverpool Street Station which was once the hub of Britain's silk industry.

Both the material, and the skill of weaving it, arrived rather late on British shores. In the thirteenth century, while Polo and his father were abroad in Asia, their compatriots in Italy were applying their inventive minds to the possibility of using machines to weave the exquisite but delicate strands. Over the next 200 years they brought their new techniques to Antwerp and western Flanders, and in the fifteenth and sixteenth centuries the great Walloon migration carried them to Canterbury, Norwich and this obscure East London suburb. The Walloons were soon joined by Dutch weavers at Billingsgate alongside the Thames, and later a wave of Huguenots came in, fleeing from persecution in the cities of the Loire. Overshadowed today by office blocks, the houses of these early immigrants still stand, their Franco-Dutch architecture perfectly complemented, on one of the lanes, by a sign which reads 'Fleur-de-Lis Street'.

The true origin of silk was one of the best kept secrets of the ancient world. About the year 2800BC, an observant peasant in what is now the Jiangsu province of China noticed that the grub of an undistinguished moth extruded a fine but very strong thread. At first the unfortunate silkworms were ripped alive from their cocoons. However, this tore the yarn, so later they were killed by steeping in hot water: a method which, though hardly more humane, allowed the thread to be unreeled to its full length of more than half a mile without a join.

Shi Ling Si, Empress of China from 2700BC and said to have been one of the most beautiful women in the East, put the infant Chinese silk industry on a firm footing by promising a painful death to anyone who revealed the secret of its origin. Her threat was never put to the test, but history records that a local princess, wanting desperately to take a worthy wedding gift to her fiancé, the Prince of Khotan, hid silkworm eggs among the flowers in her hair. (One can only hope that the prince was worth the risk.)

For three thousand years, Shi Ling Si's great secret never reached the West, yet with the coming of the Roman Empire the demand for silk soared. By the sixth century AD it was costing three-quarters of its own weight in gold, and the Emperor Justinian was being pressed to put an end to the Chinese monopoly. By chance, in the year 550, a pair of Nestorian monks arrived from the East, claiming to know how silk was made, and with the promise of a handsome reward Justinian induced them to smuggle some silkworm eggs out of China in a hollow bamboo cane. The gambit paid off: the monks returned safely with the eggs, and the monopoly was broken. Silk farms were soon thriving in Constantinople, and later in Greece and Italy. But the new cultivators, like their predecessors, guarded their methods jealously – not only on the matter of cultivating the worms, which eat only the leaves of the white mulberry tree, but also when it came to spinning. The Walloons and Huguenots of Spitalfields would have had to rely on silk spun in the Piedmont region of northern Italy; only in the eighteenth century did their descendants learn how to spin it themselves.

At a mere seven denier, silk is the finest of all natural fibres, and the technique of spinning it is quite different from those used for wool, cotton or flax. In 1717, tired of paying the exorbitant prices asked by his Italian suppliers, a London importer named John Lombe set out on an assignment which today we would call industrial espionage. Disguised as a local outworker, he infiltrated the Piedmont mills, and made off not only with their secrets but also with some of their staff. In 1718 John's brother Thomas was granted a British patent for the newly pirated design, and three years later silk was being spun for the first time on British soil.

Ironically this move, which brought about a golden age for the silk industry, was to be the downfall of Spitalfields. Spinning needed power, but in the eighteenth century the Industrial Revolution had yet to provide the choice of generating methods available today. Water was the only practicable source, and the Lombes' mill harnessed the fast-flowing Derbyshire Derwent. Others followed: around Macclesfield on the western fringe of the Peak District, and straddling the sedate but constant chalk streams of the southern counties. Many of the new mill-owners found it best to spin and weave in the same building, using country labour which, then as now, came cheaper than in London. The Spitalfields bosses hit back, cutting the wages of their own staff, and causing such unrest that in 1744 Parliament passed a 'Spitalfields Act' which set minimum pay. Within a decade, the silk industry at Spitalfields was dead – its few remaining weavers making a living of sorts by repairing old clothes, before finally quitting and moving out.

Strolling reflectively among the weavers' cottages, I am intrigued by the connection, remote though it may be, with the news from Pakistan. I decide, as a start, to visit one of the country mills that so brutally eclipsed Spitalfields. Twelve miles from my home in Hampshire I find one of the finest examples still working. There has been weaving on the River Test since Domesday times, but it was not until 1830 that the mill at Whitchurch first advertised for weavers and 'winders'. A dozen teenage girls were taken on, and by 1838 the business had 108 workers including 39 children under thirteen. The mill's first contracts were humdrum, supplying silk to insulate copper wires for an emerging electrical industry. Later, it won the honour of making the linings for Burberry's famous raincoats. Today it concentrates on special orders and some interesting short runs. Theatrical suppliers use Whitchurch silk to reproduce period costumes for stage, film and television productions; and when barristers 'take the silk' and become Queen's Counsel, many choose Whitchurch silk. So the wheel has turned full circle. As in Roman times, top people are impressing their peers with silk. And the material which feeds the looms of Whitchurch comes not from Como, or even Constantinople, but from China.

'So you're going after the old caravans?' chuckles Bill Carr, the mill manager, after listening to my half-baked plan. He eyes me mischievously. 'A sort of modern Marco Polo, eh?' Against a background of deafening looms, Bill speculates on this thought. Steadily, the waterwheel turns in the crystal stream beneath the building; and steadily Bill's face grows more flushed as the thought unfolds.

'Our silk comes ready-spun, you know – from Glemsford Mill in Suffolk,' he enthuses. 'But their agent buys it from the China National Textiles Corporation. Here, you see: the Chinese labels are on the bales.' He hesitates for a moment before coming to the point. 'I don't suppose you could find out where it comes from?'

This is just the challenge I have been looking for, and I accept it on the spot. Clutching one of the triangular yellow labels, I follow Bill past three of the mill's great tappet looms, each nearly a hundred years old and clanking like a steam engine. The shuttles whiz back and forth like cannon shots, and the operators look up only briefly from their work. In his office by the mill race, Bill gives me a contact at the Suffolk mill, and the address of their importing agent. We agree to meet again before I leave. Stepping out of the mill and back into the twentieth century, I contemplate the puzzle he has unwittingly set. Will European silk once again, as in Roman times, turn out to come from the Chinese province of Jiangsu?

How can you prepare sensibly for a journey into the unknown? Judging from the records of other travel writers, the answer seems to be – you can't. John Steinbeck packed his bags ('about four times too much of everything') with a firm conviction that his *Travels with Charley* would never happen. Eric Newby began his *Short Walk in the Hindu Kush* with boots too small and wilderness experience amounting to a weekend in Wales. Redmond O'Hanlon and James Fenton prepared for Borneo by visiting the SAS, and nearly died of fright before the expedition began. Jonathan Raban bought an old sextant from a junk shop. Robyn Davidson began her preparations to cross the Western Australian desert by 'sipping gins on the verandah, making lists which got thrown away, and reading books about camels'.

On the other hand, some of the greatest achievements in exploration have been made by professionals who prepared for months, if not years, in advance. The first ascents of Annapurna by Maurice Herzog and Everest by Hillary and Tenzing were possible only because of prodigious back-up – including, in Herzog's case, the entire staff of the French Alpine Club.

For me, the best trips fall somewhere between the two extremes of military-style organization and blind chaos. I have never favoured the meticulous packing instructions where mint cake ('one doz pkts per six man/days') sits romantically alongside ice screws and rock pitons in the Advance Base Ration Box. But I do need *some* basis for deciding what to take on the Silk Road, so I scour my notes of previous journeys to see what I missed most. After several draft lists, some bare essentials emerge:

Clothing

Boots (Zamberlan, with
  Sorbothane insoles)
Woollen socks
Desert trousers
Jacket
Cotton shirt (long sleeved)
Woollen sweater
Helly Hansen salopettes
Hat!
Down sleeping bag (Blacks'
  Snowgoose)
Dachstein mitts

Cooking kit

Stove (Camping Gaz
  Globetrotter, modified to take
  C200 cartridges, which are
  available in Turkey and one or
  two places in Pakistan)
Aluminium saucepan
Enamel mug
Teaspoon
One-litre water bottle
Three-litre water bag (an inner
  from a wine box)
Water filter ('H₂OK')
Salt, pepper, instant coffee

Medical kit

Bandage
Blister pads (lots)
Adhesive plaster
Antiseptic cream
Water purifying pills
Herbal linctus (blackberry root
  bark/catechu/gingerine/
  cinnamon and clove oil: my
  pet cure for diarrhoea)
Slippery elm tablets (for stomach
  upsets)

Flagyl tablets (if all else fails)
Fybogel and Dioralyte powder (to
  maintain body salts)
Buprenorphine and DF118 tablets
  (painkillers)
Aspirin/codeine
Paludrine malarial prophylactics

Other

Rucksack (Berghaus A.B. 70 GT)
Tent (Vango Hurricane Alpha)
Foam sleeping mat (cut in half to
  save weight)
Moneybelt
Padlock
Universal sink plug
'Gaffer tape' (to secure banging
  doors)
Earplugs (if Gaffer tape fails)
'Repel 100' mosquito repellant
'Tubigrip' bandage (to use as
  second moneybelt)
Maps of central Asia
  (Survey of India, four miles to
  one inch, 1925–30 editions,
  copied in the Royal
  Geographical Society map
  room)
Zipped plastic wallets (for maps
  and documents)
Compass
Notebooks and pens
Headtorch
Army knife
Sewing kit
Safety pins
Nylon cord (to hang washing, or to
  guy tent if stormy)
Washing kit (no towel)
Camera (Pentax ME Super, in
  padded belt pouch)
Lenses (telephoto, standard,
  wide-angle)

Miniature tripod	Turkish and Chinese dictionaries
Tape recorder (Marantz CP230, with AKG microphone, loaned by BBC)	Letters of introduction
	Postcards of home (to give away)
	Duplicate address book
Film; filters; cassettes; batteries	Passport
Candles and matches	Money ($US)

In the whirlwind of last-minute preparations, the day of departure, 24th May, comes almost as a surprise. Seemingly without warning I find that farewells are being said; toasts drunk; I am being driven to London's Victoria Station; the clock shows almost 10.45 a.m.; and the boat train is pulling out. As its last carriage clears the platform, smiling faces accompany one last wave, then my friends turn to walk back to their everyday lives.

Since 1846 Venice, *La Serenissima*, the greatest island-city-state that ever was, has been approached matter-of-factly by a bridge. At first it was simply a railway bridge, a Victorian monster which the city fathers tried (and thankfully failed) to extend over the canals and palaces to Piazza San Marco. Today it is accompanied by a road bridge, and both road and rail terminate where the city begins. If you want to penetrate further you must use boats or feet.

Robert Benchley, who visited the city just after the Second World War, cabled home after his ill-prepared arrival: 'STREETS FULL OF WATER. PLEASE ADVISE.' One must presume he got no further than the station, for Venice has two distinct systems of circulation, one for boats and one for people, and you can reach all parts by both. The canals follow the lines of ancient rivulets, largely ignoring the needs of their users; from the Grand Canal to the narrowest *rio*, they twist in cocky defiance of where you want to go. But Venice's alleyways are another matter. Products of neither planners nor Nature, they have grown by usage over the centuries, and can take you swiftly and exactly to your destination. Impractical though they sometimes seem (I have measured the Calle de Mezo and it is just six feet wide), these lanes are ideally suited to their purpose. Using them, you can cross the entire city in half an hour. Congestion there is, to be sure, when Venice's population doubles for the summer season, but 'people jams' are quickly sorted out. I have known it take longer to drive half a mile in London than to cross the whole of Venice on foot.

James Morris, in his eloquent study of the city where he used to live, described the essence of Venice as melancholia. You might not think so, grappling with the crowds in Piazza San Marco where, on summer days, there seem to be more people than pigeons. You would certainly find no lack of lustre in the blue eyes and banal smalltalk of the gondoliers, for they are showmen and have been practising their smiles for years. Morris found the melancholia most potent when he peered across the lagoon through the mists of a January dawn, when the city's sounds were muffled by a blanket of snow. In summer it is hidden – but only just. Strolling through the backstreets on the evening of my arrival, I come across a drunk, not scowling into an empty bottle as they do in other cities, but in full *sotto voce* celebration of the wonders of the world. I return later to make sure he hasn't fallen into the canal, and find him sleeping peacefully, head propped up against a cistern pump, his face creased in a hangdog look which seems to encompass the tragedies of fifty generations of Venetians.

As long ago as 1928, D. H. Lawrence noted the city's overabundance of everything. 'Too many people in the Piazza, too many limbs and trunks of humanity on the Lido, too many pigeons, too many ices, too many cocktails, too many menservants wanting tips, too many languages rattling, too much sun, too much smell of Venice, too many cargoes of strawberries, too many silk shawls, too many huge, raw-beef slices of watermelon on stalls: too much enjoyment, altogether far too much enjoyment!'

This tendency of Venice to overdo everything is one of its most trying yet endearing qualities. In summer, you can hardly move – you certainly can't relax – yet without such exuberance the city would become strangled by its sheer impracticability. Its larger-than-lifeness is what keeps it going.

Like other admiring visitors for a thousand years, I could explore Venice for weeks: poking down its alleys, nosing into courtyards, spying on the secret ways in which its people have adapted to their curious environment. But this is not supposed to be a pleasure trip. Riding on gondolas, clutching a red-ribboned boater and joining the revellers from a score of countries in their communal singing, will have to wait until another time. My sole mission in Venice is to visit the home of its most celebrated citizen, and then be on my way.

Three hundred yards from my *pensione* on Calle delle Acque, not far from the Rialto bridge, an alleyway squeezes between two shabby buildings and underneath a third. The beams above the narrow passage – a *sotoportego* – are so low that I have to duck. But the effort is rewarded. I emerge into an L-shaped courtyard, quite plain, with archways forming an exit to my left and the sound of lapping water coming through another *sotoportego* ahead. The houses surrounding this undistinguished square are bare of decoration, except for some carved sheep and griffons over one of the arches, and a small painted sign opposite. The sign reads *Corte del Milione* ('Mister Million's Courtyard') – announcing in its deadpan way that I am standing outside the home of Marco Polo.

The place is dark but friendly. A black-clad woman grins at my wide-eyed stare as she lowers a basket on a rope, in the Venetian tradition, for the postman to pop in her mail. The two *sotoportegi* form a route linking other courtyards nearby, and passers-by break out in smiles as they catch me with tape recorder and microphone, recording the place for posterity. Tourists don't often come this way, although perhaps other romantics do.

The Polo family mansion has long since crumbled to dust, and the structures in front of me are mostly eighteenth century. I have soon sampled all there is to be had of the atmosphere of Mister Million's Courtyard, and, feeling slightly downcast, turn to go.

'*Signor!*'

The call comes from the old woman with the mail-basket. She has been watching from her doorway, and now she scurries over to clutch my arm.

'*Signor, deve vedere la placca.*' ('You must see the plaque.')

She leads me through the *sotoportego* to her house's canalside face, where a small tablet has been fixed by a first floor window. On yellow stone dappled in watery reflections, I read:

Qui furono le case
di
MARCO POLO,
che viaggio le piu lontane regioni dell' Asia
e le descrisse.

('Here was the house of Marco Polo, who travelled
through the farthest countries of Asia and described
them.')

The plaque's date, MDCCCLXXXI, suggests that *Il Milione*'s home
town was rather late in recognizing him (six centuries late, to be
exact), and its beguiling suggestion that this might have been his
very house reflects a typical Venetian vagueness, or perhaps
indifference. But the acknowledgement is there. As I note it
down, my wrinkled guide tugs again at my arm. *'Mia casa è stata
sua'* ('My house was his'), she smiles, sweetly perpetrating the
lie.

Being seafarers, Venice's merchants naturally began their
eastbound journeys by ship, setting their compasses first south-
east through the familiar waters of the Adriatic, and then,
rounding the Peloponnese, either east-south-east to Alexandria
or east and north to Ayas, Antioch or Constantinople. But
modern ferries are no way to recapture the thwack of a medieval
galley's oars, so to begin my journey I take the route which
approached Constantinople by land.

This ancient thoroughfare is also well known to modern
travellers, from the hippies who nursed failing flower-buses
towards Asia in the 1960s to today's tee-shirted lorry drivers with
their 40-ton juggernauts. From Venice's Piazzale Roma it sweeps
across the lagoon towards the massed industrial gadgetry of
Mestre, then past Aeroporto Marco Polo (surely a misnomer,
unless this is a reference to the millions of lire it cost to build) to
that other former city-state – Trieste. These days the journey is
simple: an *autostrada* whisks you through the vineyards of Friuli-
Venezia Giulia and deposits you almost on the border of
Yugoslavia.

I have managed to talk my way on to a Turkish bus, full of migrant workers returning home from Paris. The driver pulls into Piazzale Roma for a rest stop, and pulls out with my remaining lire in his pocket and his last seat filled. Two hours later, we are coasting in late afternoon sunshine through the dainty limestone country of Slovenia, all forests and meadows, where women stand arms akimbo beside milking parlours, and farmers in braces scythe the edges of the fields. Although Yugoslavia now looks westward for her culture, her farming pattern comes from the north and east. European Community incentives do not apply here; the fields are small, animals draw the ploughs and carts, and the few tractors are likely to be made in Titograd rather than Turin.

There was a time when the cobbled *autoput* between Zagreb and Belgrade was said to be the most dangerous highway in Europe. Drivers are still thankful when they put this road behind them, but it is no longer cobbled, and some parts (to the relief of the local hospital staff, no doubt) have been converted into a wide dual carriageway. The horse-drawn carts of fifteen years ago have also vanished – embedded in the tarmac, perhaps. But the illusion of a modern Yugoslavia collapses when I look across a field and see a man raising water from a ditch, bucket by tedious bucket.

As our complement of passengers sense their homeland drawing closer, the mood inside the bus becomes tense with anticipation. What news there will be to exchange! What tales to tell. What reunions! After months of separation from their families, what hugging and backslapping. What parties! The atmosphere develops by degrees as we wind through the Nišava Gorge towards Bulgaria, thickening with emotion as much as with the output of thirty-two chainsmoking Turks.

It is hurriedly stifled towards midnight as we reach the border. Some of us have visas; some don't. I am among the latter. The guards here have a reputation for turning back visa-less travellers, even though every Bulgarian embassy in the world will assure you that visas are not needed for those in transit.

Two passengers are picked out and ordered off the bus. Predictably, one of them is me. A brief argument ensues.

'You don't seem to have a visa,' observes the immigration officer.

'I don't need one,' I insist. 'Look, this letter from your London embassy says so.'

'No visa, no entry,' replies the officer indifferently, and returns my passport with a shrug.

The trip has begun.

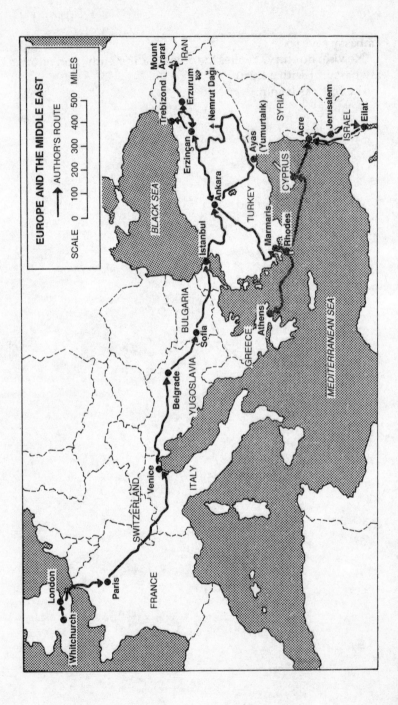

EUROPE AND THE MIDDLE EAST

↑ AUTHOR'S ROUTE

SCALE 0 100 200 300 400 500 MILES

3
Across the Bosporus

The situation is hopeless.

I have resigned myself to a tiresome trek back to Belgrade, and am about to take my luggage off the bus when the immigration officer summons me again. He has discussed my predicament with his colleagues, and if I am willing to pay some money into the nearby Bank of Bulgaria (miraculously still open at midnight) they will grant me the privilege of crossing the country without a visa.

'You're lucky,' says the bus driver as we accelerate towards Sofia. 'They usually turn the British back.'

The crossing takes just four hours. Skirting the Rila Mountains and descending the broad valley of the Maritsa, the bus tears through the night on an all but deserted road. Driver and passengers now have only Turkey in mind, and their eyes stare frantically into the blackness ahead. Fifteen years ago I found the Bulgarians kindly but sad, a desperately poor people even by the standards of the Eastern Bloc. As I leave their country in a bitter dawn, I search in vain for evidence that their lot has improved in the intervening years.

Dominating Turkey's north-western borderlands is one of the country's greatest mosques: Selimiye. To a traveller from Europe its soaring minarets, nestling amongst the dusty hills of Edirne, are a dramatic signal that one has reached the East. Finer than many of its more illustrious Asian counterparts, Selimiye possesses a purity and symmetry which make it even more impressive from a distance. If the Islamic world wished to make a statement to the hedonistic West, one feels that this great dome, with its covey of spires, should be it. I mention my thoughts to a Turk sitting next to me on the bus. 'Yes,' he says. 'It is a fine mosque.

But my people come to Edirne not to pray; we come for the greased wrestling!'

Istanbul, capital of two empires each lasting a thousand years, is approached from Europe these days by a smog-hung, six-lane highway known aptly as Londra Asfalti. How many hearts must have sunk at this degradation of the city of their dreams! If only guidebooks would mention that the road and its horrible accoutrements are built precisely on the ancient route across Thrace, down which the army of Constantine the Great marched to claim Byzantium for the Roman Empire, and along which caravans were travelling even as late as the nineteenth century, bound for western Europe with spices, silk and precious stones. Today's caravans on Londra Asfalti are of a different kind, swaying wildly behind speeding BMWs, earnest Teutonic faces at the wheel.

Although Constantinople was home for several years to his father and uncle, Marco Polo himself favoured the sea route to Anatolia and the Middle East, preferring like all Venetians to cast his fate to the wild but brief tempests of the familiar Adriatic rather than the unpredictable whims of Bulgars. Thus he never became acquainted with the city's mosques, squatting like tarantulas above the Golden Horn. Had he done so, he would doubtless have featured them in *Divisament dou Monde* (enthusing about their dimensions, no doubt, in thousands and millions). He would certainly have noted Constantinople's strategic setting, commanding the neck of the Bosporus and so controlling the flourishing trade between the Mediterranean and the Black Sea. He might also have mentioned its industrious population, cosmopolitan and worldly, but at the same time refreshingly honest and never slow to take pleasure from the simple things in life.

In spite of their qualities, 'Stamboullus' have had a pretty rough deal over the centuries. Just fifty years before the Polos Senior took up residence, Constantinople had been cruelly sacked by the Crusaders and had lost nearly a millenium's worth of accumulated treasure. Later it was regained by the Turks, but in 1453, after a turbulent two centuries under Selçuk rule, the city was besieged by the greatest army it had yet seen: that of Sultan Mehmet II. Driven by Mohammed's prophecy that this greatest of all Middle Eastern cities would one day fall into Ottoman hands, Mehmet set about fulfilling it with the help of the most powerful artillery the world had yet seen. But it was tactics rather than firepower that secured his victory. The city's defenders had thrown a chain of boats across the Golden Horn to protect their north-eastern flank, but Mehmet outwitted them, under cover of darkness, by dragging his own ships round the obstacle over-land. A deserved victory, say modern Stamboullus, who call him Mehmet Fatih, 'Mehmet the Conqueror'.

One might of course argue that they are biased. Most Stamboullus are, after all, directly descended from Mehmet's men. But Mehmet did initiate one of Constantinople's few periods of stability – four centuries during which the mosques were restored and bazaars spread and flourished on the city's seven hills. It was not until the early years of the present century that the city's fortunes once more took a turn for the worse.

Like the rest of their Empire, Constantinople suffered pitifully from the Ottomans' decision to side with the Kaiser in the First World War. After the Armistice, Turkey was on the brink of being partitioned: the Greeks had invaded Anatolia, the British and French were occupying the Bosporus shores, and from Lisbon to Leningrad it was a commonplace insult to call a man 'a Turk'.

It is a harsh fact that nations, like people, are often the better for having endured a 'darkest hour'. The nightmare of the four years from 1918, when the Turks' young leader Atatürk was struggling against impossible odds to prevent his country being swallowed up, has left an indelible mark on every Turkish mind. Those old enough to remember do so with a wince, followed by a thoughtful smile. For Atatürk not only rid Turkey of its occupy-ing troops; but slowly, painstakingly, through reforms at home and statesmanship overseas, he gave Turks back their self-respect.

In 1923, Atatürk symbolized the nation's fresh start by decamping to a new capital inland – a technique to be copied years later by countries as diverse as Brazil, Tanzania and Belize. Istanbul accepted its demotion gracefully, and set out to consoli-date its position as the financial and commercial capital. Even before 1923, the city had become all but paralyzed by congestion, a victim of its own magnificent location; and the loss of the government did nothing to stem its growth. Istanbul's traffic jams are legendary, and today's view across the Bosporus is discoloured by bands of pollution. But Stamboullus hardly seem to notice; such is their devotion to progress that they accept these things as a small price to pay for it – if indeed they think about them at all.

On my second evening there, I indulge myself in a visit to one of the dozen or so restaurants which hang suspended in the bowels of the Galata Bridge. Fifty yards to the east, fishermen from small boats swing baskets of mullet onto the quayside; and you can, if you wish, eat them fresh from the boats themselves. The men keep kerosene stoves burning in the bilges, oil spilling from the frying pans as they rock in the wake of the ferries. In between offloading their catch, they will gladly slit open half a loaf of bread and slap in a whole fish with a handful of spring onion – all for the sum of 20p.

But tonight I will be paying a bit more. I can't quite see the open water, with its ships bound for Alexandria, Odessa and Trebizond, but then neither can I quite see the rat underneath the fridge by the kitchen door. (I can see its tail, though.) With my mullet and salad I have been given a glass of deep red Anatolian wine – a peasants' claret, as rough as the land from which it comes.

The bridge above me must rank with Calcutta's Howrah Bridge as the most congested in the world. Six lanes of belching buses and tooting taxis are silenced for a mere hour each day, between 4.30 and 5.30 a.m., when the central spans are floated aside to allow ocean-going ships into the Upper Horn. For the other twenty-three hours it seems as if most of Istanbul's five million people, in vehicles or on foot, are engaged in trying to reach the other side. If you arm yourself with earplugs and lean for ten minutes on its ornate cast-iron balustrades, you can see an entire microcosm of the city's life.

One thing always in evidence, on the bridge and on all but the narrowest streets, is the *dolmuş*. Cruising boldly over cobbles and potholes, this shared taxi usually has at least a dozen occupants, sometimes as many as twenty. The name comes from *dolmak*, 'to be full', but this is misleading because the drivers never fail to find a place for one more passenger. This morning I flagged one down in Aksaray, near my apology for a hotel, and found myself hemmed in on one side by a fifteen-stone mother of four (three of whom were on her lap), and on the other by an equally stout businessman who spent the journey taking me to task for not staying at the Pera Palas. In any other car I would have been crushed; in the *dolmuş* I just sank back into the faded upholstery, relaxed to the purr of the V-8 engine, and contemplated the reflection of Ordu Caddesi's neon lights in the tail fins to my left and right – for the *dolmuş* is no less than a Chicago gangster car, disguised by several coats of paint. These Dodges, Oldsmobiles and Plymouths, none less than thirty years old, are kept in motion by backstreet mechanics who turn out spare parts to order. From a '55 Chevvy shock absorber to a '49 Buick big end, all are copied faithfully from the originals, so the *dolmuş* is never off the road for more than a few days. Only in Peru and Uruguay have I seen such collectors' pieces on the streets; in any other country they would be locked away. Not so in Istanbul! They earn their living, and by doing so each has become stamped with a character of its own. Long may they last; Marco Polo would have approved of mileometers registering so many millions.

A discreet cough suggests that I have stayed at my table too long. I look up to see the waiter sweeping the floor, and have a notion that even the rat is eyeing me shiftily. Hastening from the brightly lit restaurant, but too stimulated (either by my exotic surroundings or by the Anatolian wine) to return to the depressing district around my hotel, I climb cobbled streets on the Beyoğlu side towards the Pera Palas where my *dolmuş* companion would have had me stay. It is late, and only a few figures are about, some walking quickly in the shadows, others swaggering brazenly down the middle of the street. A shouted greeting in Spanish tells me I am near the Galata Tower, where Iberian Jewish refugees still retain their language, customs and even a synagogue amid the gaunt tenement blocks.

Emerging at Şişhane Square, I ask for the Pera Palas and am directed up another dark street. A clock is striking midnight by the time I fetch up outside its polished walnut doors.

For well over ninety years, the cream of Istanbul's visitors in both fact and fiction have arrived at the station or airport, summoned a taxi, and ordered (usually loudly in English) 'Take me to the Pera Palas!' Noël Coward and Rose Macaulay stayed here in the 1920s, followed by several of Eric Ambler's and

Agatha Christie's characters. And was it not on a balcony of the Pera Palas that James Bond, in 1957, issued the famous order 'Shaken, not stirred'? Conceived a hundred years ago by the Belgian Georges Nagelmackers to accommodate his Orient Express passengers, the hotel stunned Victorian Constantinople with its opulence, and still does. The Sheraton may have relieved it of most of its customers, but the Pera Palas is still a home-from-home for the aristocratic traveller – actual or would-be.

Ruminating mildly on the prospect of a nightcap in its velvet and mahogany saloon, I climb the steps to the pillared and porticoed foyer. A white-gloved hand enters my field of vision, followed by a tall figure in a maroon uniform.

'I'm sorry, sir. No visitors without a tie.'

This has never happened to me before. Porters in Hiltons may have raised their eyebrows a fraction as they see me marching purposefully across thick-piled carpets towards the gents. But to get no further than the revolving door is a disgrace! Too astonished to argue, I murmur my apologies and head shame-faced towards my hovel across the Horn.

My chief task in Istanbul is to visit the Grand Bazaar, and among its 4,000 shops to seek out a particular one: the carpet emporium of Mr Erdoğan Tüfekçi. It is not going to be easy. Under the great building's aisles and domes lies a warren of alleyways, several miles in all, and the bazaar has become such a massive enterprise over the years that it now maintains its own banks, mosques, police station and even a post office. I approach a *kapısı*, one of a dozen heavy-gated entrances, and duck inside.

After the pell-mell of the city streets, the bazaar is quiet and cool. A stream of people come and go – gaggles of tourists, hurrying shoppers, and an occasional businessman thoughtfully curling his moustache – but the high-vaulted ceilings with their clerestory windows somehow conduct the noise and heat away. This is, of course, no chance design. For centuries, transactions have been taking place under this roof and its predecessors every minute of the day, and the architecture ensures that they can be made in a civilized and comfortable atmosphere: a hallmark of good bazaar design the world over.

The Grand Bazaar started as a simple *bedesten*, or warehouse, where carpets were stored. Gradually stallholders and traders in other goods put up kiosks and shelters in the surrounding streets, and as trade grew the principal merchants built *hanlar* or courtyards where caravans could unload and animals be fed and watered, while their owners got on with the business of the day. Other bazaars were growing along similar lines nearby: such as the Egyptian Bazaar by the Golden Horn, which specialized (as it still does) in spices and nuts. But no other dealt in such a rich assortment of wares. The Grand Bazaar's alleyways give clues to their occupants of long ago: Jewellers' Street, Swordmakers' Street, Pearlmerchants' Street, Fezmakers' Street, the Furriers' Bazaar, Cloakmakers' Street, Oilmerchants' Street, the Gate of the Darners, and – of course – the Bazaar of the Carpetsellers. Tentatively I ask for this one, and head in the direction of a dozen pointed fingers.

I have not met Erdoğan before, but have been given his name by a fellow-passenger on the bus from Venice. Nevertheless he manages to look as if he has been expecting me.

'Come in, come in!'

I mention our mutual friend and introduce myself.

'Hello, Mister John, I'm delighted to meet you. You are from America, yes?'

'No, Britain.'

'Ah well, never mind. Sit down, please. I think I may have just the carpet for you. You will of course take *çay*?'

The shop is an Aladdin's Cave, with carpets at every turn. They are stacked chest-high in alcoves, stretched like tapestries on the walls, laid out under spotlights, stuffed cursorily into cubby-holes. Carpets from Anatolia, from Armenia, from Kurdistan; large and small, silk and wool, old and new, pristine and shabby. Some depict animals, birds and flowers, or illustrate ancient proverbs or the Koran; others consist of symbols, inscriptions, runes, or simply abstract patterns handed down through the generations. A sizeable sample of Turkey's carpet output is displayed within the confines of Erdoğan's sixty-foot-square shop.

A boy appears from nowhere with the tea, black and strong, in a tulip-shaped glass on a silver tray. I explain that sadly I cannot afford Erdoğan's splendid carpets, but that he has been recommended as a good subject for one of my radio interviews. His face drops for just a second while he considers this; then his enthusiasm is restored.

'An interview, you say? For the BBC? Why, I would be delighted. Please tell me when this will be broadcast. I must order more carpets!'

Iranians will tell you that the Persian carpet is unmatched for quality anywhere in the world; Afghans make the same claim for their own; Pakistanis, naturally enough, favour those from Pakistan; and of course any Frenchman will persuade you that a good Aubusson is unquestionably the best. But Erdoğan argues convincingly that Turkish carpets are the finest of them all. Hunched on a three-legged stool and sipping my tea, I set the tape running and he excels himself: a professional through and through. Whatever the quality of his wares – and at up to £10,000 apiece they should be impeccable – Erdoğan deserves success on the strength of his salesmanship alone.

Roman Byzantium had its Hippodrome; Ottoman Constantinople its Topkapı Palace, home and harem of a score of sultans. But the symbols of modern Istanbul are prosaic. Hotels in glass and concrete are what visitors see nowadays from the seven hills. Fast-flowing traffic mocks the arches of the Byzantine aqueduct of Valens; bank buildings in pompous granite dwarf the fourteenth-century Galata Tower, their marble vestibules a monument to the city's irrepressible economy. Istanbul's energy seems impossible to douse. It shares with Mexico City the dubious distinction of being one of the world's fastest-growing conurbations, a title which it seems grimly set to retain. As with Mexico, you cannot leave Istanbul for more than a few years and expect to recognize it when you return.

It is also one of the noisiest cities I can remember. I used to think of Quito as a rumbustious place, as night after night I lay listening through wafer-thin walls to insomniac Ecuadorians having parties. But the hubbub there came from human throats; in Istanbul it comes from a celebration of every mechanical device known to humankind. Where else would Middle Eastern rock music from a ghetto-blaster on an open windowsill strive for harmony with the cracked, over-amplified voice of a *muezzin* issuing from a loudspeaker on a minaret? Or an unsilenced, overloaded city bus grind up a hill to the accompaniment of a dozen blasts on a ferryboat's foghorn? After a few days and nights of this cacophony, I find my eyes increasingly wandering across the smog-shrouded Bosporus to the Asian shore, the minarets of Üsküdar and the hills beyond.

The completion in 1973 of a bridge between Europe and Asia took much of the traffic from the old steam ferries. But sufficient services remain for passengers who turn up at Docks 7 or 8 to be seaborne within a matter of minutes. The original steamships, some still sporting the brass nameplates of their Tyneside makers, have recently been replaced by throbbing diesel-powered craft. But I should not complain. The pistons may have gone, but there is still plenty of romance left, and even those who commute daily seem to share with the foreigner a sense of occasion in setting sail for a new continent.

The boats are fast and the crossing takes no more than twenty minutes. With a hoot and a flick of the rudder, we are alongside the Haydarpaşa quay, and I surge ashore with the homegoing throng. Of all my landfalls in Asia, this has been easily the most straightforward. For once there have been no frontier formalities – no queues of sweaty bodies in dark corridors, no prying customs officials or sullen immigration men. The crowd disperses, the ferry returns, and the quayside is empty once more.

For centuries, travellers have approached Anatolia with sinking hearts. No easy routes cross its plateau, no natural gaps pierce the ranges to north and south. From Bursa to Doğubayazít, from Bodrum to Kars, it is a land of scorching summers and biting winters, richly fertile around the occasional volcanoes, but otherwise a succession of poor to mediocre grasslands given over to Angora goats and the occasional herd of cattle.

This intimidating Turkish heartland, the 'Asia Minor' of historians, would have been eagerly bypassed by the Silk Road traders had there been any obvious alternative. Indeed, to avoid it much traffic took to the sea, and both the Mediterranean port of Alexandretta (now Iskenderun) and the Black Sea city of Trebizond owe their origins to this fear of the overland journey. But the routes to the ports themselves were far from easy. To reach Alexandretta from the east, caravans had to brave the barren country between the Tigris and the Euphrates, where warfare and robbery were rife and there were few caravanserais to offer protection and shelter. Those heading north to Trebizond had to negotiate one of the most hazardous roads of all, including a cliff-hanging section on the Zigana Pass which remained a nightmare for travellers until the present century. In his book *Armenia*, published in 1854, Robert Curzon described an encounter on this road with a Turkish caravan:

They were seated in a row, on the ledge of the precipice, looking despairingly at a number of their baggage-horses which had tumbled over, and were wallowing in the snow several hundred feet below. They did not seem to be killed, as far as I could see, as the snow had broken their fall, . . . [but] dead frozen bodies were frequently brought into the city [Trebizond]; and it is common in the summer, on the melting of the snow, to find numerous corpses of men, and bodies of horses, who have perished in the preceding winter.

Travellers took the road through Anatolia only because the alternatives were even worse. Had there been a single less perilous route, the undulating grasslands which I am about to cross would have been left to the goats and cattle. Like my predecessors through the ages, I approach this stage with some trepidation, though perhaps for different reasons. Today Anatolia is crisscrossed by modern roads, and although the passes are still treacherous, the modern traveller is more likely to come to grief in a traffic accident than by falling over a precipice. But as I step onto Asian soil, what is worrying me is not the thought of precipices, nor even any doubts about the skills of Turkish drivers, but a small headline I have just read in an Istanbul newspaper: 'BRITISH DIPLOMAT KIDNAPPED IN TEHRAN'.

The diplomat is Edward Chaplin, First Secretary at the British Interests Section of the Swedish Embassy (as the old British Embassy is now called). His abduction by the Iranian Revolutionary Guards, although brief, has been somewhat violent, and the British Government is talking about reprisals.

The incident couldn't have come at a worse time, for I am still without a visa for Iran. Three months ago, when I applied at Iran's London embassy, I was told it would be ready in a week. When I enquired after three weeks I was told it would be no more than a month. After a month I was assured it would take another four weeks at the most. And after the second month, just days before my departure, I was informed that telexes were being exchanged that very day on the subject of my still unconfirmed visa.

The telexes, if they existed, had no effect, for I left London without my visa, but with a promise that the authorization would be telexed to the Iranian Embassy in Ankara. Now, as I approach Ankara with nothing more than the embassy's address in my pocket, the last thing I want to hear is that our relations are on the rocks.

But the newspaper report is brief, and I will have to be patient until I can find out more. As I watch the ferry return towards Istanbul, I push the question to the back of my mind. A few steps from the quayside my onward transport to Ankara is already waiting – the *Anadolu Ekspres*.

Turkish trains have a reputation for being uncomfortable, dirty and slow, and I suppose this is precisely what has lured me to them. I have crossed Europe in luxury – too much luxury – and now I want to remind myself that I am in Asia, with everything that this implies. Previous Asian journeys have left me with some vivid memories: saffron-robed pilgrims by the Ganges at dawn; the sounds of people and animals in a mountain village; an encounter with a Hindu holy man. But impressions fade, and the more mundane things are soon forgotten. I want to remind myself of ordinary sights and sounds and smells. And what better way to start than on a train?

The *Anadolu Ekspres* takes twelve hours to cover 300 miles, leaving Istanbul at 8.30 each evening and reaching Ankara at the same time the following morning. Well-heeled passengers take a sleeper, but my ticket is for the ordinary carriages, and I find myself a corner opposite a family of six.

Unusually for Turks, they are gargantuan. The two men, apparently brothers, are fairly bursting from their open-necked white shirts, and their baggy black breeches suggest further mountains of flesh beneath. Only twin drooping moustaches detract from a perfect resemblance to Tweedledum and Tweedledee. The two wives (or sisters?) are slightly less rotund – or perhaps they simply hide it better beneath an endless swathe of shawls. A ten-year-old son and rather younger daughter complete the strange collection, and although chubby-cheeked these two look almost slim beside their undulating elders.

The jolly faces and ruddy complexions of the adults suggest that their portliness has been achieved by a lifetime of self-indulgence, and there is no hint of the guilt or apology which would go with this in the West. As the train rattles out of

Haydarpaşa Station, they introduce themselves with gusto: Bedir, Yücel, Ibrahim, Evi. . . . The unfamiliar names wash over me, but before I have had time to take them in, the family has already turned its attention to a more urgent matter. A tablecloth has been spread on the floor between us, and from holdalls and carrier bags a feast is being laid out. Sausages, tomatoes, olives and *beyaz peynir* (a soft white cheese) are accompanied by mounds of *ekmek* – cigar-shaped slabs of bread still hot from the oven. With broad smiles and grand gestures they invite me to join in their meal, and as each pile is devoured, more quickly appears. Finally, satiated, I hold up my hands in a plea that I can take no more. With sighs and belches they continue their own repast, and only after all the food has been consumed, mouths wiped and a watermelon divided and eaten, does the feast come to an end.

Whilst we have been eating we have left the Sea of Marmara behind, and now the train is climbing noisily towards the Anatolian Plateau. The lights of Izmit have given way to darkness, in which only an occasional glow, dim and flickering, betrays the presence of a shepherd's house among the hills. The train loses speed as the diesel struggles against the gradient. My companions doze, and by midnight, in spite of my best efforts to stay awake, I have joined them in a fitful slumber.

I dream vividly, conjuring up pictures of border guards, hotel porters and other uniformed officials in a rush of confused images as my subconscious mind tries to come to terms with travelling again. Just two weeks after leaving Britain, I am in a different world. I half-wake. My companions have slumped into semi-horizontal positions across the hard bench seats, and look for all the world like sea-elephants snoring gently. My groggy eyes take them in, and I adjust myself into a similar position before drifting back to dream this time of sea-elephants and gondoliers.

I have become used to having bizarre dreams whilst travelling abroad. I suppose they are a reflection of the only slightly less bizarre things that happen by day. My dreams are an indicator of how well I am coping with the events of the moment, for if I am ill at ease they often lag behind, conjuring up subjects from months or even years ago in an attempt to shut out what is happening now. At other times, when I am over-confident, my dreams forge ahead to become fantasies of the future. So I am quietly relieved that tonight my mind seems to be chewing over the events of the last two weeks. Having come to terms with these, it will be better prepared for new adventures. Dawn breaks across a misty plain to reveal my rotund companions and me, in a dishevelled but contented heap on the carriage floor.

Ankara is having one of its frequent summer temperature inversions, and I arrive to find a blanket of exhaust fumes smothering the lower town. Turkey's new capital is hardly a pleasant city at the best of times, for Atatürk's choice of location was inspired by political considerations rather than the thought that it might be a nice place to live. The years surrounding the First World War saw some remarkable world capitals founded – most notably Canberra and New Delhi – but Ankara can't be counted among this élite. Since 1923 two million people have made their homes on the hills surrounding the Hisar, a hilltop fortress which had previously formed the core of a pleasant Anatolian market town. Now the fortress and the old town are lost amid waves of office and apartment blocks, whose architectural style – though style is too grand a word for it – could have come from anywhere.

I have heard the city praised for many things – its fine shops, spacious streets and excellent Hacettepe University – but such flattery comes mainly from upwardly-aspiring young Turks who haven't yet lived there. And to live there is the one thing that all young Turks want to do, for Ankara represents the future. As Turkey's principal boomtown it has supplanted even Istanbul; and if, to take advantage of its opportunities, one has to live in a slum and breathe polluted air, then many Turks are happy to do so. Few Ankarans are Ankara-born, but ask where they are from and they will say not Izmir, or Samsun, or Kayseri, but *'Tabii Ankara'* –'Ankara, of course'.

The Hotel Devran lies north of the railway on the edge of the old town: the best of a bad bunch. Having complied with its odd request that 'guests must show their passports and *sing* the registration book', I set about my visits briskly. I won't be staying longer than necessary.

My first call is at the British Embassy, a gracious whitewashed mansion which overlooks the city from the airy suburb of

Çankaya. As with the other embassies along my route, I have written in advance, so the consul, Nigel Morley, is expecting me. After a few minutes' smalltalk he comes swiftly to the point.

'Edward Chaplin wasn't just kidnapped, you know. He was beaten up.' Mr Morley considers his words carefully, as if making a speech. 'The Foreign Office is going to take a hard line.'

'What does that mean?' I ask. I am not familiar with diplomatic euphemisms.

'It means we're going to expel some Iranians. I expect their Manchester consulate will be closed.' He avoids my eyes. 'There will almost certainly be repercussions in Iran. The official advice is that British people there should leave immediately.'

I know that the Foreign Office only issues this advice when diplomatic ties are approaching breaking point. It is not given lightly. I ponder on the deteriorating situation as I leave Mr Morley's office and follow his directions towards my next port of call. Descending Cinneh Caddesi, the avenue which bisects the embassy quarter, I note the nameplates on the compounds: *Syria, Korea, USSR, Mongolia, Jordan, The Libyan People's Bureau.* Finally, behind tall gates and high walls, bathed in floodlight and scanned by closed-circuit television cameras, I find what I have been looking for: *The Embassy of the Islamic Republic of Iran.*

The building is heavily guarded. It takes twenty minutes of argument and persuasion before I am finally allowed in. Belligerent revolutionary posters cover the walls: 'AMERICA, THE GREAT SATAN.' 'DOWN WITH THE USA!' Like the slogans behind him, the man at the consular desk is in truculent mood. No: he has had no message about me, either from London or from Tehran. No: he will not make enquiries. No message means no visa. Nor will he consider a fresh application. I rephrase the question a dozen times, but the answer comes back unchanged. Decidedly, emphatically, no.

The morning's efforts have confirmed my worst fears. It is now four months since I lodged my application in London. If the Iranian authorities were going to give me a visa, they would surely have done so by now. The delay can no longer be put down to bureaucratic sloth; it can only mean, as the consular assistant has so clearly told me, that the answer is no.

My last remaining hope lies in the eastern Anatolian city of Erzurum, where Iran maintains a consulate just 200 miles from the border. Heading east from Trebizond, Black Sea traders used to join the main Silk Road here, restoring their energies in the city's many caravanserais before tackling the deserts of Persia. I will do the same, continuing my exploration of Turkey in the hope that by the time I reach Erzurum diplomatic relations will have improved – but at the same time making some contingency plans in case they haven't.

As a start, I apply for visas at the embassies of Syria and Jordan; then I buy some supplies for my rucksack; finally, there remains just one more job to do. My trusty camera, veteran of two previous Asian trips and survivor of untold abuse, has jammed. After a round of enquiries I am directed to the workshop of Bay Irigün – which means, in Turkish, 'Mr Good-day'. From behind a workbench piled high with transistors and diodes, the old man smiles enquiringly over half-rimmed spectacles. A pool of light from an anglepoise, the only illumination in the room, casts a ghoulish reflection on his features as he examines the camera gravely.

'You have quite a serious problem,' he says at length. My spirits sink; but then he adds, 'Normally I would do the repair by tomorrow, but in this case I must ask you to wait until the day after.'

Mr Good-day is as good as his word. At the appointed time I return to find my camera cleaned and working, and his bill a modest one. I am impressed.

'Where did you learn to fix Japanese cameras?' I ask.

'Where we learn everything in Turkey – in the Army,' comes the acid reply.

My evenings at the Hotel Devran have been enlivened by Vasvi, a handsome Turk whose Spanish guitar and baritone voice have been soothing the nerves of the hotel's guests (if only by drowning the clamour of the traffic outside). Vasvi tells me he is a businessman, though he is so reticent about his 'business' that I have come to think of it as something of a fantasy. But on the morning of the third day he appears at my breakfast table.

'I have some business in Çeyhan. Would you like to come?'

Çeyhan is 400 miles away on the coast of the Mediterranean, just twenty miles short of Ayas, the Polos' landfall in Asia. I jump at the chance, both of visiting the one-time Genoese port of Ayas and of sharing a journey with this striking and generous man. An hour later he calls for me, and as his battered Fiat pulls up outside the hotel I see that Vasvi is even more generous than I thought. Five other passengers – three Turkish and two Dutch – are already crammed into the tiny car, and it takes some readjustment of bodies before I am safely installed.

In the suburbs, traffic is heavy and our progress is slow, but once clear of the city we gather speed, and are soon approaching the caked-white beaches of the salt lake of Tuz. After Ankara's noxious smog, the air of the Anatolian Plateau is cool and sweet, and I gulp mouthfuls as it rushes past. From my position between and partly beneath the Turks on the back seat, I gradually become aware that Vasvi's driving is appalling. We swerve past other vehicles on the narrow road, and the Dutch couple in the front seat (who, unlike me, can observe what is happening) cry out in fear. Vasvi seems not to notice. The road sweeps past the Cilician Gates and through the Taurus Mountains in a defile which he takes at speed, maintaining a running commentary on historical attractions to left and right, while each blind corner brings fresh intakes of breath from my unseen companions.

At midnight we reach the city of Adana, and I have had enough. 'Stop!' I yell, writhing beneath the Turks. 'I've changed my mind about Çeyhan. I want to get out here.' To my relief, Vasvi pulls up. I burst out of the car, and with his slightly reduced complement he roars affably on his way.

In the city centre I find half a dozen budget hotels; but it is late, and they are either closed or full. I am on the point of pitching my tent on some waste ground when the receptionist from the last one comes running up. '*Haydi gir*' ('Come with me'), he beckons. Leading me through the hotel foyer, he points to the television lounge, and gestures that I may sleep in a corner. The arrangement has only one drawback: thirty other guests are crammed into the room. The finals of the World Basketball Championships are being broadcast from Izmir, and all are vigorously cheering the television set. I join in – taking care to cheer only the Turkish team – but my eyelids droop before the final whistle, and I can't recall who won.

The next day begins promisingly, with an easy hitch-hike to Çeyhan and a *dolmuş* for the final few miles to the Mediterranean coast. Mid-morning finds me speeding down a single-track road towards Ayas. At first the outcrops and dry-stone walls are of limestone, recalling the scenery of southern Cumbria and the Yorkshire Dales, but these quickly give way to rolling wheatlands whose nearest equivalent is in faraway Canada. In fact these Çukurova coastlands contain some of the most fertile soils in Turkey, and supply bakeries from Istanbul to Erzurum. The hot summers bring rapid ripening, and the harvest is already in full swing. Under an olive tree I spy a team of twenty or more men, women and children, taking an early lunch of bread, sausage and goat's milk cheese, and to complete this rural picture the roadside cowparsley is in full bloom. The men's baggy Turkish breeches – crotch hanging somewhere about the knee – are the only evidence that I have not walked onto a film set for *Cider with Rosie*.

Suddenly the Mediterranean comes into view, bringing me back to my senses. The *dolmuş* bounces towards a promontory which bears a crumbling huddle of buildings, not much changed since Polo's time. The road comes to an end, the *dolmuş* pulls up, and as the dust settles, the driver flings open the doors for his half-dozen passengers.

'Ayas Şehir,' he grins. ('City of Ayas.')

4
'Turk, Be Proud!'

Polo was by no means the only seafarer of his day to take advantage of Ayas's sheltered harbour and well-stocked bazaar. After a decade of Genoese rule, it was already becoming the main port for the Asian caravan trade. Back home in Italy, the Genoese were shortly to declare war on Polo's compatriots, but in this remote corner of the Mediterranean they were willing to take any ship which paid its dues. Polo himself was clearly impressed:

Ayas [is] a busy emporium. For you must know that all the spices and cloths from the interior are brought to this town, and all other goods of high value; and merchants of Venice and Genoa and everywhere else come here to buy them. And merchants and others who wish to penetrate the interior all make this town the starting-point of their journey.

A Genoese fortress still guards the entrance to Ayas's small harbour, its cannon once commanding the sea passage to Alexandretta across the bay. But today fishing smacks are all that remain to be protected: a score of twenty-footers, whose rough-cast owners seem to spend more time mending their nets and playing backgammon in the quayside cafés than actually fishing. As I hump my pack down the single street, the life of Ayas proceeds around me at the pace of a somnolent Turkish donkey.

A gang of youths has been watching from a bench, and now the eldest of the group comes over and grasps my arm. 'Excuse you, my sir! My friends and I saw you arrive. We are wanting to say . . .' (he gestures grandly to the crumbling buildings) '. . . welcome to Yumurtalık!'

'But I thought this was Ayas?'

'Ayas? No: Ayas is an old name. This now Yumurtalık.' The

man searches for the right word, and, finding it, grasps my arm once more.

'Egg-town!'

When two people share as little of each other's language as Şengül and I, one doesn't expect much insight into the other's life. But some people can communicate without words, and my new friend is a master of this. Speaking mostly Turkish, but with gestures that leave no doubt as to his meaning, he indicates that I am to sleep at his house across the bay. 'My wife will welcome cooking for you!'

'But doesn't she have your family to cook for?' I ask.

Şengül shakes his head. Allah has not blessed them with a son. He uses the word for son, *oğul*, deliberately, and declares that it is a punishment for something he did as a child. I mention that I, too, am childless, though by choice rather than divine retribution. Şengül finds this difficult to believe. I am at least ten years his elder, and he tells me gravely that I should start looking for a wife. At a loss to explain, I change the subject and return to the matter of eggs.

'Ah.' says Şengül brightly. 'So you've heard of the *kaplumbağa*?'

'The what?'

'*Kaplumbağa*! Like this, no?' Making wild swimming movements, he urges me to understand, and finally I do. He is talking about turtles.

Thirty years ago, on a beach west of Ayas, loggerhead turtles took to laying their eggs in the soft sand, and Şengül assures me that they still do. *Yumurta* means 'egg' and *Yumurtalık* means literally 'the place of the egg' (it also means egg-cup). In other parts of the Mediterranean, the loggerhead has been ousted from its nesting beaches by the unremitting onslaught of tourism, but Ayas's tourist trade is still in its infancy, limited by the absence of any 'tourist class' accommodation. Relieved that in this far outpost, at least, the turtles seem to be holding their own, I ask Şengül if he will show me the beach. 'Of course! It isn't far. Meet me at six o'clock, and we will go!'

As evening descends on Yumurtalık, we approach the beach cautiously, and spend half an hour searching with our torches – to find only roaring surf, howling dogs, and empty, ghost-white sand. Disappointed, I quiz Şengül on why this should be, and he points to the welter of footprints left by the daytime bathers.

'Look at these!' he declares angrily. 'Here: you see? These people have been digging up the eggs.' He spits in disgust. 'They are *suçlular*: criminals! The more people come to Yumurtalık, the less we will see of the *kaplumbağa*.'

Şengül's house is modern, and like many in Turkey it is only half-built. From its concrete roof, reinforcing rods sprout like tufts of hair on a wart, waiting until Şengül can afford a second storey. I observe them at close quarters as I relax on his balcony in morning sunshine, devouring a breakfast of figs, yoghurt and eggs (not turtles', thankfully). Although his wife has almost certainly prepared this sublime meal, it is Şengül who brings it to me. Moslem etiquette dictates that she must remain out of sight. Over coffee, I probe Şengül about this, and he seems surprised that I should even have noticed.

As the day warms up, the few holidaymakers in this mini-resort (all Turkish, all male) don old-fashioned bathing suits and tiptoe to the water's edge. I am tempted to join them in the cool water, but I am even more tempted to look for the jetty which Şengül has described to me as 'Marco Polo's port'. After some searching I find it half buried beneath a new car park – a small sandstone pier, all but crumbling into the harbour. It is certainly old, though it doesn't look nearly as ancient as the Genoese fortress nearby. Whether Polo used it must be open to doubt. What is not in doubt is that the modern citizens of Ayas have no use at all for 'Marco Polo's port', and I suspect its rough-hewn blocks will soon be carted off for other purposes – possibly even to help with the second storey of Şengül's house.

In the thirteenth century, as today, travellers heading east from the Mediterranean were plagued by man-made hazards as well as natural ones. The year 1272 saw a bitter battlefront developing across northern Syria and Iraq, as Mongol armies spurred on by a crusading Prince Edward (later Edward I) confronted the Moslem forces of Sultan Baibars. So when in that year Marco Polo, his father Niccolò, his uncle Maffeo and a caravan of tough Anatolian ponies set off on their three-and-a-half year journey to Beijing, they began by taking a north-westerly direction, the way I have just come. Through Adana they rode, past the Cilician Gates, and only when they were safely on the Anatolian Plateau did they turn north-east towards Sivas. By keeping well inside Mongol territory, they hoped to avoid the ever-shifting war zone.

The warmongers these days may be different, but the Middle Eastern traveller has to pick his or her route just as carefully. Like the Polos, I am making my way towards Sivas, but by a more southerly route which will take me across the Euphrates, providing a glimpse of the forbidden territory beyond and also taking in the remarkable mountain of Nemrut Dağı.

'Remember Yumurtalık!' laughs Şengül, slipping a bag of fresh figs into my pack as I trudge up the road.

Walking and hitch-hiking back to Çeyhan, I arrive just in time to catch the daily bus to Urfa on the road to Iraq. Unlike the smart Mercedes vehicles which ply further west, this is an ancient model, rough-looking, and its occupants look ancient and rough too. But they are an amiable crowd, and the old-timer next to me points out some of the more noteworthy features along the way. He seems particularly taken with filling stations: each time one comes into view, he nudges me conspiratorially and croaks 'Güzel!' ('Pretty!') in my ear.

The E–24 between Adana and Gaziantep is one of the most foully congested roads I have ever encountered. Winding over the Akyokuş Pass, it was built for animals, carts and perhaps the occasional *dolmuş* heading for Syria or Lebanon. Since the Gulf War closed Iraq's seaports, this previously little-used highway has played host to convoys of road tankers of every shape and size, day and night, as Iraq tries desperately to get its oil to world markets. They are unmistakably Asian vehicles: rusty, filthy and (judging by the number jacked up by the roadside) not in the best of condition. On downhill stretches, some scream along in bottom gear; others freewheel wildly, their drivers grappling with the controls. Occasionally a pile of wreckage in a ravine suggests that one has not reached its destination. My bus joins a convoy and I hope for the best.

At Gaziantep the roads to Syria and Iraq part company. Against a backcloth of sand-coloured houses, carpeting a hillside of sand, a sand-swept bus station advertises services to '*S. Arabistan, Suriye, Lübnan, Ürdün, Iran, Irak, Kibris*'. Our driver announces that we will spend an hour here, so I stroll through the town, looking for a café in which to pass the time.

At first, people seem to be going about their business, but after a hundred yards I notice that several passers-by have turned to follow me, and the number swells until by the time I reach the main square I am at the hub of a teeming crowd. They are not exactly hostile, yet at the same time not quite friendly. One of the throng begins to interrogate me in thickly accented Turkish. I shrug my shoulders and smile, but am beginning to feel just a little nervous, when suddenly a young man bursts through the scrum.

'Quick! Follow me!' Pushing the others aside, he ushers me across the street and almost drags me into a tea-room.

'Come; sit down. They won't bother you here.'

My new-found ally, who looks no different from the men in the crowd outside, orders tea in Turkish. Then, turning to me, he continues in English, with a hint of an accent that I have heard somewhere before.

'Not many foreigners come to Gaziantep – apart from truck drivers, of course. But you needn't worry; they were only curious.'

But now it is I who am curious. 'Where did you learn English?' I ask.

'Oh, in Melbourne. Lots of our people went to Australia in the 'fifties. I was born there.'

'Really? So you're Australian?'

'No, Turkish. That's why I'm here. I've come to do National Service.'

It is scarcely credible. Fifty years after his death, on the other side of the world, Atatürk's 'children' are being groomed to fight for a country upon which they have never set eyes. Whatever the case for National Service – and in Turkey, shielded by NATO, it is a debatable one – such mindless patriotism makes me uneasy. But my concern would not find much favour in Turkey. Across the street, astride a bronze stallion in heroic pose, Atatürk rides atop a marble plinth. Beneath pawing hooves are inscribed the words: *Türk! Ögün. Ne Mutlu Türküm Diyene.* ('Turk! Be Proud. What Joy to Him who says "I am a Turk".')

It is time to go, and I move to pay for the tea. 'No, no,' insists my friend. 'It's my round.'

Birecik, Urfa, Hilvan. Darkness; more convoys; a landslide; forked lightning over distant mountains. I doze restlessly in my seat, in between a change of buses at Urfa and a breakdown in the middle of nowhere. Sleepily, I watch the sun rise as we cross the

Euphrates. Beyond the bridge a string of peasants is winding its way along the road: nut-brown, wild-haired men leading donkeys loaded with mattresses, veiled women carrying the younger children, grandparents hobbling with sticks or perching precariously on top of the loads. They remind me that I, too, will be on foot again soon; for the bus is approaching Kâhta, gateway to the ancient kingdom of Commagene, and to one of the strangest mountains on earth.

For nearly two millennia, Nemrut Dağı was just one of several 7,000-foot peaks in a little-visited part of Anatolia – neither as lofty, nor as celebrated, as the other mountain of the same name on the distant shores of Lake Van. It was in 1881 that a visiting German geologist heard from shepherds that the mountaintop was covered with statues. The visitor picked his way up its rocky slopes, and could hardly believe what he saw. For the stone gods which festoon the summit of Nemrut Dağı – Hercules, Zeus, Apollo and Hermes – are endowed with some of the largest heads on earth.

You might say that the biggest head of all was that of their creator, King Antiochus I. Commagene had been a kingdom for only sixteen years when he came to the throne, and it was destined to become part of the Roman Empire just a century later. Admittedly, Antiochus had impeccable credentials. Descended on his father's side from the Persian royal family, and on his mother's from Alexander the Great, he was undeniably well connected. But his rule extended over no more than a few valleys, and his 10,000 subjects could not raise even a bodyguard, let alone an army. Incredibly, during his short reign, Antiochus chivvied them into performing one of the greatest civil engineering works of the age, and culminated the project by filling the prime position (between Hercules and Zeus) with a statue of none other than himself.

The old Dodge minibus pulls out of Kâhta's bus depot, springs groaning. Inside, it is crammed with women, children and pigs, but I have been invited to join half a dozen men among the baggage on the roof. Crossing the River Cendere by an arched Roman bridge, we continue on a deteriorating track towards the village of Eski Kâhta.

The track becomes steeper, and the minibus, grinding up it in bottom gear, finally comes to a halt. Villagers survey us sullenly from the hillside above. A dozen passengers decide to continue on foot, taking with them the pigs. With cries of encouragement, the rest of us push, heave and almost lift the vehicle over the remaining boulders and onto the patch of beaten earth which forms the *meydan* or village square. A football match is hurriedly abandoned to make way for us, and the exhausted complement sit about gasping as the driver unties the load from the roof. Steam hisses from the radiator; then, as the engine cools and the passengers drift away, silence returns.

The setting is sensational. Eski Kâhta itself is perched on a saddle above the Kâhta Çayi river, but higher still, on an outcrop whose face falls sheer to the water, sits the extraordinary castle of Yeni Kale. This was the site of Antiochus' capital, and a more impregnable position one cannot imagine. I spend two hours among its ledges and passages before retiring to a dirty and overpriced guest house in the village.

For the last decade, visitors have been able to drive almost to the summit of Nemrut Dağı on a cobbled road, but I have decided to follow the original path on foot. Almost a month after starting my journey, I can at last look forward to the pleasure of walking in awesome country, alone, a light pack on my back, following a rough track towards a mysterious destination. As I leave Eski Kâhta, I can already sense the joy of thirst quenched at a spring; an unexpected meal at a village house; and finally, as night falls, the prospect of finding a place to pitch my tent and rest my exhausted legs. I am not disappointed. An afternoon of steady climbing leaves me so elated that even getting lost fails to douse my spirits. After wading through wild oregano for several hours by torchlight, I reach the summit car park at midnight, too triumphant to sleep.

Of Nemrut Dağı's two dozen statues and carved reliefs, half face the rising sun and half the setting sun. For a reason best known to themselves, tour guides encourage their clients to team up with the former and marvel at the dawn. Shortly after 3.30 a.m. I am woken by the first minibus struggling up the mountain-side, and for the next two hours a procession of headlights approaches, each vehicle depositing a dozen irritable passengers until the sky pales to reveal more than a hundred shivering figures on the east terrace. The atmosphere is like that at Machu

Picchu, Peru's lost city of the Incas, when the tourist train comes in. I hate the forced conviviality of such occasions, and stroll away quietly to spend the sunrise in the company of the sunset gods on the far side. One of the heads here is said to bear a resemblance to Elvis Presley, but after looking at it from all angles I have to say that only the most devout Elvis fan would see the likeness.

The Polo caravan, threading its way across the Anatolian Plateau, gave Nemrut Dağı scarcely a glance as it headed for Sivas. The Polos' sights were now set on the region they knew as Greater Armenia:

This is a very large province. Near the entrance to it stands a city called Erzinçan, in which is made the best buckram in the world, and countless other crafts are practised. Here are the finest baths of spring water to be found anywhere on earth. The inhabitants are Armenians and vassals of the Tartars. There are many towns and cities, but the most splendid of these is Erzinçan.

Entering this region from the desert of south-east Turkey, I am glad to see vegetation again – but with the greenery come clouds and rain. Between Zara and Erzinçan the Silk Road took to the uplands, climbing steeply between the peaks of Köse Dağ and Bey Dağı. Until recently the modern road followed a gentler route to the north, thirty miles longer, but more suitable for the underpowered lorries and buses of the 1960s. Today it is back on its original line, using embankments and cuttings to ease the gradients which plagued earlier travellers. But the journey is still a formidable one, through bleak country with a reputation for foul weather. Approaching the 7,000-foot Kızıldağ Pass in an Iran-bound juggernaut, I see deep snow patches lining the road. For a few minutes the cab is strafed by hailstones. Shepherds cower under boulders, their flocks marooned in the teeth of the squall. Looking at my diary, I notice it is midsummer's day.

In 1939 Erzinçan, a fine old city graced with more than fifty mosques, was hit by one of the worst earthquakes in recorded times. Forty thousand people perished in the rubble. The rebuilt town is uncompromisingly modern, but with a curiously time-worn air, its dusty boulevards paced by sallow, despondent figures who give the appearance of struggling beneath unfathomable burdens. This may be close to the truth, for as well as its appalling tectonic history the city is the home of Turkey's main police and military training centres. Whether by Nature or by politics, both young and old in the streets of Erzinçan have probably been displaced from their homes.

If anyone visits Erzinçan by choice, it is for the hot springs or *ekşisu* that they come. The word means literally 'bitter water'. It appears on the front of the No. 12 bus which plies hourly from the Town Hall to the foot of the Keşiş Mountains. Here, I tell myself, I should find Marco Polo's 'finest baths of spring water to be found anywhere on earth'.

The springs are certainly there – and they have grown a little since Polo's time. Around them, the city fathers have built a spa, with swimming pools, drinking fountains, a miniature train, and picnic tables under the eucalyptus trees. Worldly though he may have been, I suspect the old Venetian would turn in his watery grave if he could observe the scene that greets me as I step off the bus. It is Sunday morning, and half the population of Erzinçan is at the springs: men and boys splashing merrily in their boxer bathing shorts, women and girls sitting demurely and pretending not to see. Few foreigners come this way, and a crowd soon gathers round me. As in Gaziantep, I am powerless to stop the swelling numbers, but here at least the throng is good-natured. Small boys shove and jostle to test the stranger with their schoolroom English. The familiar calls of "Allo!', 'What yura nayam?' and 'What tiyam ees eet?' are followed oddly by 'You are Aleman?' and 'From Fransez?'. The possibility that an English speaker might be from Britain doesn't seem to have crossed their minds.

After sharing in a dozen picnics I run for the bus, chased by fifty cheering children. The baths may still be 'the finest on earth', but the company is not for me.

Trebizond! The name shines temptingly from the map, beckoning to me from the south-east corner of the Black Sea, just a bus ride away. Though the city is now known as Trabzon, I am pleased to see that its old name still takes precedence on the map. It is a pivotal point on the great journey to the East – one of the few places that seems to have left an impression on all who have passed through. So when I hear that a bus is leaving for Trebizond this very evening, I make straight for the bus station, and before long am clutching a ticket.

The world boasts perhaps half a dozen cities whose reputations are so legendary that they must inevitably disappoint. I'm told that Samarkand and Timbuktu are like this; so, approaching Trebizond through the night, I can't help wondering if it will turn out to be just another Turkish town.

Philip Glazebrook offers a timely warning in *Journey to Kars*:

I suspect that Turkey has always looked as though it would have been perfectly wonderful if you'd come twenty years ago. The disappointments are brought about by the mis-preparation of your mind for what really exists; yet it's the mis-preparation – the treasure trove buried in your mind under certain place-names in early days – which draw you there in the first place. Perhaps if I'd known what it's really like in most of Trabzon nowadays, I wouldn't have come. Only by not knowing, by refusing to listen, by insisting on setting out with pickaxe and secret map, can you hope to find Trebizond.

Will my pick strike gold? Stepping from the bus in a grey dawn, I face a battery of prefabricated warehouses, and doubt it. It is 4.30 a.m.; not a soul is about. I shoulder my pack and leave the horrors of the port, taking a cobbled street which rises between crumbling tenements towards the city centre on the hill.

Founded 800 years before Christ, Trebizond was already flourishing (under the name of Trapezus) when Xenophon arrived with his 'Ten Thousand'. The emperor Hadrian – fated, it seems, to be remembered for his engineering projects rather than his governing skills – built the city's first artificial harbour; and over the next 1,800 years it grew to be the Black Sea's principal port. The Polos favoured the Mediterranean for shipping goods to and from the East, but theirs was the last generation to do so. Warfare and political instability in the Euphrates and Tigris valleys had, by the 1840s, diverted most of the east–west traffic to Trebizond – a business said to have been worth £1 million a year. From the west came the products of a budding Industrial Revolution; from the east such exotica as leeches, rhubarb, arsenic and, above all, opium. It was the latter which gave Trebizond its reputation for intrigue and vice.

I nose about the alleys of the still sleeping city. 'The bazaars of Trebizond contain a good deal of rubbish,' wrote Robert Curzon in 1849, 'of both the human and inanimate kind.' A woman leans from a second-floor window and hurls slops from a bucket. Some things, at least, haven't changed.

It is still only 5.00 a.m. when I come across a café owner removing his shutters, and although I have intended exploring rather than breakfasting, the smell of fresh-baked bread sweeps away my resolve. There is no menu. The proprietor vanishes into the kitchen and reappears with a plate containing a slab of butter, a dollop of whipped cream, a dish of honey, and bread rolls too hot to touch. These are quickly followed by *çay*: not in the usual tiny glass, but in a half-pint mug, with a jug of milk by its side. This is clearly someone who knows his customers' needs. I decide that I'm going to enjoy Trebizond.

In *The Towers of Trebizond*, Rose Macaulay observed that the local azalea honey has a strange effect on the brain. Xenophon's Ten Thousand went quite beserk after indulging in it, and the honey on my plate may have something to do with what happens next. Full of hot bread and *bonhomie*, I leave my pack with the café owner and head for the Kale, the walled Byzantine citadel which Mehmet Fatih (the same Mehmet who so deviously conquered Istanbul) called the only truly impregnable fortress anywhere in the world.

The Kale occupies a bluff between a pair of ravines that tumble down from the coastal mountains to the Black Sea. Its fortifications crown the cliffs in much the same way as those of Edinburgh Castle cap Castle Rock. The Selçuk leader Aladdin Keykubad lost a whole army trying to scale these crags, and I decide hot-headedly to have a go myself. To be fair to Keykubad, the rock has been provided with foot- and hand-holds since his time, and one part seems to be used by today's ravine dwellers as a short cut into town. Also, I don't have the inconvenience of defenders pouring boiling oil on me. But I still feel incorrigibly pleased with myself when, after an airy scramble, I swing over the top with no more than a few scratches to show for it. Mehmet the Conqueror was wrong!

In the records of Trebizond's shipping agents, arsenic and opium have long since given way to more humdrum products such as television sets, computers and the local specialities of Ordu hazelnuts and Rize tea. However, in an ironic re-creation of medieval trade patterns, Iran once more receives most of her European consumer goods through here, and will continue to do so until her sea routes become secure once more. Trebizond's port authorities must be confident that this won't be for some time, because behind the decrepit warehouses where I entered the city they have invested in an expensive new container terminal.

The Zigana Pass, Trebizond's link with the East, has been terrifying travellers for centuries, and I look forward to seeing what it entails. Curzon may have had to lift his ponies across icebound ledges; Wolff may have tunnelled through snow; Glazebrook may have considered the ride 'a helter-skelter you can't get off'; but on this fine June morning the journey looks quite straightforward. The bus is modern, the driver prudent, and as we climb through first beech and then pine forests into the Pontic Alps I find it difficult to visualize the mudslides which occasionally sweep vehicles and their occupants into the River Değirmendere far below. At 6,000 feet we enter cloud, so I am denied the Black Sea vista which has gladdened the hearts of so many westbound travellers. But I have no complaints. I have no complaints even about the greasy mutton stew which is dished out at the summit café – an obligatory meal, it seems, for I am the only passenger who fails to consume my bowlful. The mist is cool and clinging, and I savour the respite from the dust and heat. All too soon we are bouncing down towards Bayburt on the other side.

'And on the route from Trebizond to Tabriz,' wrote Polo, 'is a fortress called Bayburt, where there is a large silver mine.'

He was right about the position of the fortress, but my fellow passengers assure me that he was wrong about the silver mine. 'There are no mines in Bayburt, Mister John. Not coal, nor lead, nor silver, nor gold.'

But all is not lost.

'Mister John!'

'What?'

'This town here. Look at its name!'

'Gümüşhane?' I ask, squinting at the sign.

'Yes. Gümüşhane.'

'Well?'

'Don't you see? *Gümüş*, silver; *hane*, house! If you're looking for a silver mine, you should start here.'

Stepping off the bus, I decide that Gümüşhane is the most

improbable mining community I have ever seen. It has the air of an Alpine or Pyrenean resort, and the inhabitants I talk to are not miners but hoteliers and restaurateurs. I am still fifty miles from Bayburt, and am about to board another bus when an old jeweller assures me that there is a *gümüşmaden* (silver mine) up the hillside. Of all people, he should know. He takes my pack for safe keeping while I set out to look for it.

The hills surrounding the town are not exactly picture-postcard material, but neither do they give the impression of mining country. No spoil heaps scar the slopes; no winding gear disfigures the horizon. Despite several hours of searching the grassy uplands under a scorching Anatolian sun, I find no evidence of the elusive *gümüşmaden*. Months later, I am to discover that both the mine and the original town – several miles from the present one – were abandoned following an earthquake in 1916. But for the time being I will carry on to Bayburt in ignorance. After taking some photographs as mementoes, I clamber back down to the town, and walk straight into trouble.

While I have been aloft observing Gümüşhane, it seems that the Gümüşhane police have been below observing me. They are waiting at the jeweller's, all hung about with guns, binoculars and walkie-talkies, when I return.

I've been told that when facing grim Turkish police sergeants, only two things need be said. The first and most important is what a fine man Atatürk was (which is true); the second is that Greeks are cads (which isn't). It is sound advice. Setting aside my actual feelings on the subjects, I try it in my stumbling Turkish, and soon we are drinking tea, all smiles again. To my relief I am excused an explanation of what I was doing on the hillside with my telephoto lens. I ask the sergeant if I may photograph him in front of his impressive array of patrol cars, and such is his empathy for a fellow Greek-hater that he almost agrees.

A late bus takes me to Bayburt – and indeed beyond, for in the dark it has continued a further two miles towards Erzurum before I manage to scramble forward and ask the driver to stop. The walk back, in pitch darkness above the fast-flowing Çoruh Nehri river, proves so tricky that on successfully reaching the street-lights I turn to admire my achievement, step into a manhole and nearly break my neck.

Bayburt's hotels have long since closed for the night, but I am offered a room in a tumbledown bar by the river. Looking at the clientele, I wonder what else I will be offered. Washing at this establishment is done in the river itself, and as I return from my ablutions I notice a sign swinging reassuringly above the door. It reads *Otel ve Garaji*. This means not 'hotel with parking space' but 'hotel and bus station' – which perhaps explains why the bus driver was so reluctant to stop. I try to creep unnoticed to my room, but the floorboards produce Hitchcock-style sound effects, and I am shamed into joining the drinkers at the bar. One of them speaks French, and in spite of his intoxication we are having a lively conversation when somebody points out that I haven't touched my glass of *raki*. *'Vous devez le boire tout d'un coup,'* explains my friend. 'You have to drink it all at once.' I glance nervously at the liquid in the tumbler before me, which looks and smells exactly like Esso Blue. I turn to my tormentors. I beg, I plead; but my feeble excuses only fire their enthusiasm all the more. *'Bois! Bois!'* Seeing that there is no escape, I pull myself upright and down the stuff quickly before I lose my nerve. Inside me a fireball explodes. I panic momentarily as my stomach suffers what must surely be second-degree burns. The others thump my back vigorously in congratulation. But as shock gives way to anaesthesia, I watch the room start to spin and feel my lips freezing into a smile. I mutter something about bedtime, turn towards my room, and crumple gently, drunkenly, to the floor.

Eighteen hours and a hundred miles later, I reach Erzurum with a headache and some misgivings. Erzurum will be a turning point on the trip. One way or another, my future course will be decided here.

On the fifth floor of a shabby office block I find the Iranian Consulate. I manage to see the consul, but he is unable to help. He has received no authority, either from London or from Tehran, to issue me with a visa. Furthermore he cannot pursue it for me, for he is forbidden to telephone his superior in Tehran. To my surprise, he agrees to give me the man's number. 'But don't say you got it from me.'

The consul then gives me the news I have feared most. Relations between Britain and Iran have been all but broken. Tehran has expelled its remaining British diplomats, leaving the Swedish Ambassador to look after British interests. The Iranian

Embassy in London is to close in a few days' time. The consul shrugs his shoulders. What can he do? If foreign governments put obstacles in the way of Iran's revolution, their subjects must take the consequences. The British businessman Roger Cooper is doing just that, he reminds me, having already spent two years in a Tehran gaol on charges of spying. The consul raises his eyebrows as if to suggest that I might be a spy too – though on what evidence I cannot begin to imagine.

I spend an exasperating afternoon trying to contact the consul's superior at the Ministry of Foreign Affairs. Government officials the world over make a point of being difficult to pin down, but Tehran's switchboard operators are the best filibusterers I have ever come across. After spending several pounds on phone calls, I am told that the number given me by the consul does not exist.

I have one last hope. I feed my remaining change into the telephone and ask for the Tehran office of London Oriental Carpets, a business run by an Iranian friend, Nick Oundjian. Nick lives in London, but by a stroke of luck he is visiting Tehran, and it is he who answers the phone.

I explain my predicament. 'I'm not surprised you couldn't get anyone at the Ministry,' replies Nick. 'Iranian time is two hours ahead of Turkey's, and they will already have closed for the Islamic holiday tomorrow. But don't worry. I've got to see them about another matter on Saturday. I'll ask them to look up your file.'

Heart racing, I thank him and put down the phone. It is a small hope, but it is hope. Will Nick be able to pull the necessary strings? Today is Thursday; I will find out in two days' time.

If travel is character-building, then waiting for visas is even more so. To occupy my time, I climb the hills around Erzurum, and search in vain for some beauty in the town. I re-read the books in my rucksack; I trim my beard, hair by hair. I talk about every subject under the sun with those of Erzurum's citizens who speak English, and listen to monologues from several who don't. I redouble my efforts to learn Turkish, memorizing every word in my phrasebook for which I might conceivably have a use – including *Dalgalı perma istiyorum*, 'I'd like a curly permanent wave'. But despite these efforts, the impasse with the Iranian authorities is whittling away at my zest for the trip, and I feel listless and lonely. My loneliness is not for lack of company; for

12

no Westerner in the East is ever alone for more than five minutes. But the company of strangers sometimes simply emphasizes one's isolation. What I need now is not company, but companionship: someone to relax with, to laugh with, to cry with – even to squabble with. So much for the thrills of solo travel.

I remind myself that I am not the first to have fallen foul of Middle Eastern immigration officials. Philip Glazebrook, travelling in Turkey in 1980, was moved to write:

Frontiers are among the 'ordeals' of romantic travel, or should be. To achieve a proper relationship with them – and to promote frontiers from mere lines on a map into real barriers which require penetrating – maybe it's necessary to cross them secretly, with false papers if not a false nose.

At last, on Saturday evening, Nick telephones to tell me my fate. A ruling of 21st June has decreed that no further British passport holders will be allowed into Iran. There will be no exceptions whatsoever. Today is the 27th; I am just six days too late.

For a moment my enthusiasm for the Silk Road utterly expires. I stare at the telephone in disbelief. Misinterpreting my silence as a disconnection, Nick hangs up, and it is left to the manager of the hotel whose phone I have been using to find some comforting words. He rises to the occasion by pointing to my camera. 'Şunu müsadere edermişler; seni müsadere edermişler,' he suggests mildly. ('First, they would take that; then, they would take you.')

He is quite right: Iran, at the moment, is probably one of the most perilous places I could have wished to be. In the eyes of the Revolutionary Guards, my notebooks, camera and BBC tape recorder would surely have been grounds for detention, and with no diplomatic assistance I might well have joined Roger Cooper in Tehran's Evin Gaol. Perversely, these thoughts sober and cheer me, and I determine to see as much as possible of the enchanting border country before tackling the question of an alternative route.

According to the map, Turkey extends for a further 200 miles east of Erzurum, taking in the salty waters of Lake Van, the thyme-scented grasslands around Mount Ararat, and the south-western slopes of the Little Caucasus on the border of Soviet Georgia. But the map is deceptive, and wise visitors to this region speak cautiously in the company of local people. Hitch-hiking east of

Ağrı on the road towards Iran, I am picked up by an agreeable man returning home to Doğubayazıt. After some minutes listening to my eulogy about the hospitality of Turkish people, he turns to me and scowls, 'I'm not a Turk; I'm a Kurd.'

The disaffection of Turkish, Iranian and Iraqi Kurds for their mother states is hardly surprising, when you consider how they have been treated over the years. Since the abortive Kurdish revolt of 1925, successive governments in Ankara, Tehran and Baghdad have reacted brutally to the slightest hint of insurrection. In 1930 and again in 1937, activists were sought out and executed. More recently, both sides have started to adopt more lethal technology: the guerrillas attacking with remote-controlled grenades and bombs, the government forces replying with air strikes against their hideouts in the hills. To anyone from the British Isles the stories have a depressingly familiar ring; like the Northern Irish, the people of the Kurdish lands – whether Iranians, Iraqis, Turks or Kurds – seem doomed to a conflict without end.

Nor are these people alone in their predicament. Their northern neighbours the Armenians have, if anything, been even more abused. Like the Greeks, Serbs and others subjugated by the Ottoman sultans, the Armenians saw towards the end of the last century an opportunity for independence. Why they failed to achieve it is hard to say: perhaps it was the lack of outside support, perhaps a failure of leadership. But in the 1890s and again in 1915, the sultans massacred them mercilessly, deporting many of the survivors to the wastes of Mesopotamia. After the First World War, Turks and Russians horse-traded the Armenian homeland with its depleted and demoralized population. The Russians acknowledged the Turkish occupation of Kars, while the Turks recognized Russian claims to the Caspian coast and its fertile hinterland of Azerbaijan.

Out of these sublime but bloodstained grasslands rises Mount Ararat – the highest Middle Eastern peak outside the Caucasus. It is not only by far Turkey's highest mountain, but also her most majestic; and over the ages its volcanic symmetry has caught the imagination of generations of storytellers. At the height of the Flood, Noah's Ark was supposed to have run aground on its upper snowfields, and expeditions are mounted regularly – though so far unsuccessfully – to look for it.

I can never pass a mountain that looks climbable without itching to give it a try. Anticipating this, I have already asked in Ankara for permission. The gentleman at the Ministry of Sport laughed at my request. 'We never process applications in less than two years,' he replied merrily. 'It keeps the numbers down.'

From Doğubayazıt's main street, the Hotel Ağrı Dağı looks quite reasonable, but a closer inspection shows it to be missing something. Beyond a deceptively normal lobby, tell-tale tufts of reinforcing rods sprout among weeds. Until the finishing touches (like floors and ceilings) have been put to what will undoubtedly one day be a fine establishment, guests are accommodated in a shed. It is rather more spartan than the builders' cabin nearby, with which it shares a tap. But for 48p a night I don't expect the Ritz, and the glimpse through my window of dawn rays catching the snows of Ararat makes up for a night on a springless bed.

A local guide, Ahmet Çoktin, offers not only to arrange instant permission for me to climb Ararat, but to take me up himself. I don't doubt his sincerity, for the Çoktin family is rumoured actually to own half the mountain; but Ahmet's fee of 500,000 lirasi (about £350) is rather beyond my means. When I explain this to him, he shrugs his shoulders good-naturedly, and confesses that he is quite relieved at my decision: he wouldn't have wanted to be responsible for anyone with crampons as blunt as mine.

Four young Germans have also been looking at Mount Ararat with longing eyes. I have already met them in Ahmet Çoktin's office, where they were no more able to afford his fee than I was, but over Turkish beer we resolve to make an attempt on our own. Being close to the Soviet border, the mountain is heavily patrolled, and someone suggests we should disguise ourselves as Turkish peasants. But Turkish peasants don't wear crampons – even blunt ones. (Around Doğubayazıt their costume seems to be denim skirts and bell-bottoms.) So my companions and I simply don our climbing clothes, take a taxi to where a track heads towards the lower slopes, and set out to see how far we can get.

The answer comes within an hour. Following us along the track, a plume of dust slowly transforms itself into an army jeep. As it pulls up beside us, I happen to be pointing my camera at a stork which has made its nest on top of a telegraph pole, and in the cause of photography I carry on. Perhaps this isn't the wisest thing to do, because an army sergeant bursts out of the jeep, and for the second time in a week I find myself under arrest.

My co-conspirators and I are hustled into the vehicle, to a barrage of Turkish abuse. The sergeant's words are too rapid for us to follow, but the gist is clear, and a rough translation would be: 'Bloody tourists! We put up signs all round the mountain, and still you come. I joined the Army to fight for the honour of Atatürk; but all I ever do is arrest tourists!'

We are driven back to Doğubayazıt and into the barracks. An armed guard accompanies us to the commanding officer's building, and for a moment it seems as if we are in serious trouble. We sit in a row, looking contrite. At length the officer appears, and to our great relief speaks fluent German, so my friends quickly explain that we are tourists, not terrorists, and at my suggestion add the bits about Atatürk and Greeks.

The commanding officer spouts irately, and for a moment I wonder whether in their anxiety my companions have got their pieces about Atatürk and Greeks the wrong way round. But suddenly we are dismissed. *'Gehen Sie weg!'* he bellows. We scoot before he can change his mind.

There is no question about it; it is time to move on. Iran and the Soviet Union bar my way to the east; Iraq and Syria (which has also now refused me a visa) to the south. Luckily there are twice-weekly ferries between Greece and Israel, and cargo ships continue to call at Israel's Mediterranean and Red Sea ports. There is just a chance that I may be able to persuade one of these ships to take me east.

A week after the incident on Ararat, I am back in Mediterranean waters, stepping from the Marmaris quayside onto a morning ferry bound for Rhodes. Behind me, a pine-clad amphitheatre cradles a sparkling bay. In a waterfront café a fisherman is lighting his first cigarette of the day, his half-mended net forgotten as he stares thoughtfully at the ferry's retreating stern. Across the sand-blown street, almost hidden beneath a bronze Atatürk in heroic pose, a marble plinth reads: 'Turk! Be Proud. What Joy to Him who says "I am a Turk".'

5
Detour

On a morning when the water's iridescence is unusual even for the Aegean, the ferry with its forty or so passengers creeps towards the open sea. The Bay of Marmaris, twelve miles across, has a shore so crenellated that its true splendour can only be appreciated from the bay itself. Insect-like, the little craft emerges from the port, and as the horizon broadens I begin to see why these waters have inspired poets and storytellers through the ages. From the shore, crags rise vertically for 300 feet or more, before giving way to thickly forested slopes and the occasional sun-bleached meadow. In the straits where Jason's *Argus* once steered its perilous course, sleek yachts now scythe through the water, their radar reducing the skipper's task to an occasional check on a screen.

The neck of the bay is narrow. Cliffs loom overhead, and the echo of the engine bounces back from pinnacles on which goats graze. A goatherd watches us from a foothold only slightly less precarious than those of his animals – and he is the last Turk I see, for in a moment we have burst upon the Mediterranean. The mainland recedes, and through the haze beyond the ferry's pitching bow an even more dramatic sight emerges. Ramparts flanked by massive towers cradle a harbour whose name would have been familiar to Marco Polo. Behind them, pitched roofs and palm trees rise in casual contrast to the stern minarets of the land I have just left. Within an hour we have docked in Rhodes.

In spite of its impressive fortifications, this is an island which has suffered more than its share of invasions over the years. As early as 305BC Demetrius the Besieger, the Macedonian warmonger, was battering its town walls with a nine-storey assault tower rolled forward on trunks of oak. The Romans invaded and butchered; Venetians and Crusaders occupied and fortified. By Polo's time the stronghold had fallen to the Genoese, and the ships of his countrymen would have called there only *in extremis*.

But the worst was still to come. In 1522, after a siege lasting nearly six months, Süleyman the Magnificent overwhelmed the island with an Ottoman force said to include 300 ships and no fewer than 100,000 men. The Ottoman occupation lasted for 400 years; the more recent occupations by Mussolini and Hitler seem, by comparison, both short-lived and tame.

These days the forces invading Rhodes bring not assault towers but beach bags. In July – the height of the season – they seem to outnumber the defenders, and I walk the shady streets in shock. Luckily Rhodians are more sanguine. As Paul Theroux has observed of the Cornish, they are a farming people and treat their visitors like livestock – feeding us, fencing us in, and getting us to move occasionally to new pastures. We are cumbersome burdens, a headache for most of the time, but at the end of the day there is profit in us.

As I stroll among the pleasure-seekers, my thoughts have already turned to Pakistan. Banned from Iran and Syria, I have only one course of action if I am to reach the East by land and sea. As I join the assorted Israelis, Cypriots, Europeans and Americans climbing the ramp of the Haifa-bound F/B *Paloma*, I have to admit that it is an option of last resort.

I am comforted by knowing that the Polos had a false start too. Marco might never have joined his father Niccolò and uncle Maffeo on their second journey, had not the spring of 1269 brought news to them in St Jean d'Acre (now the Israeli city of Acre or Akko) that Pope Clement IV was dead. Kublai Khan had ordered the brothers to return to China with tangible evidence of the religion called Christianity, of which they spoke in such glowing terms. Amongst other things, the Khan had asked for oil from Jerusalem's Holy Sepulchre, which only a pope could provide. But after two long years in Venice, with still no sign of a papal election, the Polo brothers grew impatient and set out again, this time with the seventeen-year-old Marco. Passing hurriedly through Acre, they continued to Ayas, only to be told that Pope Gregory X had finally been elected and wanted to see them forthwith. A fortnight later, the adventurers were back in

Acre for a third time. Happily, on this occasion, luck was with them. The new Pope happened to be visiting the city, and was quick to recognize this opportunity to spread the word of God beyond Christendom. He gave the Polos the presents they sought, wrote a message to the Khan, and sent them on their way.

By a happy coincidence, today's ferries land their passengers across the bay from Acre, so on disembarking I make off immediately to see the scene of the Polos' comings and goings. The city's outskirts are modern, but the Crusader fortress at its heart encircles the mosques, souks and passageways of an almost perfect medieval Arab town. Eight hundred years ago the harbour would have been crowded with Venetian and Genoese galleys, for this was the premier Levantine port. The Crusades were at their height, and on cobbles shaded by silk awnings the aristocracy of medieval Europe could be seen. Ludolph von Suchem, a contemporary of the Polos, reported kings, princes and noblemen strutting 'with golden coronets on their heads, each . . . with his knights, followers, mercenaries and retainers, his clothing and his warhorse wondrously bedecked with gold and silver, all vying one with another in beauty and novelty of device, and each man apparelling himself with the utmost care.' According to von Suchem, Acre was also the home of 'exceeding rich merchants of all nations, who from sunrise to sunset brought merchandise thither from all parts of the world, and everything that is wondrous and strange used to be brought thither because of the nobles and princes who dwelt there.'

The Polos were lucky. Their stays in Acre coincided with a rare lull in its turbulent history. Eighty years earlier, Richard I had been routing its Arab defenders in the Third Crusade; twenty years later, the Mamluks were to seize it amid appalling bloodshed. Phoenicians, Assyrians, Romans, Persians, Byzantians, Genoese, Arabs, Ottomans and British have all at one time or another occupied this inconsequential promontory just 400 yards across. Others, such as Napoleon, were only driven back in brutal fighting. Ayas and Antioch may have been the ancient Middle Eastern gateways; Istanbul and Trabzon more recent ones; but Acre, for all its small size, has been a prize for Middle Eastern conquerors for the best part of three millennia.

Today's aristocracy still tethers its boats in Acre's picturesque harbour, but they look rather different from the vessels of Polo's time. The razzmatazz of today's waterfront, too, would have been absent then. But in the walled city Polo would have recognized the remaining caravanserais, some of which still take in travellers (one of the best ones is a youth hostel). And amongst many other architectural reminders of old Acre, he would have been delighted to discover a Pisa Square, a Venice Square and even a Marco Polo Street.

The Polos undoubtedly got to know Palestine well during their sojourns in Acre. The region is not mentioned in *Divisament dou Monde* for the simple reason that most of his readers would have been familiar with it, by hearsay if not personally. It would have been like telling Londoners about Southend.

Sadly, my acquaintance with modern Israel is briefer. As I scour the ports for ships, my impressions are limited to stacked containers, crumbling concrete, and detritus of both the vegetable and the human kind. Ships there are in plenty, but none can take me onwards. In Haifa, most are heading for the western Mediterranean. At the Aqaba Gulf port of Eilat, too, it seems that hardly any are going my way. I have a hopeful moment in Eilat, when a Greek captain hints that he may be able to take me as far as Aden. Unfortunately, his cargo is classified, so first he must telephone for permission from his Piraeus headquarters. I wait by his side as the call goes through. To my frustration I can make out little of what is being said, but eventually he turns to me with a shake of the head.

'Pchaa,' he declares angrily. 'They say I can't take you, just because I am carrying bombs!'

In the heart of the Arab Quarter of Jerusalem, where the street known as Ma'Alot Hamidrasha crosses Beit Habad, a persistent enquirer will find the Tabasco Tea Rooms. Its elderly clientele of bygone years has given way to young Palestinians slumped over the beer-stained tables, and the wailing of the *muezzins* is now drowned by the over-amplified sounds of Dire Straits. Overhead, dormitories echo to the cries and shouts of commerce in the surrounding alleyways; but it is a distant sound, for the walls are old and thick and the windows small. Arriving filth-encrusted from the desert, I take a shower and a bed and relish the sense of peace after the turmoil of my brief tour. Modern Israel, it would seem, makes few concessions to its biblical past. At Nazareth, I found apartment blocks covering the hills where Christ grew up; on the Sea of Galilee, fishing smacks have made way for speedboats and sailboards; at Beer Sheva, scrapyards ring the town. Only in the Golan Heights, the West Bank and Sinai, those barren lands so fiercely fought over, does the thorn bush linger undisturbed.

But in Jerusalem – whatever your background – you can forget the present and absorb yourself in history. Jews focus their attention on the Wailing Wall, part of a retaining buttress of Herod's Second Temple. Moslems pray at the Dome of the Rock, or at Al'Aksa Mosque where Mohammed is said to have seen Paradise in a dream. And Christian pilgrims come to the Church of the Holy Sepulchre, where Christ was once said to have been crucified and buried. Modern wisdom places the exact spot elsewhere, but sixteen centuries of tradition have made the Holy Sepulchre venerable in its own right. Certainly this was where the Polos would have come to collect their holy oil. And whatever one's own feelings on the matter of religion, it would be an obtuse visitor who did not feel humbled by this city which has more significance for more people than any other square mile on earth.

I spend three nights at the Tabasco Tea Rooms, and it is with the greatest reluctance that I pull myself away. Returning to Haifa, I continue my depressing round of the shipping companies. None can offer the slightest help. An assistant at the Port Manager's office smuggles me through to the quayside and introduces me to half a dozen captains, and I savour this wisp of hope. But the wisp disappears, as one by one the captains tell me their destinations: Naples, Marseilles, Antwerp, Liverpool, London, New York. In trade, as in culture, it seems that modern Israel looks firmly to the West. Banned from Moslem ports, her ships rarely pass through the Suez Canal, and eastbound foreign vessels seldom call.

'Why don't you try Piraeus?' suggests the helpful manager of Zim Lines, one of the firms I have been pestering. 'You might find a Pakistani ship returning home.'

Climbing the ramp of the *Paloma* just two weeks after I descended it, I feel rather as the Polos must have done as they returned under Papal summons. It has been a frustrating fortnight, with not a jot of eastward progress to show for it. The trip seems becalmed. But in spite of the disappointments (or perhaps because of them) I have learnt a lot: so it is in good spirits that I watch Mount Carmel recede. Perversely, I am still hopeful that my luck will take a turn for the better.

In Piraeus, the Port Authority Captain is sympathetic, but unable to tell me where any of his ships are going (although he seems to know where they have come from). However, I leave his office clutching the addresses of no fewer than thirty shipping companies in the streets behind the port, and this piece of paper is to keep me occupied for the next three days.

Athens street-signs never fail to thrill me. My base (a mattress on a balcony) is down ΟΔΟΣ ΑΡΙΣΤΟΤΕΛΟΥΣ, Aristotle Street, whilst other signs point to ΑΓΓΕΛΟΠΟΥΛΟΥ and ΨΥΧΙΚΟ – Angelopoulou and Psychiko. I also peer at brass doorplates bearing less lyrical names, like *Transmed* and *IntraEurope Express*, watched from the street corners by beady-eyed kiosk newsagents who peer inquisitively from apertures in their arrays of magazines, looking like hamsters which have just nibbled a peephole. I decide to give *Splosha Marine* a miss, but towards the end of my list *Christos Tsamis – Shipping Consultant* looks promising, and I make an appointment to see him.

Christos Tsamis is a lean, athletic-looking man – the sort you might expect to meet jogging in his lunch hour. Even before he speaks, his eyes tell me my mission is hopeless. 'Five years ago I might have been able to help you,' he commiserates. 'But since the hijacking of the *Achille Lauro* our insurers have put a new clause in their policies: no casual passengers.'

I can understand their point. Why should a cargo vessel take on board an unannounced stranger, a possible saboteur? At best, such a passenger might become sick and require medical attention at sea; at worst, a seasoned terrorist could blow up the ship.

'Besides,' says Christos Tsamis, 'I don't believe there have been services to Pakistan from here since – let me see, now . . .' He crosses the office and consults a file. 'Since 1982.'

I stroll back towards Aristotle Street, wondering how Polo would have tackled the problem. A born opportunist, he would undoubtedly have lost no time in booking a flight. The temptation is strong. Athens offers possibly the widest choice of discounted air tickets in Europe. In the space of a few blocks south of Syntagma Square, thirty or more travel agents compete fiercely for custom in what can only be described as a 'bucket hypermarket'. It is 23rd July. If I am to stand the slightest chance of crossing the Pamirs before the snows come I will have to reach the Chinese border by mid-September. The more I think about it, the more obvious becomes my next step. Ignoring the reproachful looks of the hamster-newsagents, I hasten my footsteps in the direction of Syntagma Square.

How easily old habits return! Within an hour of landing at Karachi Airport I am up to my ankles in cow dung, striding towards the city centre with a swarm of youngsters running alongside me. 'What your nay-am?' 'Where you-a from?' 'You play-a cricket?' The questions come in a flood, as they do whenever a European face makes an appearance on the streets of the Indian subcontinent.

It takes me two hours to reach the city, and although the perspiration is making rivers down my face I enjoy every moment. The pungency of the gutters vies for my nose's attention with the fumes from elderly motorized rickshaws, and both in turn are ousted by drifting smoke from a wood fire. Gaily painted lorries hoot delightedly at me. Children wave from rotting verandahs; water buffalo pout from storm-flooded fields. Dogs yelp, pigs snort. I am back in Asia, and the welcome is ear-splitting.

From humble origins as a fishing village and *dhow* port, Karachi has grown into a sprawling agglomeration – the leading commercial centre of Pakistan. 'Karachi, thou shalt be the glory of the East!' cried Sir Charles Napier when he became Governor of Sind Province in 1843. 'Would that I could come and see you in your grandeur.'

Grandeur is not a word I would associate with Karachi, though the British did leave behind some fine buildings, such as the Empress Market, larger than Covent Garden and dedicated to Queen Victoria just a hundred years ago. As for the rest, I fear Sir Charles would have been disappointed. Karachi's nine million residents live in undistinguished suburbs, overcrowded and occasionally strafed by savage violence, when the mutual hatred between Mohajirs and Pathans erupts in the alleys and streets. Only the small foreign community has managed to create safe

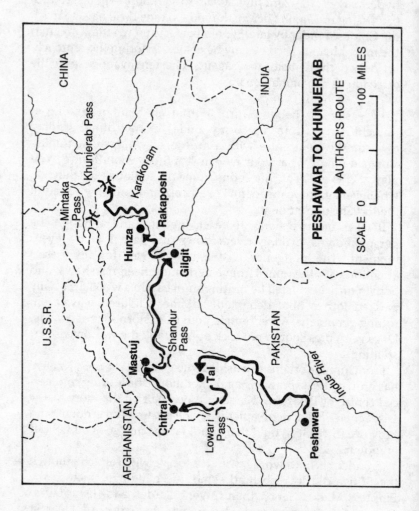

and bearable surroundings for itself out of the scrubland and swamp.

A glance at Pakistan's coastline shows how inevitable it was that a major seaport should develop here. The Indus has always been an artery for trade, and the city occupies a narrow strip between the marshes of its delta and the great deserts of Sind and Baluchistan. Yet curiously I can find only one passing reference to a port in ancient times. While silks and other high value goods were being carried across Asia overland, an embryo spice trade was already developing between the South China Sea and the Persian Gulf. Flimsy vessels hugged the coast, calling at every port as they made their cautious journeys round the Bay of Bengal and the Arabian Sea. Passing the mouth of the Indus, they took shelter in a harbour by the name of Barbaricon, and an old map shows this to be exactly where Karachi lies today.

Being seafarers, the Polos naturally considered making their journey this way too, but when they saw the vessels at Hormuz they changed their minds:

The ships are very bad, and many of them founder, because they are not fastened with iron nails but stitched together with thread made of coconut husks. They soak the husk till it assumes the texture of horsehair; then they make it into threads and stitch their ships. It is not spoilt by the salt water, but lasts remarkably well. The ships have one mast, one sail and one rudder, and are not decked; when they have loaded them, they cover the cargo with skins, and on top of these they put the horses which they ship to India for sale. They have no iron for nails; so they employ wooden pegs and stitch with thread. This makes it a risky undertaking to sail in these ships. And you can take my word that many of them sink, because the Indian Ocean is often very stormy.

Vessels stitched in this way continued to be used until the turn of the present century, so it is intriguing to read the Venetian's disparaging views. One would have thought that with hindsight he would have considered them – with all their faults – less perilous than his journey overland.

July will soon turn to August; my deadline for crossing the Pamirs is drawing closer; but I am still off course. I take a last look at the Arabian Sea, its surf languid in the summer breeze, before turning back towards the Silk Road and another sea, beyond China, 4,000 miles to the north-east.

North-west of Karachi, the route I had originally intended to take emerges from Iran, and threads its way through salt pans and bleached mountains to the Baluch capital of Quetta. This frontier city, close to Afghanistan and accessible only via high and difficult passes, seems an appropriate starting point for what will surely be the most demanding part of the trip. From Karachi it is a two-day journey, first across the Sind Desert to Jacobabad, then on to Sibi at the foot of the Brahui Mountains, and finally through the Bolan Pass. At this time of year the region around Sibi is one of the hottest in the world – definitely not a place in which to linger. For speed, if not comfort, the best way to cross this abominable desert is by train.

At first sight Karachi Cantonment Station appears to be preparing for some kind of siege, but on closer inspection I realize that this is its normal state. In Pakistan, it is sometimes difficult to remember that you are in a Moslem country and therefore seeing only half the population of any one place. The other half, being female, is required to stay at home. I wonder how the staff of Karachi Cantonment Station would cope if this were not so. As it is, eight ticket clerks are facing several hundred travellers demanding tickets. The queues extend out of the station concourse and into the street. Linear and orderly for most of their length, they become bulbous at the front, like grotesque onions, as more and more people lose patience and charge the ticket windows. Only the insistence of Ali, the servant of some friends with whom I have been staying, secures my ticket to Jacobabad and gets me to my train. 'It is my privilege to be helping you, Mister John,' he calls through the moving carriage window.

Karachi's square-set, mud-and-concrete houses soon give way to desert. On the occasional riverbank naked children wave at the passing train. Goats, oxen, buffalo and a herd of Arabian camels run from its approach. An old man squats impassively by the tracks, his *kamiz* and turban so caked with mud that he is almost invisible against the surrounding waste. At the many wayside halts, food and drink vendors peddle fried rissoles to be washed down with glass upon glass of hot sweet tea. At Sehwan beggars board the train, three to each carriage, in a well-practised routine. I give two rupees to a woman with four toddlers in tow, and her eyes sparkle. But one of my companions takes me to task. 'You should have given her one rupee only,' he admonishes.

Arriving in Jacobabad at midnight, I find that I am the only passenger alighting, and as the train rattles on its way I am left to savour the sounds of the desert night. The familiar drone of the crickets is punctuated by an occasional throaty gurgle from an unseen frog. Along the platform, shrouded figures on charpoys snore in rumbling harmony. Somewhere in the darkness a horse whinnies. Lulled by these gentle sounds, I give quiet thanks that I didn't book through to Quetta and stroll off in search of a bed.

Of the routes into Baluchistan, the Pass of Bolan is the most popular yet the most notorious. Alexander the Great retreated this way, and by the first century BC the first of several waves of Shaka invaders were funnelling through it from their Afghan homelands to subdue earlier settlers on the Indus plain. Nineteen centuries later, the British used the Bolan in their ill-fated campaign which was to culminate in the First Afghan War, and for the remainder of the British time in India it was guarded every bit as jealously as its more illustrious neighbour the Khyber to the north. In some ways the Bolan was actually more dangerous than the Khyber. The sixty-seven-mile defile is peppered with out-crops, offering perfect concealment for anybody planning an ambush – and history books and graveyards tell us that many have done just that. Add to this a tendency to flash floods, a fierce desert climate with an annual temperature range of more than 110 degrees Fahrenheit, and some of the most severe earthquakes recorded on earth, and you have the essence of the Bolan Pass.

'A bus to Quetta, *sahib*? Today? You must be joking, *sahib*, it is a holiday.'

Although for more than twenty years now a motor road of sorts has covered the 180 miles between Jacobabad and Quetta, the fiercely independent people of Baluchistan prefer to conduct their lives as if it wasn't there. Scouring the bazaar, I quiz the driver of every vehicle. 'Quetta, *sahib*? Sorry, *sahib*. Not today, not tomorrow. Sit down please, *sahib*, and take some tea.'

Deciding to take a few steps in the right direction, I walk to where the road leaves the town and prop my pack against a rock. After some minutes a jeep emerges from the haze. It pulls up, smothering its occupants and me in a fine dust. No, it is not bound for Quetta, but for twenty rupees the driver will take me to a junction perhaps fifty miles along the way.

I accept his offer and am soon at the turn-off, a group of shacks at a bend in the road. The jeep disappears. It is hotter than ever. Dusty faces peer shyly from doorways. The sun scorches my arms. I pick up my pack and start slowly down the road.

After what seems an eternity, the sound of an approaching diesel engine makes me turn hopefully, but the army lorry speeds by without stopping. A short while later I step behind a boulder to take some respite from the sun, and curse as a pick-up tears past.

It is a long half-hour before a third vehicle approaches, but it stops immediately and the driver beckons me into the back. We bounce along for some miles and then, to my dismay, turn in to a police compound. Am I about to be arrested again? Happily not. Station Commander Mohammed Taqi rises from his charpoy, salutes, shakes my hand and speaks in faultless English. 'Quetta, you say? Why yes, we should have no difficulty in getting you to Quetta. I will stop the first vehicle that comes. But first, I do hope you will join me in some tea?'

Commander Taqi is a colonel's dream of what a well turned-out officer should be. Shining from his bulging forehead to his brass-buckled boots, he makes the next hour pass almost unnoticed, enquiring politely but in detail about my journey and my opinion of Pakistan. A Punjabi, he finds little to inspire him in bleak Baluchistan, and I wonder what such an obviously able man has done to deserve this posting. A feud with a superior, perhaps? A bribe taken in a moment of weakness? Sadly I am not to find out, for a shout from the gatehouse announces that my lift has arrived.

The lorry is waiting by the police barrier, its engine ticking over, tassles and chrome glinting in the afternoon sun. Four Baluch faces eye me unsmilingly from under coiled white *pugris* in the wooden cab. It is clear what they think of this arrangement. I throw my pack on top, and climb in.

As soon as we have left the police post, my hosts brighten up. 'Police – *aach!*' snorts the driver, spitting in disgust. As none of the four speaks more than a smattering of Urdu or English, our conversation is somewhat limited, but using gestures and grunts I explain that getting the police to do my hitch-hiking is not something I have indulged in by choice. From this moment we are friends.

Like most of Pakistan's lorries, this was once a Bedford, but its original cab has been replaced by a taller and wider structure of timber, so that only the Bedford's chassis, engine and bonnet remain. The load-carrying part of the vehicle is contained within a high-sided superstructure edged in carved oak, and this extends over the cab, thrusting forward like the prow of a ship. Inside the cab itself, the seats have been replaced by a padded bench at a level which enables it to straddle the engine. The arrangement is splendidly comfortable, and its only drawback is that neither driver nor passengers, peering down through the original Bedford windscreen, can see more than a fraction of the road ahead.

Electric cables hang inside the cab like a fishing net set out to dry, with little apparent relationship to the functions of the vehicle. But by touching particular leads the driver can sound a choice of klaxons, make the cassette system burst into life, or illuminate arrays of coloured lights around the vehicle. As we crawl towards Quetta he demonstrates each function in turn. I am impressed, but it occurs to me that anyone watching this flashing, tooting lorry from the cliffs opposite will assume its occupants to have been touched by the desert sun.

The driver and eldest passenger introduce themselves as Tabar Lut Khan and Basheer Khan: creators, owners and drivers of this kaleidoscope on wheels. The remaining two are of lesser order, their duties to clear boulders from the road ahead and to keep the radiator topped up from wayside streams.

High summer means low water in the Bolan River, so on stretches where the road is under repair (or not yet built) we drive along the riverbed. Down amongst the jetsam, the power of the Bolan's infamous flash floods becomes dramatically apparent. Trees, boulders and twisted vehicles form tide marks to left and right. At one point several hundred tons of steel girder bridge have been carried downstream, to be smashed like matchsticks at the foot of a cliff. The river has also taken a terrible human toll over the years, adding to the carnage wrought by military campaigns. In 1841 half a British platoon – 33 men and 101 horses – was wiped out as they camped on a gravel beach.

Beyond the village of Mach the gorge opens out, and at last I appreciate what has drawn so many people to tread this treacherous ground. For the first time since arriving on the subcontinent my eyes see green. Grasslands are dotted with villages and farms, and distant hillsides are cloaked with the darker green of trees. By the roadside are camped a group of *powindahs* – black-turbaned nomads who brave the pass each spring when the Sind Desert becomes unbearable. Now, at the end of July, they are already preparing for the return trip, rounding up camels plump from summer grazing to be loaded with their scanty belongings and assembled into caravans.

Quetta, a dull town in a dazzling setting, is reminiscent of Erzinçan in faraway Turkey, and a moment's reflection tells me why. Like Erzinçan, Quetta suffers regular and severe earthquakes. Like Erzinçan, it has been razed and rebuilt within living memory (the last decimation was in 1935, when 23,000 people died). And as in Erzinçan, its inhabitants are well aware of their precarious perch on life. But there is a further dimension to Quetta's problems. For the past decade the people of Baluchistan and the North-West Frontier have played host to the largest assemblage of refugees the world has ever seen. The thought intrigues and horrifies me. I am keen to see how the Baluch have responded to their uninvited guests – and am to find out sooner than I realize.

On Jinnah Road, pungent and spicy aromas are emerging from an Afghan restaurant. Its charcoal stove has been set up to overlook the street with just this effect in mind. After my journey from Jacobabad I am ravenous, and the enticement is too much. I duck in.

As my eyes grow accustomed to the dim light, I make out low tables and the rich patterns of Afghan rugs covering walls and floor. Fans revolve lazily overhead. Seeing an assortment of sandals by the door, I take off my own shoes, thinking how incongruous they look among their leather-and-tyre-rubber neighbours. A six-foot Afghan in full tribal costume of *shalwar*, *kurta* and *pugri* beckons me to a corner where I sit on the floor, remembering just in time that I must keep my feet and left hand out of the way to avoid offending the other customers, who are giving me welcoming nods through the gloom.

The meal is a spectacular testimony to Afghan cooking. As well as my own *pilau* of vegetables and rice, I am offered the tastiest morsels from other people's plates. They keep arriving: small chunks of tender lamb, passed on saucers from hand to hand. I acknowledge each with an appreciative nod towards its source, sometimes an Afghan, sometimes a Baluch, smiling toothlessly from a corner or from behind a pillar. I am also showered with eighteen-inch rounds of hot *nan* – Persian-style unleavened bread – the pile growing faster than I can eat. And when the meal is over and we are all smacking our lips, fingerbowls of rose-scented water are passed round, followed by glasses of sweet lemon tea.

Some of the customers have propped rifles alongside their sandals by the door, and now they shoulder them one by one as we walk out into the blinding afternoon light. Copied from turn-of-the-century British and Russian designs, these lethal contraptions are still turned out by the hundred from backstreet workshops on the Frontier – a celebrated case of industrial espionage, which neither the British nor the Russians have ever been able to stop.

My new acquaintances, Baluch and Afghans together, stroll with me as far as the bazaar. I am moved by the apparent comradeship between them, but as we part company I wonder if it has been for my benefit. I am to find out sooner than I think.

6
North-West Frontier

If it were possible to arrange such things, a small plane chartered for an hour or so from Quetta's diminutive airport would reward you with one of the most breathtaking flights on earth. Imagine yourself heading north, and passing first over irrigated fields, followed by dry hill country blending into barren mountains. Directly below, you would see sinuous ribbons of metal and gravel marking the Khojak Pass, where road and rail thread their tortuous paths towards Afghanistan. As your aircraft cleared the range, a plain would come into view, drier and more desolate than before, with the skyline punctuated by a second chain of mountains – the Tobakakar – marking the border of Afghanistan. At this point the aircraft would bank sharply to the east – for even imaginary planes cannot cross this frontier unobserved – and yet another dusty wasteland would be revealed. Then, from the cockpit window, your eyes would pick out, not twenty miles from the frontier, a welter of tracks and mud dwellings that teem like an ants' nest. This unlikely hub of human activity, just visible through the desert haze, would be the refugee camp of Surkhab.

Eighty thousand Afghans have flocked into Surkhab during the course of its eight-year existence. They are desperate people, often carrying their entire worldly possessions on their backs. Some have set about building huts from the desert earth; others live beneath tattered canvas draped over bamboo poles.

Not having access to a plane – except in the imagination – I approach Surkhab by the more traditional means of the back of a lorry. Hitch-hiking from Quetta, I encounter countless vehicles laden with refugees, but the drivers are reluctant to stop. A white face spells trouble here. Finally, in desperation, I wind a khaki shirt around my head in passable imitation of the Afghan *pugri*, and a few minutes later secure my lift.

The lorry's cab door announces that the vehicle has been donated by West Germany – to whom, is not clear. During the rough four-hour journey its twenty or so occupants settle down on flour sacks and sleep, shuffling wearily to life as the first buildings appear. The camp consists of a single street, four miles long, and we stop every few hundred yards to pick up or let down passengers, or simply for the crush of people and animals to let us through. Occasionally, amongst the huts and shelters, a more permanent enterprise can be seen: a cement building, perhaps, or one of brick. At three points along the way knots of people are gathered round water taps, the only concession to modern living in this primitive place. To left and right the desert waits, ready to repossess, as it inevitably will, this pathetic human invasion of its territory. But today the people have other things on their minds.

'*Kandahar Mujaheddin: Zindabad!* Long live the Mujaheddin of Kandahar!'

Stepping down from the lorry, I am instantly recognized as a foreigner, and the cry goes up. The crowd is inquisitive rather than hostile, and I feel quite safe, particularly once I have established myself as British and sympathetic to their cause. But the very size of the throng makes it difficult to move, so when I am invited to take tea in a hut, I quickly accept.

The building is of wattle and daub, furnished with faded carpets and lit by a single small window at the back. The tea is *qahwa* – green, bitter and unsweetened – and it is served to me in the Afghan style with a bowl of sugared almonds by its side. My host has invited a group of men to join us. We settle down on rugs, a dozen mud-caked, khaki-clad figures sitting cross-legged in the gloom.

The men roll cigarettes and talk in Pushtu, grinning in my direction through gold-capped teeth. A youth is brought in, given a babble of instructions, and ushered to my side.

'My name is Fazall Mohammed,' he begins hesitantly, 'and these are my uncles. They ask you, please, to tell people that we desperately need ammunition for the *jihad*.'

The *jihad* is the Afghans' so-called 'holy war' – the resistance led by Mujaheddin (freedom fighters) against the Soviet occupation. Now, in 1987, it has been continuing for nearly eight years.

Despite heinous atrocities and untold casualties on both sides, the resistance shows no sign of abating, and international calls for a Soviet withdrawal have yet to find receptive ears in Moscow.

'Is the *jihad* carried on from here?' I ask.

'Of course. The *jihad* will be carried on wherever there are Afghan people. We want our country back!'

'How much longer can you keep going?'

Fazall is thoughtful for a moment before replying simply, 'Till we win.'

I spend the evening with Fazall's hospitable family, assailed and appalled by their descriptions of how dying Mujaheddin are ferried from the 'front line' to the Red Cross teams in Quetta. Driven by loyalty and faith, they are groomed to fight to the death; and from the perspective of mid-1987, it seems as if many more may have to die before Afghanistan is independent once more. Despite a comfortable charpoy, set out for me by Fazall, I sleep fitfully under the desert stars.

Back in Quetta, a message is waiting for me at the Allah Wala Hotel. Would I please contact Mr Haleem Aslam of the Narcotics Control Squad? The note has come from the Excise Office on Allamdah Road. At first I am inclined to ignore it, but, suspecting that Mr Aslam will eventually find me anyway, I decide to find him first.

'Ah, *sahib*,' says a friendly Punjabi from behind mountains of excise correspondence. 'Mr Aslam is presently taking tea. You will find him at the Café Baldia on Shara-e-Iqbal.'

The Café Baldia turns out to be a pink and mauve painted bungalow opposite the District Court. Its street frontage is occupied by a bakery, but at the rear I can make out a shady tea garden, surging with robed and turbaned tribesmen in animated discussion. A pall of tobacco smoke rises through the trees. I approach gingerly, but am quickly hailed by one of the few customers who is not a Baluch or an Afghan. The plump Punjabi comes forward, bows, shakes my hand, introduces himself as Haleem Aslam, and leads me to a table where two others are seated.

None of the men looks the part. Aslam himself is middle-aged and balding, his flesh squeezed into a faded shirt and slacks clearly bought in leaner years. His colleagues are of slighter build, of indeterminate origin, and similarly dressed but with the incongruous addition of turbans. Surrounded by several dozen six-foot frontiersmen, we make a comical quartet. Uncomfortably, I survey the laden ashtrays on the table in front of me and ask as casually as possible why they have sent for me.

'We know you have been to Surkhab,' begins Aslam. 'The camp is closed to foreigners – but no matter.'

He pauses to observe my reaction. I wait impassively.

At length he continues. 'You seem to make friends quickly. People trust you. In fact, would it be stretching a point to say that you have something of a *rapport* with our Afghan brethren?'

I glimpse what is about to come. Again Aslam pauses and again I say nothing.

He offers me a cigarette. 'You will have heard of our problem with the heroin smugglers. Two thousand kilogrammes came through last year. And that was just the amount we intercepted. . . .'

I once read that a kilo of good heroin could be picked up on the Afghan border for a mere £300. In London or New York, the same stuff would have a street value of £1 million. If Aslam and his men are seizing £2,000 millions' worth of heroin every year in Quetta alone, how much more must be slipping through unnoticed? The very figures are dizzying. In 1986, under pressure from Washington, President Zia launched an offensive on the drug traffickers. The penalty is no longer merely life imprisonment; it is death.

'We would like your help,' says Aslam, fixing me firmly with his eye. 'Merely to make enquiries, you understand, and to tell us what you find. You will be well rewarded, I can assure you. And of course your protection is guaranteed.'

Your protection is guaranteed. Aslam speaks the words with a conviction I do not share. I am sorely tempted to accept his offer: to learn more about the frontier's hidden economy, which possibly contributes more to its wealth than the official one. Yet I would be dabbling in a matter which is none of my business, and my ignorance could be dangerous. With so much at stake, can my protection really be guaranteed? I somehow doubt it. A mission such as this might well mark the end of the trip – if not the end of me.

'I expect you'll need time to consider,' says Aslam, reading my thoughts. 'Come and see me at the Excise Office whenever you wish. And now, Mister John, you will of course take tea?'

I spend a good deal of my night at the Allah Wala Hotel mulling over the idea of working for Aslam, and by morning I have made up my mind.

I will not be seeing him again.

For more than fifty years, every Monday morning promptly at 10.00, a narrow-gauge train used to steam out of Bostan Junction, a few miles north of Quetta, heading for the town of Zhob. The 1987 timetable shows it still to be running, but the stationmaster at Bostan Junction shakes his head.

'I'm afraid we've had some problems with this service, sir. They are what you might call engineering difficulties. Tribal rebels blew up a couple of bridges.'

The stationmaster points across the tracks to where the train sits forlornly in a siding. Already streaks of rust have appeared on the locomotive, and the green and white paintwork of the wooden carriages is peeling in the desert sun.

'It will be running again shortly,' he suggests optimistically. 'Why don't you have a cup of tea?'

Zhob – originally named Ford Sandeman after Sir Robert, who commanded the British forces in the Third Afghan War – can also be reached by road. But it is a long journey, not to be taken lightly, through territory where government control is minimal and tribal laws prevail. As well as the usual hazards of crossing deserts, travellers periodically suffer the indignity of being held up at gunpoint. Foreigners are considered good booty. As hostages, they can command ransoms of a million rupees or more, as against only 50,000 for a local dignitary – an interesting observation on human values.

For this very good reason Zhob has for many years been closed to foreigners. But unlike the forbidden areas I have come across so far, it isn't much guarded or patrolled. The road from Bostan Junction stretches invitingly into the desert: the same route, it would appear, as that used by the early overland traders between Peshawar and southern Persia. As I stand wondering what to do, a convoy of modern traders comes bouncing into view, headed by a station wagon with two Pathans riding shotgun on the roof.

They stop without my asking and beckon me on board. I climb up immediately, before they – or I – can change our minds.

The journey, although excruciatingly slow, passes without mishap, being punctuated only by frequent stops for prayers. The Pathans enjoy themselves hugely, alternating their lookout between roof and running board, and warning me of bandits behind every bluff. As we pass a police post, they cover me jovially with a blanket, but to the relief of us all the post is unmanned.

It is late evening when the convoy arrives in Zhob. The streets are empty and the few streetlights have long been switched off for the night, but my companions lead me through the blackness to a *muzzaffar khan*, a Pathan inn. The innkeeper eyes me doubtfully, but is finally persuaded to give me a primitive room. I am too exhausted to complain about the pile of rubbish by the door, or about the family of cockroaches which has made its home there. Closing my eyes and my mind to the watchful insects, I sleep deeply until the morning.

Buying supplies next afternoon in the bazaar, I feel ridiculously conspicuous amongst Zhob's dusty citizens. Predictably, as I try to buy a bus ticket to leave the town, a policeman taps me on the shoulder.

'You must come with me!'

In the police station waiting room, a faded notice reads:

FORT SANDEMAN FIVE-YEARLY CRIME STATEMENT

Murder	0
Riot	0
Hurt	0
Dacoitry	0
Robbery	0
Burglary	0
Theft	0

Musing on this enviable record, I await my turn for questioning. Has Zhob's low crime rate, I wonder, anything to do with the methods of interrogation used by Zhob police? I am soon to find out. After two hours and four cups of tea, the constable on duty escorts me to a waiting jeep. 'The Superintendent wants to see you,' he says briefly.

We drive across the town and pull up at a guarded compound. Stout iron gates swing open to reveal a timber and stucco bungalow, crumbling a little, but by the standards of Zhob quite grand. The Superintendent, a broad-shouldered Baluch, extends his hand warmly and introduces himself. 'Superintendent Kasi,' he beams. 'Call me Ghafoor.' I search the man's lined face for the anger and irritation which I was expecting, but find only a roguish twinkle of the eye. 'I suppose I should reprimand you for being here,' he continues, reading my thoughts. 'But to tell the truth, I'm delighted you've come.' He smiles reflectively. 'Not much happens in Zhob.'

Servants are hovering, and Ghafoor Kasi sends them off to prepare food. He whispers to me conspiratorially, 'Would you care for a whisky?'

My evening with Ghafoor is delightful not just for its unexpectedness. For the next five hours, oiled by the contraband whisky, our conversation ranges from tribal matters to national politics. Ghafoor's own Kasi tribe is from Afghanistan, but he himself grew up in Quetta and has taken a keen interest in Pakistani affairs. Many years ago, Ghafoor's brother was murdered – along with many hundreds of others – on the orders of President Bhutto, so not unnaturally he favours the greater stability of the Zia regime, despite the undeniable repression. We debate the merits of military versus civilian rule, and of Zia's call for a more fundamental interpretation of the Koran. Neither Ghafoor nor I give a moment's thought to the possibility that within a year Zia himself will be gone.

Ghafoor attributes many of Pakistan's problems to partition with India. 'It was forty years ago, but we are still suffering the consequences,' he declares sadly. 'I hear the Indians are too.'

I mention my visit to Surkhab, and my horror at the refugees' plight. 'Aha,' snorts Ghafoor, 'but do you know what those people were up to before the Russians invaded?'

I confess that I don't.

'Fighting!' he growls, eyes flashing. 'Always have; always will. It's in their blood.'

He pours another whisky.

'Mind you, the tribes on this side of the border are no better. Even the convoys get ambushed if the word gets round that a VIP is aboard.' He smiles wryly. 'That's why we pulled you in. After wandering round the bazaar as you had been, you wouldn't have stood a chance on the bus you were trying to catch.'

I blush as I recall the tap on the shoulder.

'Don't worry,' Ghafoor assures me. 'No harm done. You will stay here tonight, and tomorrow we'll put you on the plane to Dera Ismail Khan.'

A plane! I groan inwardly. Another flight is the last thing I want to take. On the other hand, despite Ghafoor's hospitality, Zhob isn't the sort of place in which a foreigner would want to stay longer than necessary. 'Is there no way I can get out by road?' I ask.

'Not if you want to continue this escapade of yours. In fact, not under any circumstances.'

Ghafoor must have noticed the defiance in my eye.

'I'll be taking you to the airport myself,' he says firmly. 'Now, do have another whisky.'

The flight is a short one, and I am pleased to see that Dera Ismail Khan is to the east rather than the north: I will not miss much of the Silk Road. Ghafoor has been called away, but his chauffeur drives me to the airport in the jeep. After ten minutes, he turns down a track and pulls up by a tin shed. 'Air-a-port, *sahib*.' And with a salute he is gone.

My departure from Zhob Airport borders on farce. The Twin Otter taxis bumpily to a halt beside the shed. Propellors still turning, its complement of three passengers – including myself – step aboard. As we do so, the terminal manager and his security guard (the airport's sole staff) stand to attention as if, at the very least, a minor prince were passing through. By mid-morning I am in Dera Ismail Khan, and nightfall finds me in Bannu, less than a day's journey from my next port of call.

Peshawar, city of spies, smugglers, racketeers, refugees, freedom fighters and relief workers, lies just inside Pakistan at the foot of the Khyber Pass. Officially billed as the seat of government of the North-West Frontier Province, unofficially it is

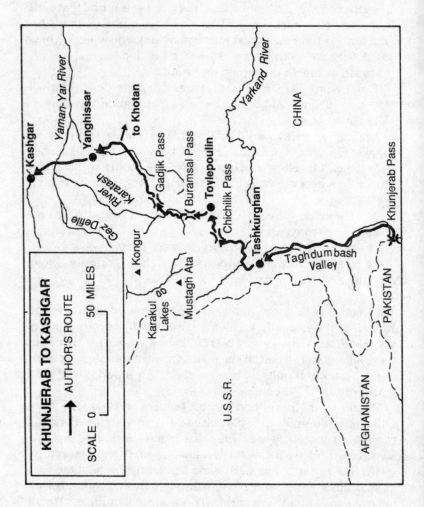

more notable as the Pakistan headquarters of the world's major intelligence services and drug trafficking rings. It is a city of intrigue, and knows it. In Qissa Khawani, the Street of the Fortune Tellers, the aroma of hashish hangs like a cloud. In the *lassi* or milk bars, rough Pathan fingers can be seen dismantling 'Red and White' or 'K-2' filter-tips and re-rolling them with the added ingredient of the day. Satisfaction is etched on their faces as they inhale the weed, like the expressions of those tweedy men in Condor tobacco advertisements. It seems comical to me that these robust characters should at the same time be quaffing milky drinks.

Peshawar is said to have more spies per square foot than anywhere else in the world. The Soviet KGB, its Afghan equivalent the KHAD, the Pakistani Special Branch and the American CIA are all well represented, as are dealers in contraband of every description from rifles to refrigerators. The Mujaheddin also have their headquarters-in-exile here. Needless to say, foreigners are watched closely and their movements monitored, for although Peshawar does receive genuine tourists and travellers, by far the majority of its visitors are on business with Afghanistan.

A friend has recommended the Khyber Hotel, a hippy hang-out of the 1970s conveniently placed between Saddar Bazaar and the Cantonment. The hotel takes some time to find – not least because its sign has fallen down – but my effort is rewarded. Rooms look onto an open courtyard, sheltered from the midday sun by a large awning, dragged diligently across bamboo poles each morning by the elderly caretaker or *chowkidar*. Few names have appeared in the registration book since my friend passed through three years ago; but the *chowkidar* nevertheless watches attentively while I fill in the various columns. Then, with the air of one who has done this a thousand times before, he leads me silently to an upstairs room, returning a moment later with a large teapot. '*Milluck chai, sahib,*' he says simply.

The teapot is leaking from a crack down one side. On the ceiling a fan is revolving, but too slowly to shift the sodden air. Across the courtyard lies a beam which snapped, I'm told, in the earthquake of 1984. Later I will discover the Khyber's remarkable plumbing – another feature remembered fondly by past visitors – whose only drawback is an all too frequent absence of water.

Generations may come and go, wars may be won or lost, but one is left in no doubt that the Khyber Hotel will continue to welcome guests to its collapsing rooms.

Outside in the bazaars, Peshawar's shops are brazenly ramshackle. Some combine shop with workshop, and if you peer into these you can make out leatherworkers, woodcarvers or copper-inlay wallahs hammering industriously in the gloom. As in most cities, the shopfronts are disfigured by cables and fluorescent tubes – but glance up to the floors above, and you may catch glimpses of an elegant architectural past. Exquisitely carved balconies hang crazily over the pavement, stacked one upon the other on pillars encrusted with a dozen coats of paint. In Andarshahr, the Jewellers' Bazaar, the buildings conspire to blot out the sky. But emerging at its western end you are confronted by the forbidding walls of Bala Hisar, the fort which for 150 years has protected the city's merchants from their covetous and trigger-happy neighbours in the mountains to north and west.

Through the shady alleyways swarm waves of tall Pathans, robes billowing, the occasional chubby Punjabi or thickset Chitrali almost unnoticed in their midst. '*Paise, paise?*' You turn and nearly trip over a bald, crippled ancient, a Wazir perhaps, his hand thrust belligerently in your face. Behind him strides a Sikh, instantly recognizable by his flowing beard and huge coiled turban. In Chowk Yadgar, where several lanes meet, a group of women swathed in the Pathan *burqqa* size up Swat blankets and Kaghan shawls in a haberdashery before moving in close formation to scrutinize the pungent contents of a vegetable stall. Moneychangers sit cross-legged on their safes. A water buffalo urinates in a gutter. A parrot squawks angrily at passers-by in what was once known as the Street of the Partridge Sellers. And behind it, like another lost migratory bird, the bewildered face of a Westerner appears momentarily through the crowd, only to disappear again in the relentless flow.

It is 6th August, an important date in the Moslem calendar. The Festival of Eid is about to begin. For a week now the streets have been all but impassable as the people of Peshawar prepare for three days of prayer and feasting to commemorate Abraham's sacrifice of a ram instead of Isaac. Every family, rich or poor, re-enacts the event, using a sheep, goat, ox or buffalo specially fattened over the previous weeks. On the eve of the festival the chosen beast is garlanded, daubed with coloured dyes, and led through the streets to its final resting place, where for twenty-four hours it will have the time of its innocent life. Family and friends gather to pat, pamper and cosset the animal, and present it with the finest grasses and oatmeal. At every corner, you can see sheep munching happily, eyes full of ovine contentment. The next morning – *slit*. The gutters run with blood as the carcasses are carried off and butchered. I have witnessed sacrifices before, and am told that they bring about a quicker and less agonizing death than the techniques of many Western slaughterhouses. But the ritual still sickens me. The only mitigating aspect of the Eid celebration is that much of the meat is given to the poor.

Nevertheless, my enforced rest is a timely one. Public holidays can be a nightmare for travellers, since the world about them comes to a complete, if temporary, halt. But after ten weeks on the move I am more than ready for a break, and I spend the time in and around Rawalpindi, renewing an acquaintance with an old friend and securing a visa for my entry into China.

The twin cities of Rawalpindi and Islamabad, three hours from Peshawar down the Grand Trunk Road, muster a combined population of well over a million. They have all but merged, but it would be wrong to imply that they are a single metropolis. They are as distinct as two cities can be. Rawalpindi, two thousand years old, exudes energy at every turn, its alleyways literally bursting with activity. Islamabad, on the other hand, at a mere twenty-five years of age, has so much space to spare that I fear it will always look half-finished. A purpose-built capital, it is the pride of Pakistan, but has as much life as Blaenau Ffestiniog on a wet Sunday.   •

In my experience each Chinese embassy has its own ideas about visas. In London they insist that you obtain a letter of introduction from Luxingshe, the Beijing-based China International Travel Service, a reply from whom may take a month or more. In Hong Kong, few questions are asked, and visas are issued almost on the spot. Having suffered already at the hands of immigration officials, I approach the Chinese Embassy braced for the worst, and can hardly believe my luck when I am given a visa the very next day – efficiently, courteously, and with hardly the batting of an oriental eye.

*

To appreciate mountains at their best, it is important to approach them as slowly as possible. I have never been one of those who can't rest until the summit is reached. For me, the joy is in the anticipation, as distant ranges become individual peaks, until finally the towering mass of one's chosen target emerges. With this in mind, on my second morning back in Peshawar, I am up early, combing the station for a bus to the valley of Swat. More than a hundred vehicles are gathered there, for Peshawar is one of the crossroads of Asia. After emerging from Afghanistan through the Khyber Pass, the Grand Trunk Road continues its dusty way east to Lahore and, in happier times, to Delhi. The Silk Road branch which I have been following sweeps in from the no-man's-land to the south, and from Peshawar heads north towards the Karakoram and the Pamirs.

It takes the best part of an hour to find my bus. This is not because the destinations are written in Urdu; translation is done simply and ably by the army of youngsters who follow my every step. The reason for the delay is that I am being constantly distracted by the buses themselves. Pakistan's public vehicles are folk art. Not a square inch of bodywork is unembellished, not a potential attachment point unhung with garlands, badges or chains. Their function as a means of transport is distinctly secondary, which perhaps explains why so many spend much of their lives lying drunkenly by the wayside. Pastoral scenes are favoured for the rear, with symbols of speed and/or destruction down either side. Occasionally the themes become intermingled, so that skyrockets appear to be showering bombs on cattle grazing peacefully in alpine meadows. Add to this, for each vehicle, many yards of hand-worked chrome strip and an extraordinary array of lights and horns, and you have a genuine transport of delight – an audio-visual show on wheels.

After the enervating heat of Peshawar, each mile of the ascent brings fresh energy to my jaded body. Slowly, tantalizingly, the bus grinds past dizzying drops towards the Malakand Pass, where in 1897 a thousand Sikh infantry under British command held off ten times that number of tribal warriors in one of the Frontier's more distinguished campaigns. From the summit, reached after a full hour of climbing, I can make out the pine-clad slopes of Swat, topped by cool meadows rising to dark bouldery peaks. Incongruously, they remind me of the Pyrenees. The silk traders, reaching this valley after months in central Asia, imagined they had found Paradise. Coming from torrid Peshawar, I can easily see why.

From Khalam in the upper valley, logging trucks ply the last few miles of dirt road alongside the foaming Swat River to a village by the name of Utror. From this roadhead, guidebooks tell of a path leading over an 11,000-foot pass towards Dir and Chitral. My companions on the bus have warned of pillage and rape in these hills, but on my first day I meet only hospitable shepherds who invite me into their huts to share meagre rations of *roti*, butter and sour sheep's milk. Back among mountains and trees, a sketch map in my hand, some basic provisions in my rucksack, pine cones crunching beneath my feet, I feel content. For the first time in weeks I find myself looking forward to the journey ahead; seeing it as something to be savoured instead of just a series of hurdles. At last I am in my element, and I bask in the simplicity of putting one foot in front of the other.

Suddenly he is upon me. Hatchet raised and face contorted in wrinkled menace, the woodsman lets flow a torrent of Kohistani abuse as he stands blocking my path. Fending off his raised arm, I try to reason with the old man in my limited Urdu as I look for a means of escape. He lowers his arm but stands his ground. Speaking in English provokes no reaction, so I make a guess at what is most likely to divert his attention from my neck. I take out my camera.

The effect is sensational. The man freezes to attention, the hatchet set on his shoulder like a rifle, and salutes. My film is finished but I press the shutter anyway, and as he hears the click his face breaks into a satisfied grin.

Over the pass, at the hamlet of Tal, the village schoolteachers are horrified that I should have come this way alone. 'The people up there are animals,' they warn. 'That old man was harmless – we often see him around the village – but some of them are quite mad. You're lucky they didn't shoot you. You must come back to the schoolhouse before they play any more tricks.'

Tal's six teachers are trying against heavy odds to instil some education into a people who see no point in it. The girls' school has already had to close – the parents of the valley have forbidden their daughters to attend – and now the boys' classes are facing rising apathy and truancy. Harsh winters and short summers have relegated education to a low position in the villagers' order of things, and the teachers confess readily to the hopelessness of their task. But they are a positive and spirited band – as is the village's police force, to which I am quickly introduced. I find them smoking and playing cards, having apparently given up trying to police a valley whose laws are delivered and enforced much more effectively by the village elders.

Both teachers and policemen, however, are proud of their community, and after several cups of tea I am taken on a conducted tour. As characters pop out from their houses to be introduced, I discover what it is like to be a VIP. The situation is so absurd that I catch myself folding my hands behind my back, Prince Philip style. Then, after making a 'guest appearance' at the school's daily English lesson, I join a task force to investigate why its water supply has dried up. The school is served by a metal pipe which threads its way through fields and terraces from an intake a kilometre up the valley. After an hour's search we find the cause of the problem: a joint has fractured, and water is spewing into the soil. Deftly, with no more than cloth, polythene and a strip of rubber, the teachers bind the fracture. Incredibly, the seal is tight; and after watching it for a few minutes to be sure, we return to the school in high spirits.

A rough track links Tal to the Chitral road, and on my second morning in the village the sound of a pick-up announces that a rare delivery of goods and mail has arrived. The police bundle me aboard – relieved, no doubt, to have me off their patch without further mishap. My teacher friends wave politely from the roof of their parody of a school, looking as if with very little persuasion they might jump on board too.

Fifteen miles from the Afghan border, 5,000 feet up in a valley surpassing all that I have seen so far, lies the oasis of Chitral. Its single-street, single-storey bazaar is bordered by terraced wheatfields, its higher slopes clothed in orchards of apricot, apple, walnut and mulberry. The hardworking people of this modest town give no hint that just under a century ago their ancestors conducted one of the most famous sieges in the history of warfare.

In those days (and, indeed, until the recent provision of a small airstrip) Chitral was cut off from the rest of the world for six months out of every twelve. In 1885, fearful of Russian intentions in the 'Great Game', the British made a deal with Aman-ul-Mulk, the Mehtar of Chitral, and established a Political Agent in the district. They needn't have worried; the Russians were occupied elsewhere. But when, ten years later, a series of unfortunate coincidences led the British garrison to hole up for the winter in the Mehtar's fort, the Chitralis rose in defiance. Nobody gave much for the troops' chances: nobody, that is, except a certain lieutenant-colonel called James Kelly.

John Keay, in *The Gilgit Game*, has described Kelly as 'a fragile-looking Irishman in the evening of an undistinguished career'. He was weak. He was pushing sixty. But he was in the right place to bring 250 Gilgit Scouts and a couple of five-hundredweight guns over the Shandur Pass to Chitral's beleaguered troops. How they succeeded, through shoulder-deep snow in temperatures so low that the mercury sank off the bottom of the scale, is one of the legends of the Indian Army. The fort still stands in their memory.

Eastbound silk traders used to reach Chitral via a notch of a pass called Lowari, and continued up the Mastuj River under the shadow of Tirich Mir to a second, higher col. This was the Shandur – the same pass over which the Gilgit Scouts were to struggle centuries later with their cannon.

Polo said of the region:

This district, and the whole country, is very cold. . . . On the top are wide plateaux, with a lush growth of grass and trees and copious springs of the purest water, which pour down over the crags like rivers into the valley below. In these streams are found trout and other choice fish. On the mountaintops the air is so pure and salubrious that if a man living in the cities and houses built in the adjoining valleys falls sick of a fever, whether tertian, quartan or hectic, he has only to go up into the mountains, and a few days' rest will banish the malady and restore him to health. I vouch for this from my own experience.

Lest anyone should think this was some kind of health retreat, he added later:

No birds fly here because of the height and cold. And I assure you that, because of this great cold, fire is not so bright here nor of the same colour as elsewhere, and food does not cook well.

My route to Gilgit, like Polo's, lies over the Shandur Pass. A jeep track now follows the Mastuj River for the first sixty miles, and the route is covered daily by a vehicle known locally as 'The Wagon'. Many of the earth's remoter communities are blessed with such a thing. Often their only motorized link with the outside world, the services are known by the vehicles' brand names: in Latin America *la Toyotá,* in the Indian subcontinent the Suzuki, in ex-British Africa the Land Rover, and in south-east Asia the Jeep. Apart from throwing an intriguing light on the market penetration of various motor manufacturers, these names provide an instant clue to the type of vehicle to be expected. 'The Wagon', however, holds its secret until just ten minutes before departure, when a cloud of smoke engulfs the bazaar, and out of it emerges a blue Ford Transit van.

I presume it is a Ford because that is what is written on the back. But welding operations on various parts of the bodywork over the years have altered its shape somewhat from that of its cousins on the roads of Europe. This vehicle has led a long and full life. Its personality shines from every corner: from the hand-beaten front wing panels to the single rear light. Close encounters on the Mastuj Road are, literally, written all over it. Furthermore, it is decorated inside and out in the best tradition of Pakistan. Chrome garnishes the sills and radiator, tinsel dances from wing mirrors, and plastic flowers bedeck the interior in such profusion that the driver's visibility is reduced to a few square inches front and rear. Other features not found on Western production models include an ingenious linkage between left and right seat belts, which enables them to be stretched across the entire width of the cab to provide a headrest for driver and front-seat passengers. This arrangement is preferred to the conventional use of the belts, presumably on the premise that any accident on the Mastuj Road is likely to be fatal anyway. The final touch is a cassette system featuring no fewer than eight speakers, which guarantees ear-splitting entertainment to take passengers' minds off the very real dangers of the journey ahead. This, in brief, is The Wagon.

As the vehicle draws up, a ragamuffin leaps down from the running board, yelling its destination with gusto. 'Mastuj, Mastuj-aa! Mastuj, Mastuj-*aa*!'

The Wagon already seems full. Indeed, I would have declared it full with half the number of passengers I find grinning down at me, not to mention the sacks of flour, rice and indeterminate substances, the three canisters of *ghee*, the four chickens and the goat. However, all move over to make room for me (the goat with some reluctance) and after a brief circuit of the town to make absolutely sure no more passengers can be found, we are away.

It is a moot point whether travelling like this is better than walking. I concede that it is faster, though taking into account the stops for vehicle maintenance and repair, social calls and essential recuperation/resuscitation of the passengers, the difference can't be great. Certainly, the effort expended to keep bruising to a minimum must be every bit as great as that required to walk the distance with an average-sized pack. All that can be said for vehicles like The Wagon is that they never fail to cement relationships by the time the journey is over. United in such adversity, I have known complete strangers stay friends for years.

The outskirts of Chitral mark the end of the paved road, and we spend the rest of the day jolting over gravel – sometimes on the valley's upper slopes, sometimes at the edge of the foaming water. In view of the instability of the area, some of the turns are plainly suicidal, and indeed the road has taken its toll in travellers' lives. But the Mastuj is not a valley where choices abound, and a brief inspection in each case confirms that the route the road takes is the only possible one.

I search for an end to the marching ranges. But each twist of the valley merely reveals more peaks, more cliffs, more scree. The land is parched, and occasional rainstorms often cause flooding as the water struggles to drain away. The villagers cope with these flash floods by evacuating their flimsy homes; the road engineers by punctuating the fragile surface of the track with wide, concrete-lined depressions, through which the floodwaters are guided by carefully positioned breakwaters. (These dips are known as 'Irish bridges', though my Irish friends claim no knowledge of them.)

As the day wears on, the road deteriorates and the 'Irish bridges' multiply, so I am thankful when, in late afternoon, The Wagon approaches a row of tumbledown stone huts and judders to a halt.

'Mastuj, *sahib*,' smiles the driver wearily.

A meal and a bed will be arranged for me in one of the huts, but before introducing myself to the incumbents I tiptoe to the river for an hour's contemplation of this extraordinary landscape. Although essentially a desert, the Mastuj valley contains ledges on which a thin soil has become established, and these shelves can be pinpointed by the streaks of green they make on the valley side – part natural, part cultivated by painstaking effort over the years. Mastuj occupies a patch of greenery rather larger than most, where two rivers come together in an explosion of white water. In the oasis itself water gurgles through a network of miniature channels, irrigating terraces of barley which already, in late August, are almost ripe. I sit in the shade of apricot trees groaning with fruit – so laden, in fact, that the village children fell fifty apricots with one thwack of a branch, and come running to give me handfuls. By my side are banks of sweet-smelling rosemary: not cultivated, but a natural resource to enliven the villagers' diet of chapattis and *dal*. Some of the houses are deserted. Their occupants have left to spend the summer on high pastures, for they cannot subsist on these ledges alone. But the doors of their houses (where they possess doors) have been left unlocked in the gesture of trust that is normal among people unsullied by a wider world.

Back in the village, I am introduced to Asghar Ali, a schoolteacher from further up the valley. Asghar Ali is returning home. His village is on the way to the Shandur Pass, and we agree to walk together. 'I hope you are an early riser, *sahib*,' he warns. 'I'm leaving at 4.30 a.m.'

The first hint of sunrise has yet to show as Asghar Ali and I creep out of the village; but we are far from alone. Like all people without electricity, the villagers of Mastuj rise and retire early, and shadowy figures are already making their way to the fields. We walk briskly in the chilly dawn. Hemmed in on all sides, the valley will not see the sun for another two hours, but when it does the temperature will soar. A wise traveller in Pakistan will always make an early start – even in the mountains.

Until fifteen years ago, there were no vehicles beyond Chitral, nor any track on which they could drive. I ask Asghar Ali about those days, and he smiles. 'They were dreadful! I attended school in Mastuj, so I used to do this walk all the time. It's about ten miles; that's three hours each way. When my father visited Chitral, he would be gone for days.'

Left: The summit of Nemrut Dağı in eastern Turkey is littered with 2,000-year-old statues which lay undiscovered until 1881.

Above: A Kurdish shepherdess watches goats graze the grasslands near Mount Ararat, a landmark for Silk Road travellers since before the time of Christ.

Left: *Burqqa*-clad women in Peshawar.

Left: On Pakistan's North-West Frontier, a rifle is a man's most cherished possession, and is lovingly maintained and passed down from father to son.

Below: Fellow traveller on the Shandur Pass.

Left: Clinging to the cliff face, some parts of the old Hunza Road are less than two feet wide.

Right: A Manchu fort dominates 2,500-year-old Tashkurghan, one of the oldest caravanserais on the Silk Road.

Left: The snows of Rakaposhi feed the streams of Hunza – the land James Hilton called Shangri-La. This was my last stop before China. In the Mir's palace, I speculated on the journey ahead.

Below: Even at low water, river crossings were sometimes hazardous and always cold. Here, a Hunza man approaches Passu.

Tajik women – 'the most sumptuously dressed on the Silk Road'.

Descending the Karatash.

When irrigated, the soils of the Taklamakan yield abundant harvests. This stallholder was one of several hundred at Kashgar's Sunday market.

Letter-writers still do a brisk trade outside Xinjiang's post offices.

Left: A Bactrian camel is worth eight yaks, nine horses or forty-five sheep.

Below: Reconnoitring the route through the Pamirs.

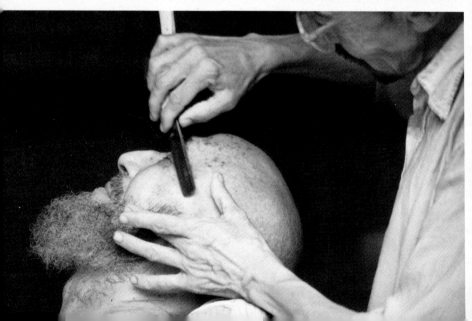

Left: Noodle-makers at work. Marco Polo introduced the noodle to Italy – where it became spaghetti.

Below: Tianchi ('The Heavenly Pool') leaves a lasting impression on the desert-weary traveller. At the head of the valley, Bogda Feng.

Left: Close shave in a Kashgar side-street.

Right: My home by Lake Tianchi – a Kazakh *yurt*.

Left: Recording an interview in Turfan's bazaar. People were surprisingly candid in front of the microphone.

Below: The Great Wall in the Taklamakan Desert.

Below: Silk Road travellers entered China's heartland at Jiayuguan, the 'Jade Gate'. For the Chinese, it used to mark the westernmost outpost of civilization.

The morning passes quickly, and by eight o'clock we are breakfasting at Asghar Ali's school. I dawdle over the meal, luxuriating in the rest and shade, but Asghar Ali agitates. 'You must make haste, *sahib*. The sun is already high. Soon it will be too hot to walk.' Forcing myself to my feet, I bid him a reluctant farewell, and before long am treading on rocks too hot to touch. I yearn for the shade of Mastuj's willow and mulberry trees. Sprawling briefly beneath an overhanging boulder, I write in my diary:

This walk is agony and ecstasy. Agony is tramping up an endless road in the searing sun; ecstasy will be when I find a stream tumbling down from the snows, and can toss the ice-cold water over my head, and drink, drink, drink. Agony is knowing that I still have more than twenty miles to go to the top of this wretched pass; ecstasy will be when I make that final upward step.

Later, another entry appears in barely legible scrawl:

It's 3.00 p.m., and the ecstasy has had to be postponed. The last ten miles have been devoid of streams, and my water has run out. In spring and autumn, I suppose, local people would have been around to warn me of this dry section, but in high summer they are up aloft with their animals. It's ridiculous. In the river 200 feet below me, a thousand gallons a second are thrashing their way towards Chitral and the plains. But the water is gluey with sediment, and would probably be undrinkable even if I could reach it.

An old man approaches and falls in with my stride. Although well over sixty, he keeps up with ease, and takes my mind off my thirst by singing as we march along. In return I regale him with some songs of my own, and will be forever thankful that no one else is nearby to hear my spirited crooning, complete with waving of arms, towards this old-timer of the hills.

At 5.00 p.m. my patience is rewarded. A bubbling stream of clear spring water flows beneath a pathside willow tree before tumbling through the terraces of Laspur, the final village before the summit. I splash and gulp luxuriously, closing my mind to the track twisting up the mountainside above me. All I can think of now is water, shade and rest.

An hour later, fully refreshed, I cast about for somewhere flat to pitch my tent. The search is both fruitless and needless. I quickly discover that precipitous Laspur possesses no flat land, but also that its hospitable people have no intention of letting me spend the night in a tent. I am frogmarched to the Rest House.

When they say 'Rest House' my heart sinks, because in India and Pakistan rest houses are often rather well appointed, their purpose being to provide accommodation for officials on government business. Such luxury I can do without. But on inspecting this Rest House I decide that no self-respecting government official would willingly stay there. A low building of hard-baked mud reinforced with straw, it blends into the mountainside and is clearly very old. It is a *muzzaffar khan*, a caravanserai. In the days of the Silk Road, travellers weary from the Shandur Pass would have regained their strength in just such an inn – perhaps this very one.

The *chowkidar*, an old Chitrali, gives the impression of having been expecting me. A kettle is boiling, and he has already set out tea things on a wooden tray. Bearing it aloft, he ushers me to a room, lights a candle and is gone without a word. The first thing I notice is that the room is blissfully cool. The second is a hen, clucking reproachfully at me from a rafter. It is some time before I take in the rest of the surroundings, because the room has no windows. Were it not for a small hole in the roof, it would be completely insulated from the harsh world outside, admitting neither light, nor heat, nor sound.

The furnishings are sparse. Two charpoys, seemingly every bit as old as the inn, grace the north and east walls. Lying on one of these, I drink my tea from an equally ancient table whose tablecloth is a grubby pink towel. Propped in a far corner is a rather newer charpoy, perhaps ten years old, which doesn't seem yet to have been brought into use. In the centre of the room is a hearth. Like everything else, it is covered in dust; yet the room doesn't seem unclean. The casual approach to housework is somehow in keeping with the inn's location and purpose.

The *chowkidar*, whose robes and face also boast a layer of dust, returns with plates of chapattis and steaming *dal*. He settles down on the charpoy outside and chatters amiably in Chitrali while I eat. Neither he nor I can understand a word the other is saying; but this doesn't seem to matter in the slightest, and an eavesdropper on our conversation would think we were old friends. The man picks up my notebooks and scrutinizes them, then settles down to read a colour magazine I have been sent from home. His wrinkled features become animated as he leafs through articles about wrecks off the Scilly Isles, the plight of the African rhinoceros, and white-water rafting in Sweden. Despite his remote posting, he is clearly a man of the world – a traveller in spirit, if not in fact.

It is curious how your appreciation of a place varies with the effort you have put in to reach it. Even by the standards of the North-West Frontier, this building is almost derelict. But after the purgatory of getting here, it has all the qualities of Paradise. I brush the dust from my feet, stretch my dog-weary body on the charpoy, mutter my gratitude to the *chowkidar*, and drift gently to sleep.

The Shandur Pass, at 12,500 feet, is neither high nor steep. The polo teams of Chitral and Gilgit pit their skills against each other regularly on its grassy summit. For six months of the year it is blocked by snow, but when I emerge panting after my four-hour climb from Laspur a scene of pastoral luxuriance meets my eyes. Underfoot the spongy sward is peppered with cornflowers of the palest blue. To left and right the slopes are dotted with sheep and goats; and ahead, a cluster of larger black blobs warns me that I am about to encounter my first yaks. Here, too, on the shores of an emerald lake, I will meet the inhabitants of those empty houses in the valley below. Swathed in sheepskin against the bitter nights, they spend their summers in makeshift huts of stone and brush-wood, watching their animals grow fat on pastures as lush as any in the world.

Eighty-five miles now separate me from the Chitral bazaar where I climbed aboard The Wagon three days ago. A troop of soldiers guarding the redoubt at the watershed inform me that Gilgit is still 142 miles to the east. But the way is downhill, and as I descend into the first hollow I catch myself leaping from rock to rock in imitation of the infant Gilgit River beside me. Considering that the nearest first aid is several days' walk away, this is irresponsible, to say the least, and after a few tumbles I force myself into a more sober gait. But I am intoxicated by these valleys, whose stoic people are managing to eke out a living against almost impossible odds. For the next four days I remain lightheaded, and even the denser atmosphere as I descend towards Gilgit does little to cool my excitement.

Seldom has such an unprepossessing town been blessed with such an eventful history. In the eighth century, long before the Silk Road brought its fertile valley to the attention of Westerners, Gilgit was being fought for by Chinese and Tibetans. Later, Hindus from the south and east occupied the town for a time, before being ousted by the Moslem ancestors of Gilgit's modern inhabitants. From 1877 to 1881 the British maintained a small agency here, replaced in 1889 by a more substantial one which became their listening post on Russian activity in the Pamirs. Set in a glade by the Gilgit River, the little fort quickly achieved fame; for not only did it have the distinction of being the most far-flung outpost of the British Empire, but in 1891 its paltry force of Gilgit Scouts saw off the Dards of Hunza in one of the most exciting campaigns of the British Raj.

More recently, in 1947, the Gilgit Scouts were again in the headlines when the Indian Air Force tried to bomb the town. At the height of the raid, the Scouts' band of bagpipers showed their contempt for the invaders by performing full-blast on the airfield runway. Sadly, history doesn't record what refrain they chose.

Today the town is peaceful: almost too peaceful, one feels, for a place which is supposed to be the commercial and military hub of northern Pakistan. True, the airport runway has been extended and metalled, a modern hotel built and some tourist shops set up; but for most inhabitants life is still a matter of what the next harvest will bring.

I settle in Abdul Karim's Tourist Cottage, which has been providing a dilapidated but popular base for expeditions to the region for more than twenty years. On a long table beneath walnut trees I plan my next move.

Should a foreigner in Pakistan tire of eating chapattis, *dal* and greasy mutton, there is a surprising choice of alternatives available for the price of a few extra rupees. Fresh vegetables abound in all but the smallest bazaars, and contrary to first impressions they do find their way into the kitchen. Further-more, when the visitor's stomach becomes queasy – as it often does – every shop from the meanest stall to the grandest city emporium carries a supply of Eno Fruit Salts and Woodward's Celebrated Gripe Water ('Important to Mothers') to put it at ease. I have never seen anybody actually buying these remedies, any more than I have ever seen a Pakistani shopper purchasing

Habib's Milluck Powder or Ahmed's Banana Cream Biscuits ('Crisp and Fresh'). But since crossing the Shandur Pass my guts have capitulated to the diet of the hills, and I comfort them with fresh tomatoes, Habib's 'milluck' and an occasional teaspoonful of fruit salts to help Nature's remedy take its course.

It is on my third day in Gilgit that I meet Taj. Some Western geologists staying near the Tourist Cottage have led me to his home behind the bazaar, and we are ushered into a simple living room furnished with cushions, rugs, and a single small table. Abdul Khaliq Taj is a Shia writer and poet who came to Gilgit many years ago in search of inspiration. Today he is a well-known radio broadcaster. As one of his sons serves cups of curd, I ask Taj about his life in this sleepy corner of his country, and am surprised at his reply.

'Yes, Gilgit people are certainly behind the times, but they are forward-thinking too,' he insists. 'They are not nearly as bigoted as in the cities.'

We go on to discuss Western and Islamic morals: the Western idea of 'love marriages'; the Koran's decree that a man may have up to four wives, but a woman only one husband; and how divorce in Pakistan is the prerogative of the man. 'This is really indefensible,' says Taj emphatically.

He sweeps back a lock of carefully groomed white hair. 'But things are changing. For instance, I assure you that I shall not dictate whom my sons should marry.' He smiles. 'I shall merely *interfere!*'

The electric bulb in the small room flickers and goes out. A paraffin lamp is brought in. Taj's slight features become animated as he warms to his theme.

'The Koran can be interpreted in many ways. The fundamentalists get all the publicity, but there are others who favour a more liberal interpretation. It is ridiculous, for instance, that my wife cannot walk alone in the streets of her home town.'

I mention some cities in my own country where this might also be unwise.

'You see!' he cries triumphantly. 'It is we men who create these problems. Really, Mister John, we should be locked away!'

Tea is brought, and the paraffin lamp casts a ghostly light over our seditious debate until it is time to go.

'Your journey is long, Mister John, and you will have plenty of time to consider the things we have discussed. Please find some space for them in your book.'

I walk home through darkened streets, and reach the Tourist Cottage without resolving the strangest thing about this unusual evening. For the entire three hours his wife remained hidden in another room.

By the time it reaches Gilgit, the Gilgit River has acquired a huge volume of water from tributaries draining several hundred square miles. A hundred and fifty feet of glutinous, foaming current separates its boulder-strewn banks. Twenty miles further downstream this torrent disgorges itself into the even greater flume of the Indus. But first, just below the shaky suspension bridge leading to Gilgit's bazaar, it receives the grandest and most famous of its tributaries. The Hunza River rises in permanent snowfields on the Chinese border, and is nurtured by several major glaciers before tumbling past the terraces of Karimabad into the shadow of Rakaposhi. Here it plunges into one of the greatest chasms on earth. The waters twist and thrash in their effort to find a course between the jumbled boulders, some of which are so hemmed in that they lie in permanent shade. More than a river, for much of the year it is a raging stream of mud. At its peak in July it is said to carry a million tons of sediment every day.

The reason is not hard to find. This is the heart of the Karakoram, the 'crumbling mountains', home of no fewer than twelve of the world's thirty highest peaks. In geology as in life, such magnificence usually spells youth, so it is hardly surprising that this is the youngest of the earth's mountain ranges. And it is still rising. Most geologists now agree that the continents float and drift, and that in the Karakoram we are witnessing the collision of the Indian subcontinent with the main Asiatic mass. The force can be compared to that of a vehicle being driven into a concrete wall. The wall may crack and give, but it is the lesser mass, the vehicle, which crumples. In the Karakoram the line of impact is thought to run roughly from Hunza to Ladakh, and recent measurements along this line suggest that India is ploughing into Asia at the reckless speed of thirty millimetres per year.

In the Hunza gorges, generations of Silk Road travellers have flirted with this monster of a stream, coaxing and dragging their bucking animals along a path at one moment 300 feet above it, at the next almost within range of its muddy spray. Peter Fleming and Ella Maillart, returning from Beijing in 1935, described the gorges as the last great hurdle on their nine-month, 5,000-mile journey. Eric Shipton also regarded them with respect. With typical understatement he recounted, in *Blank on the Map*, the following incident from the 1937 Shaksgam Expedition:

Below Hunza, a great landslide had occurred a few days before. This dammed the river, which, when the dam burst, swept away the road and caused much havoc, somewhat impeding our return to Gilgit.

One bank carries the old Hunza Road; the other, since 1970, has been occupied by the masterpiece of civil engineering known as the Karakoram Highway. Started by the Pakistanis and completed with the help of the Chinese, this 650-mile strip of tarmac was built at the cost of hundreds of lives on the Pakistan side alone; in China, where work is still continuing, the toll will be higher still. Bombarded by rockfalls and threatened by glaciers, it is kept under repair by the Pakistan Army's 'Frontier Works Organization'. Bulldozers labour continuously to sweep away the debris (or, if the landslide is too great, to squash it with their caterpillar tracks) and platoons toil over drums of boiling bitumen to repair the battered surface. The Army boasts that no fault, even a glacial surge, is allowed to close the road for more than twenty-four hours, and so far this pledge has been kept.

For three days I observe this wonder of the world from across the river. Gilgit people have assured me that I can get at least halfway to Hunza on the original path, if I am willing to wade across the side streams where bridges have been washed away. Along most of its length the path is wide enough for animals to walk two abreast, but in places it narrows to less than a couple of feet. At three points makeshift bridges were built across cliff faces where no ledge could be cut, and I am relieved to find these still in position, because for twenty miles a return to Gilgit would be the only escape. As it is, my greatest difficulty comes where a glacier cuts the path. I tread cautiously on its veneer of rubble, since a slip would land me in the river. There are no cemeteries for the dead here; anyone going over the edge is instantly swept away.

Beyond the village of Chalt, the old road crosses a suspension bridge to join the new. Between here and Hunza, I have the chance to experience at first hand what has been described as one of the world's most terrifying bus journeys. I have scarcely reached the tarmacadam when a bus stops for me. The gorge becomes progressively more constricted, until the nearest safe ground seems to be on the opposite side of the defile. The road is hewn out of the cliff face, its rock ceiling threatening to decapitate unwary passengers on the roof. The river below is unseen but keenly felt – especially when squeezing past other vehicles. It is said that this section was built by lowering workers on ropes to drill holes and place explosives. A sign warns drivers to beware of rockfalls, but fails to suggest what they should do if they encounter one. As we pass the danger area, a second sign invites us to 'relax'.

A member of the Royal Geographical Society's recent Karakoram Project pinpointed a further hazard:

Drivers aim their vehicles directly at oncoming traffic, which by definition is driven by incompetent fools. With cries of *Inshallah!* (the Will of Allah) the oncoming infidel is either forced off the road, or at least caused to take violent evasive action. Of course, the belief that God is on your side is strengthened if your vehicle is bigger than the one ahead. At the moment of truth, however, the driver with the stronger nervous system is he who does not care if the route he is taking goes to the gates of Heaven or the next checkpost.

The strategic importance of this road accounts for the rash of police checkpoints along it, but little can explain the lifelessness of the checking officers, who are supposed to stop vehicles and note any foreigners aboard. To help in this they are supplied with smart registration books, which make splendid reading for anyone with an hour to spare. Since the growth of tourism the officers now wave through much of the traffic, stopping mainly the long-distance buses. The book is passed through the bus windows and the required information inserted by the passengers themselves. At one post I find myself following an adventurer called Ziggy Stardust; at another, a trio whose occupations are given as butcher, baker and candlestick maker. Captain Kirk, Johnny B. Goode and Margaret Thatcher have all passed this way, not to mention a certain Inspecteur Clouseau – on the track, no doubt, of another '*bömb*'.

When not entering my name in these books or glancing

nervously ahead or upwards, I listen to the conversations of my fellow passengers, and find myself, amazingly, understanding them. They are speaking Urdu, but their talk is similar to that of the Nepalese with whom I once spent some months. The link is an odd one. Although written in the Arabic script, Urdu is in fact an Indo-Aryan tongue from the same group as Hindi and Nepali. To a Nepalese ear the chatter in the bus would have a familiar ring, but Nepali- and Hindi-speaking people can't read Urdu newspapers or books, because their language is written in Devanagari – an entirely different script.

Emerging from the canyon, the bus picks up speed along a terraced hillside shimmering with wheat and barley. Some of the crop has been scythed and lies in golden bundles, waiting to be threshed and winnowed. Gusts of wind from Rakaposhi's snowfields bend the trees, and in the orchards children run to gather apricots which are falling like rain. Women walk unveiled by the roadside; for we have arrived in the northernmost of Pakistan's ancient kingdoms, the land James Hilton called Shangri-La. With a last flourish of his steering wheel, the driver deposits a layer of dust on a posse of Hunza's citizens as the afternoon bus from Gilgit slews to a halt.

For centuries isolated by impossible terrain on all sides, Hunzakuts live almost entirely on the fruits of their small but fertile valley, and have succeeded in creating the kind of society towards which many of us are still striving. They favour cooperation rather than competition, each family growing just enough cereals and fruit to feed themselves, under the watchful eye of their sovereign, the Mir. In summer, a Hunzakut's breakfast, lunch and dinner will consist of one of the valley's twenty-two varieties of apricot, while in winter they supplement their *roti* with flour milled from fruit stones. This simple diet, coupled with a hard, healthy lifestyle, may be why Hunzakuts have the highest life expectancy in Asia. One man, who died recently at a supposed age of 120, had persuaded the editors of *The Guinness Book of Records* that he was the oldest person in the world.

As Moslems, Hunzakuts claim to be teetotal, but are known to be keen secret drinkers. Wine is made in quantity from Hunza grapes, and the much-acclaimed 'Hunza Water' is no less than brandy distilled from mulberries. Add to these another local feature – hedgerows made from marijuana plants – and you can see why Hunza's weatherbeaten characters go about the fields with a spring in their step.

At the Karimabad Hotel I am amply fed and watered, and decide to stay for a couple of nights to regain my strength. It occurs to me that I should feel guilty about this wanton laziness, but I don't. Occasional rest days are as vital to the traveller's well-being as good food and clean water. So I spend the day drinking glass upon glass of 'milluck chai', and, as if in retribution, a dust storm passes over during the afternoon, taking with it the flimsier parts of the hotel. To a contact lens wearer, windblown dust is a harbinger of unfathomable misery. I dive for my bed and cover myself with a blanket until the storm has passed. My host thinks I have quite left my senses.

My room-mates in the Karimabad Hotel are Andrew and Dave, a couple of likeable Englishmen forced down from a climbing trip by a bout of illness which struck Andrew on the lower reaches of the Hispar Glacier. He suspects amoebic dysentery, and spends most of the first night being sick in the toilet next to my bed. The next day he confesses to being not only sick but homesick.

'How long have you been away?' I ask.

'Five days,' he declares sadly.

Dave, who has helped his friend down from the glacier, is quite willing to stay with him until he is fit again, but Andrew feels a spoilsport. By the second morning he has come to a decision. 'I'm going home,' he announces.

I can understand his feelings. Eight years ago, in Rio de Janeiro of all places, when I was new to travelling, I watched a plane take off with a friend who was returning to Europe, and although I was in the pink of condition I found myself desperately wanting to go home too. A couple of weeks later, when the journey had taken a turn for the better, I recalled my earlier wish with disbelief. I am sure that Andrew would do the same, but he has set his heart on going home and I don't try to dissuade him. His sickness and depression remind me how lucky I am. Not only have I stayed healthy so far, but for several weeks now I have felt completely at ease with my surroundings. Whether hitch-hiking on a mountain road, or arriving late at night in a strange city, or setting out on foot up a valley which may or may not take me where I want to go, I have been excited by the challenges of the trip. Sometimes, walking alone, I have burst into song or danced a jig, simply to give vent to the pleasure of being precisely where I happen to be. I have talked to other travellers about these unexplained surges of well-being, but few seem to share them. They come, I suppose, with time and confidence. They are certainly worth cultivating.

I am on the brink of China. As Dave and Andrew board their bus for Gilgit and home, I start walking north. The Hunza River remains as powerful as ever, and with the rising altitude the landscape becomes even more austere. At Gulmit the Karakoram Highway disappears beneath debris brought down by the Gulkin Glacier, and an army bulldozer is ferrying pedestrians through the meltwater. At Passu the Batura Glacier, thirty-five miles from source to snout, has torn away part of a concrete road bridge and deposited it neatly to one side. Traffic is light, and when a cargo jeep offers me a lift I quickly accept. Bracing myself against the bitter slipstream on the tailgate, I am rewarded with a grandstand view of peaks in three countries – China, Afghanistan and Pakistan – as we roll up to the border post at Sust.

It is 5th September. The Khunjerab Pass, though still tantalizingly hidden from view, is just two hours away. Beyond lie the Pamirs, and a new challenge. Will I be able to cross them before the winter snows arrive? At best it will be touch and go.

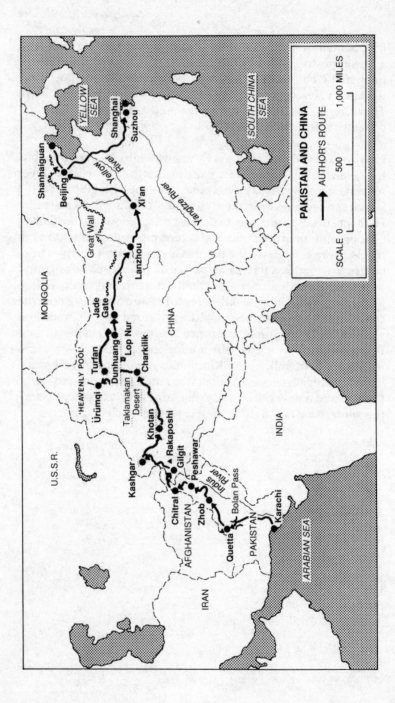

PAKISTAN AND CHINA

→ AUTHOR'S ROUTE

SCALE 0   500   1,000 MILES

7
Into China

The Pakistan–China frontier is of surprisingly recent origin. Though the Khunjerab range has always been a cultural barrier, the Hunzakuts and Tajiks whom it separates have never expanded sufficiently to define a mutual boundary. In a region of appalling communications, people understandably look downstream for their contacts with the outside world – the Hunzakuts to Gilgit, the Tajiks to Kashgar.

But towards the end of the nineteenth century, the 'Great Game' being played by Britain and Russia demanded that this inhospitable region be explored, surveyed and opened up. In 1891 a detachment of Russian officers with thirty Cossacks raised the Tsarist flag in the Little Pamir, establishing a fifty-mile frontier along the crest of the Hindu Kush and posing a direct threat to Britain's monopoly on Hunza's external affairs. The British responded in the fashion of the day by sending expeditionary forces, first to subdue the Hunzakuts and then to establish once and for all where India's frontier should be. Sir Mortimer Durand, having carried out the latter task in the summer of 1893, reported that the British need have no fear of further Russian advance; the roads over the passes were hardly wide enough for a caravan in single file, let alone a military force.

As it happened, events on other fronts were soon occupying military minds in London and Moscow, and for the next seventy years the Pamirs saw only the occasional missionary, diplomat or adventurer. In 1947 the British abandoned the Indian subcontinent, and during the next few years the Chinese consolidated their sovereignty over Xinjiang. But the Russian threat – real or perceived – continued to dominate affairs on both sides of the divide. So when, in 1960, work started on a highway across this so-called 'roof of the world', it was to be a military road. A quarter of a century was to pass before it would be open to all comers.

With these thoughts in mind, I prepare for surprises as I wedge myself into the back of a pick-up for the fifty-mile crossing to China's Pirali border post. The first thirty miles are indeed sensational, the jeep bouncing and sliding across steeply angled boulder slopes as it struggles to gain height. But the summit, which I had romantically imagined to consist of a notch in an otherwise impenetrable divide, turns out, like the Shandur, to be a broad plateau, its slopes rising gently to snowfields perhaps 500 feet above. The actual watershed is distinguished by a couple of roadside slabs, announcing in Urdu and Chinese that we are passing from one country to the other. The inscriptions do not mention that, at 16,188 feet, this is the highest paved road in the world. But in these gentle alpine meadows the road somehow does not seem out of place. We could almost be in Austria.

Camel drivers crossing the Pamirs always used to favour the Mintaka Pass, a few miles west of the Khunjerab, and when we give a lift to a Tajik shepherd I attempt to ask him why. He answers in wild gestures. The Mintaka is lower, he seems to be saying, though steeper on its northern side. But the deciding factor appears to have been that the Khunjerab leads into deep canyons on the Pakistan flank – now dynamited by the road engineers, but in earlier times impassable. The Tajik makes a motion to indicate camels immersed up to their necks.

A mile into China, the surfaced road comes to an end, and we bounce over rough gravel for the remaining fifteen miles to Pirali. A barrier decrees, in four languages, 'ALL VEHICLES HALT'.

I approach the immigration building with some apprehension, because a rumour has been circulating that only travellers with a special endorsement on their visas will be allowed to enter China here. The Chinese Embassy in London knew of no such rule, but when I pressed them they admitted that they hadn't been aware the Khunjerab route was open at all. To be turned back now would be unthinkable. Everything depends on the man behind the desk, in a smart People's Liberation Army uniform a size too big for him, who is going through the passports of those ahead of me, slowly, meticulously, with not the hint of an expression on his broad oriental face.

A British family is ahead of me in the queue, and I ask how long they have been waiting. Two hours, comes the reply. The four of them are surrounded by luggage, including a large video camera on which all eyes have been fixed since I entered the hall. The father is taking seriously his role as guardian of family and possessions, and is showing signs of strain. He snarls at everyone, especially those with questions about the video equipment. But as a fellow countryman I am singled out as a friend rather than a foe, and we all settle into conversation. They are a *pot-pourri* of everything that is British: well-spoken, well-heeled, and totally at odds with this desolate place. We talk about cricket, *The Archers*, and long-forgotten visits to Tunbridge Wells. When I mention what is uppermost in my mind – the present and the immediate future – they politely but firmly change the subject.

The situation at the counter is deteriorating. Some Pakistanis have been refused entry and are creating a scene. They shout at the immigration man in broken English, hurling insults which bounce ineffectually around the room. Eventually, raising clenched fists in a last gesture of defiance, they storm out. The immigration man continues inspecting the pile of passports as if nothing has happened.

It is my lucky day. An hour later I emerge blinking into the sunlight, clutching my passport with its treasured entry stamp. The rumour was false; I am free to continue. My British friends have also been admitted, and take off in a station wagon which, miraculously, has come to meet them. I join a collection of local vagabonds aboard the bus to Tashkurghan.

With furious blasts on the airhorn, the driver, a plump Han Chinese, is summoning her remaining passengers from the dining shed. Such is the urgency of her volleys that the tables are left littered with half-consumed bowls of noodles, to be discreetly devoured by Tajik children waiting in the wings. With engine screaming, the bus crawls fifty feet in first gear, then halts. Driver and conductor vanish into a compound. As ten minutes become twenty and then thirty, we abandon the vehicle one by one and return disconsolately to the now empty tables. Tashkurghan, four hours away, is not going to be reached before dark.

The sun is setting when the bus once more collects its passengers and lurches down the rutted road. I peer into the void. Viewing from the right-hand side is impossible because the scratches of years have made the windows opaque, but on the opposite side they have lost their glass altogether. I pull out my sweater and balaclava, settle down on the left side, and watch my first Chinese night descend.

In contrast to India and Pakistan, the land north of the Himalayan watershed is a plateau. Never less than 10,000 feet high, and rising in places to 17,000 feet, it extends for more than a thousand miles. The Himalayan chain and its outliers form a barrier to the Indian Ocean monsoons, so the region is in effect a mountain desert. My eyes are greeted by a landscape of stones. Stones cover the hillsides, spilling over to choke the riverbeds. Stones form the road. The horizon, where it is not of snow or ice, is of stones.

Marco Polo arrived on the Pamir plateau by way of Wakhan – now part of Afghanistan – and in doing so has provided us with one of the few precise references to the ancient route:

When the traveller leaves Wakhan, he goes three days' journey towards the north-east, through mountains all the time, climbing so high that this is said to be the highest place in the world. . . . The plain, whose name is Pamir, extends fully twelve days' journey. In all those twelve days there is no habitation or shelter, but travellers must take their provisions with them.

The path from Wakhan, and hence from Herat and Iran, joins the Tashkurghan road at an unsigned turn-off just sixteen miles from Pirali. This animal track was one of the three main branches of the Silk Road in central Asia, but the junction provides no clue to its significance. The bus hardly slows.

I have been looking for signs of life amongst the rubble, and am about to give up when suddenly a group of wild camels appears to the north-west. There are twenty of them, prancing and cavorting in the evening light, and I lean from the open window to watch adults and young at play. They haughtily ignore the bus with its plume of dust, a momentary intrusion into their natural world.

Xinjiang is the home of the last truly wild camels on earth. In the Middle East and India the Arabian camel has long been domesticated alongside the ox and water buffalo, but here on the high Steppe its Bactrian cousins still roam free. They migrate with the season and mate in January and February, so that after a fourteen-month pregnancy their young are born among the opening flowers and melting snows of the Pamir spring.

Unlike its Arabian counterpart, the Bactrian has two humps, and is also blessed with other features to help it survive the harsh conditions of central Asia. Most prominent of these are the double rows of thick lashes that protect its eyes from the searing Taklamakan sandstorms – arguably the only agreeable things about a beast famous for its mean temper and tendency to bite and spit.

In truth, though, the people of central Asia have cause to be grateful for this odd creature which Allah has set amongst them; for, despite its temperament, it is uniquely adapted to its role as 'Ship of the Desert'. The camel's low metabolic rate enables it to go without water for two weeks in summer and up to three months in winter, when it may lose a third of its body weight without noticeable ill effects. A thirsty camel presented with water will drink as much as twenty-five gallons, a quantity which would easily kill any other creature.

Contrary to popular belief, the camel's water is stored throughout its body, and not just in the humps, whose main purpose is to provide the food on which it survives when grazing is thin. So the state of the humps is a good guide to the condition of the animal. Firm, upstanding humps signify a well-fed beast; floppy or flimsy ones a camel to be avoided.

Another clue to a camel's well-being is the quality of its coat, and in the Bactrian case this is particularly important since it relies on a thick covering to survive the Xinjiang winter. The shaggy beasts I have just spotted have little to fear in this respect; in readiness for autumn they have already acquired a fleece lush and brown from end to end. The same woolly growth sprouts from their enormous padded feet, and tufts of it crown the dome of each hump. The Bactrian camel's fleece makes superb blankets and rugs, and is so highly prized that owners have to guard their animals night and day to stop their neighbours making off with hunks of wool. When spring comes and the wild camels rub their moulting coats against trees and bushes, enterprising villagers roam the Steppe to collect the scraps. Small wonder, then, that the camel is the most valuable of all animals in the Pamir herdsman's life. I learn later that a single beast is worth eight yaks, nine horses or no fewer than forty-five sheep.

Christina Dodwell, in *A Traveller in China*, tells how the House of Dodwell trading company once used Bactrian camels to carry Chinese tea to Russia, where it was prized for its mellow yet full-bodied flavour. Later, when railway trains replaced the camel caravans, the firm's Russian customers complained that Dodwell's tea had lost its distinctive taste. Investigations showed that the missing ingredient was camel sweat, absorbed into the tea through its hessian wrappings over a journey of several months; the sweat-free leaves were decidedly inferior. Immediately, Dodwell's consignments were packed with old camel hairs in the bags; the flavour returned to the tea, and the company's reputation was restored.

The bus continues through the blustery night, its occupants huddling deep into their greatcoats as squalls burst through the glassless windows. I scan the blackness ahead and eventually spot the red beacon on the skyline which marks our destination. The slowly blinking light atop the mast of Tashkurghan's radio station is known to all who live in the valley, and has been a welcoming guide for many a recent traveller. By contrast, the town's single street is in darkness. The arrival of electricity has not altered the habits of two thousand years, and Tashkurghan's citizens are clearly tucked up in bed.

A town called Tashkurghan was described by Ptolemy as being one of the most important caravanserais on the road to Seres, the land of silk. Was it this, or one of its two namesakes in Afghanistan and near Tashkent? We cannot be certain. But we do know that the Chinese writer Huen Tsang rested here for five days during his seventh-century wanderings, and the Manchu fort which he described can still be seen. Unfortunately the same cannot be said of the *tash kurghan*, or stone tower, which gave the town its name. Nevertheless, as I step down into the darkened bus depot, I am conscious of being one of a long line of Pamir travellers who have sought refuge here. Like others before me, I gratefully accept the greasy soup and rough mattress that are offered, and am quickly asleep.

I awake to find that the bus has already departed on its two-day journey to Kashgar, leaving me alone to explore the town. Old Tashkurghan (or what is left of it) consists of forty or so undistinguished mud buildings and a mosque at the foot of a gravelly bluff. Overshadowing them to the west is the Manchu fort, also of mud; and to the east lie the damp and fertile water meadows which are the *raison d'être* for the town. During the brief Pamir summers these meadows are as busy as Tashkurghan itself, for they serve not only as grazing grounds but as park, swimming baths, fuel bunker and launderette. Cattle, camels, sheep and goats vie for space with boys bathing, men fishing, and women washing clothes or collecting dung for winter fires. From the bluff, it resembles a green carpet rolled out on the valley floor and then sprinkled with toy figures and animals.

The broad main street is the Chinese Government's contribution to Tashkurghan. Lined with tall chenar trees and flanked by schools, public buildings and a cinema, it was laid out in the 1950s, when Beijing was striving to make its mark on the newly established Xinjiang–Uyghur Autonomous Region. The buildings are of a pattern seen throughout China: square and soulless, proclaiming their functions in proud Chinese characters on the crumbling concrete of their outer walls. As a concession to autonomy the signs are also written in the Uyghur script, but the gesture is a hollow one, since Tashkurghan's townsfolk are not Uyghurs but Tajiks.

The problem with the minority people of China's western regions is that they have absolutely nothing in common with the Han Chinese who control their destiny. Their languages are of Turkish origin, their religion Islam, and their rough Caucasian features would not attract a second glance in the backstreet cafés of Istanbul. For their part, the Han Chinese cannot comprehend why they are hated so vehemently by these people for whom they have done so much. It is true that the minorities' living standards have improved greatly under the Chinese. But some of the minority languages are no longer taught in schools, which means that a growing generation of children will find their written heritage inaccessible. Minorities in Wales, Spain, New Zealand and the Soviet Union have been driven to violence over just such issues; but the Uyghurs and their fellow-minorities of Xinjiang have raised no more than the occasional skirmish. Whether this is due to their affable disposition, the futility of their cause, or simply because a charismatic leader has yet to emerge, is debatable.

Behind the dingy counter of Tashkurghan's bank, I am

surprised to find not sullen Chinese but smiling Tajik women, and while I wait in the inevitable queue I have an opportunity to study their costumes: surely the most sumptuous on the Silk Road. The ensemble consists of a bright tunic over a matching skirt – usually maroon, though occasionally orange. But the centrepiece of the Tajik outfit, and what distinguishes it from those of the neighbouring Uyghurs and Kirghiz, is a dashing silk headscarf wrapped twice around the head and allowed to cascade enticingly over the shoulders. Coupled with the natural rosiness of the Tajik face, the combination of style, material and colour is masterly.

For all their Tajik cheerfulness, the bank clerks seem unable to move the queue. Each clerk has an abacus, and much time is spent clicking the little balls up and down in what appear to be elaborate calculations. It is only when, finally, I get close enough that I realize they are nothing of the sort. Far from reckoning up interest and computing conversion rates to several decimal places, the clerks are using their gadgets to add six and three, eight and ten, sixteen and five. I watch in disbelief. Out in the bazaar, simple stallholders do such sums in their heads without a second thought. Why not here? This pantomime (which I am to see again in banks, post offices, department stores and all institutions run by the Chinese) has the makings of a clue to the Chinese psyche. I reflect on the dire warnings of previous China travellers. *They don't think like we do. They are callous. It is as if they are from another planet.* Something tells me that these observations may share their roots with the scene before me now. Casting about for an explanation, I remember once being told about the Taoist theory of *yin* and *yang*.

The Ancient Chinese believed that all the phenomena of the universe – objects, forces and events – were manifestations of an overall guiding power which they called the Tao. The Tao governed movement and change, and hence also growth and decay; and at the same time was itself changing – waxing and waning from year to year.

The idea undoubtedly came from watching the movements of the sun, moon, planets and stars, and the changing seasons – all of which follow more or less measurable cyclical paths. But the Taoists, led by the philosopher Lao Tzu, applied the concept not only to natural phenomena but to some of the most complicated and elusive aspects of the human condition. Thus they believed that whenever a force or relationship reached its extreme, it would eventually reverse direction and move towards the opposite extreme. This belief encouraged caution during periods of abundance, and optimism when times were hard: necessary attitudes among people who, for much of the time, were struggling to make ends meet.

Yin and *yang*, the two elements which make up the Tao, originally meant simply the shady and sunny sides of a mountain. But gradually they came to encompass many related conditions: *yin*, the dark, receptive, female, maternal characteristics, *yang*, the bright, strong, male, creative elements; *yin*, contemplation and rest, *yang*, movement and activity; *yin*, compassion; *yang*, logic.

The interplay of these opposites was supposed to control both natural phenomena and the progress of people and societies. It was a dynamic relationship, in which first *yin* and then *yang* elements gained supremacy, only to reveal within themselves the seeds of the opposite which would ultimately rise to replace them.

The idea is persuasive. In the West, our well-documented obsession with science and technology for the last 400 years is symptomatic of a male-dominated *yang* society, and this is amply confirmed by social records and simple observations. In China and Japan, on the other hand, societies have traditionally been dominated by *yin* influences. The experiences and mentalities of people in these and one or two other eastern countries – after centuries of conditioning – are, I think, at the root of the rift between East and West. They explain the most basic distinctions between us; many of the misunderstandings; and, incidentally, why the *yin* Chinese find it so difficult to grasp the *yang* subject of mathematics.

These thoughts, though hardly relevant to my present problem, liven up the endless wait to receive my Chinese money, and I jot them down until I have more evidence to go with my theory. By the time the money is finally handed over the bank is closed, and I am led by a Tajik, still smiling, to leave by the back door.

*

Tashkurghan has seen quite a few changes in recent years, and its people think of it as quite a modern town. Doesn't its cinema – seating nearly 300 – show films on general release? Haven't the stuffed birds and animals in its Pamier [*sic*] Exhibition Hall been commended in the newspapers of Kashgar? Tashkurghan's citizens also direct me proudly to the new bazaar nearing completion in a sunny side street, where the first stallholders are already sitting optimistically amongst their wares. At one stall the last planks are still being hammered in, but it has already been stocked with saddle tack, ironmongery, herbal remedies, rock salt, spices, silk in various colours, jewellery, rope, needles, thread, kindling, rakes, hoes, scythes, sunflower seeds, plastic shoulder bags, textile dyes, rolling pins, meat cleavers and a couple of watermelons. Next door, the blacksmith is at the same time a cobbler: horseshoes and rubber heels lie side by side on his bench.

To the northbound traveller, whose senses have been assaulted by the maelstrom of Pakistan, Tashkurghan is a dream come true. Horses and donkeys still easily outnumber motor vehicles; people have time to stop and talk beneath the chenar trees lining the main street; small boys chase hoops with whipping sticks; and pervading everything is a glorious silence, a pre-industrial peacefulness, broken only by the blacksmith's hammer and the occasional passing cart.

At Tashkurghan, modern road and Silk Road part company. My plan is to follow the old path to Kashgar, weaving a 120-mile route over three passes before descending to Yanghissar on the edge of the Taklamakan Desert. What will be my chances on this difficult stretch? On the positive side, I am in good physical shape, and have acclimatized well to the higher altitudes since leaving Peshawar. Tashkurghan's height of 11,000 feet hasn't affected me at all. One or two people have cautioned that my route will cross uninhabited areas, but their warnings haven't been based on personal experience. Eric Shipton reported friendly Kirghiz nomads between Tashkurghan and Yanghissar in 1940, and with luck their children or grandchildren will still be there.

On the negative side is the Army. Soldiers abound in Tashkurghan, and the barracks buzz with exercises and parades. China's *entente* with the Soviet Union doesn't seem to have penetrated here. Again, Eric Shipton's 1940 experience was a salutary one, for in spite of full diplomatic credentials he was threatened at gunpoint and placed for several days under house arrest. My own chances of slipping through unnoticed must, at best, be slim.

My maps are an unknown quantity. From my limited research I know that the main features are more or less correctly shown. But on foot one can be led astray by comparatively minor errors, and I have not put the maps to this kind of test. My only consolation is that even after sixty years they seem to be the best available; the maps produced by the Chinese themselves are appalling.

Another worrying question is whether I will be able to cross rivers. Catherine Macartney, a familiar figure in Kashgar during her husband's time as the first British Consul there, reported difficulties with swollen streams west of the city in 1902. Eric Shipton wrote of similar problems in the Gez Defile during his wanderings with Bill Tilman in 1947. More recently, Chris Bonington and his liaison officer Liu Dayi only just managed to cross the Konsiver River to reach the base camp for their 1981 ascent of Mount Kongur. Three years later, Christina Dodwell's inflatable canoe capsized in the same torrent just a few miles downstream. But these occasions were all in high summer. Can I pin my hopes on a subsiding water level as winter approaches?

I decide to confide in Liu Gun, an English-speaking policeman at Tashkurghan's Public Security Bureau, who has befriended me. Liu Gun ushers me into his office and listens while I explain. He scrutinizes my photocopied maps, then looks me straight in the eye.

'There are three problems with your plan,' he says. 'First, your route is through a wilderness area. No one goes that way these days, and nobody lives there. I think you may have trouble finding food and directions.'

Summoning more conviction than the occasion deserves, I tell him that I have been in such situations before, and am not worried about going hungry or getting lost.

'Then I must tell you that a second problem will be the Army. You see from the map that you will be close to the Soviet border, which is heavily patrolled. Ten years ago, any foreigner found in that area would have been shot. Now you will simply be arrested.'

I say nothing.

'The third problem is that I am absolutely forbidden to allow you to leave Tashkurghan except by the main road. . . .'

My spirits sink, and I curse myself for having been so frank about my intentions. But looking up, I see that Liu Gun is smiling broadly.

'. . . So it will be as well if I don't see you go,' he concludes.

On the morning of 8th September I load my pack with as much of the bazaar's produce as I can carry, and walk to the end of the main street. The water meadows beckon in bright mountain sunshine. Liu Gun and his colleagues are nowhere to be seen. Giving the Public Security Bureau a wide berth, I set out along the old road down the Taghdumbash Valley, and am soon clear of the town.

For the first ten miles, old and new roads run side by side. A construction crew call over from the new one, and invite me to share their lunch of noodles and peppers. They are a spirited bunch, but impeccably polite, and if they have the slightest interest in what a foreigner is doing on foot so close to the border, they are too courteous to show it. On the new road lorries pass at regular intervals, grinding their way painfully towards Tashkurghan. On the old one I meet only an ancient Tajik with a donkey carrying freshly scythed grass. The man's cheerful 'Nǐ-hǎo' is accompanied by a whiff which takes me back to British summer days, when lawns have been mown and the air is sweet and still.

In mid-afternoon I come to the end of the wide valley, and the two roads go their separate ways. The motor road heads up a side valley towards the Karakul Lakes; my way follows the Yarkand River which at this point enters a deep defile. As with the road to Wakhan, there is no hint of the significance of this junction; yet the routes will not come together for another 200 miles.

As I hoped, the rivers and streams are running well below high water, and I am glad now to have arrived so late in the season. The first ford comes no higher than my thighs. But as the gorge deepens to a mere slit in the mountains the Yarkand River becomes fast and turbulent. I eye it nervously, looking for opportunities to cross, and hoping fervently that I won't have to. My map tells me that I should follow this river for perhaps fourteen miles, then strike north up a side valley towards Chichiklik Dawan [*sic*], the first of three passes between here and Kashgar. A path is shown as following the north bank, and sure enough I am on a track of sorts. It even has some faint tyremarks in it. I wonder dreamily what kind of vehicle could penetrate such a gorge. . . .

Without warning, the army jeep is upon me. I hear and see it simultaneously as it rounds a corner a hundred yards ahead, spitting stones. I dive for the nearest boulder and flatten myself behind it, heart pounding as the jeep bounces closer. I feel like a character in a spy thriller. It occurs to me, belatedly, that a European face in these parts would probably be taken for a Russian one. I hold my breath as the jeep comes alongside and stops. Surely they must have seen me as they rounded the bend?

But I am lucky. The jeep's incumbents merely want to relieve themselves. Some do so straight into the river; one comes up to my boulder and urinates against the other side. After a brief exchange of banter they clamber back into the vehicle and are gone.

I wait several minutes before emerging. It has been the closest of shaves, and had I been caught I could have blamed no one but myself. I resolve to be more vigilant in future.

After a night by the river under a full moon, I come to where my map shows the side stream leading to the Chichilik Pass. At first I can see no sign of it, but a passing Tajik points out a small valley some distance ahead. He seems to know the pass well, and isn't in the slightest concerned either about my presence here or about my intention of crossing it. '*Iyi şanslar*,' he says in Turkish. ('Good luck.')

Approaching from the other direction in 1935, however, Peter Fleming was less casual about the Chichilik, as he disclosed in *News from Tartary*:

At the end of the valley we began to climb less gradually, and soon came to a big stony corrie with a dark green lochan in it. Snow, beaten ice-hard by the wind, armoured the peaks around us. The pass itself was at the top of a steep, forbidding slope of screes, and up this, picking its way awkwardly among the boulders, our caravan began to wind in zigzags. The Turkis stabbed the wretched ponies midway between eye and nostril with long iron skewers which they carried for the purpose; this let a good deal of blood, and though it looked a barbarous and cruel practice it undoubtedly made the animals' breathing easier at high altitudes. Our Turkis always did it on passes and, judging by the amount of blood with which the boulders of the Chichiklik [sic] were spattered, it was a universal custom.

Sitting in my tent at 14,000 feet, I can easily visualize such scenes. Beyond the tentflaps the horizon is a line of snowcapped peaks; behind and below, the valley up which I have come is a moonscape of boulders. In no direction is a human being to be seen. I feel undeservedly privileged to be here: the first Westerner, by all accounts, for forty years.

The next morning finds me scrambling amongst more boulders across ground still deep in shadow and coated with a heavy frost, as I head up a small chasm which I hope will lead me to the Chichilik Pass. I am confused: the terrain bears no resemblance to the contours on my map. But the way ahead is flanked by rock walls, and I have no choice but to continue upwards in the hope of reaching more open country. I emerge into mountain sunshine and my spirits begin to lift. But a few minutes later a shadow falls momentarily across my path, and I look up to see a griffon, the largest of all Asian vultures, circling steadily, deliberately, less than a hundred feet above.

The last running water is now far behind, so I am anxious not to be lost for too long. I am also impatient to see the Chichilik, possibly the most famous of the Pamir passes. It was here, in 1940, that Eric Shipton saw a pair of snow leopards at not fifty yards. They contemplated him for a moment, then ambled on across the snow, quite unconcerned. Of the same pass, Polo observed:

This is said to be the highest place in the world. The pasturage is so good that a lean beast grows fat here in ten days. Wild game of every sort abounds. There are great quantities of wild sheep of huge size. Their horns grow to as much as six palms in length and are never less than three or four. From these horns the shepherds make big bowls from which they feed, and also fences to keep in their flocks.

The animals he described are fat-tailed sheep, so called because they store the fat from their summer grazing in a woolly rump where the tail should be. Like the camel's hump, this protrusion waxes and wanes with the seasons and provides an indication of the animal's state of health. In spring the sheep look quite normal, but now, at summer's end, they are waddling across the hills like geriatrics promenading by the sea. Like me, Polo encountered the flocks in their summer state, and he went on to describe them as being 'as big as asses, with tails so thick and plump that they weigh a good thirty pounds'. But we must remember, of course, that he had a salesman's gift for exaggeration.

Suddenly I hear a cry. It is a piercing whistle, the last thing I expected on this remote hillside. I peer round a bluff and find myself face to face with a family of Siberian marmots. Looking for all the world like golden weasels, these are among the largest of the marmot species, measuring three feet or more from nose to tail. They are still common in central Asia, but are shy creatures and rarely seen at close range. We stare briefly at each other, immobilized in our surprise, before they dive for their burrows and are gone.

At last I am on the Chichilik Pass. Standing on the saddle at its head, I appreciate for the first time the scale of this massive trough through the heart of the Pamirs. A panorama has opened up to the west and north, as far as Mustagh Ata, the 24,700-foot mountain that was once thought to be the highest in the world. My map shows it to be more than twenty miles away, but in the thin, clear air I can make out individual crevasses on its upper snowfields. More importantly, I can now see where I lost my way. Below me, in a broad stony plain, is a blue-green lake: possibly the lochan described by Fleming.

There is no sign of the track which should lead me through the great trench ahead, but instinct tells me that I am back on course. A fierce and extraordinarily biting wind has sprung up, blowing first from one quarter, then from another, sometimes with such force that it whips dust into my face and I brace myself, eyes tightly shut, until each gust dies down. I recall that in 1947 Shipton encountered a similarly sudden and violent tempest some miles to the north. Shipton's was short-lived, and thankfully so is mine. But I make quick work of the descent, and mid-afternoon finds me crossing a grassy meadow towards a shepherds' encampment by a stream.

The camp is made up of half a dozen *yurts*, the circular felt-covered tents of the Kirghiz people. I approach warily, for I have not encountered Kirghiz before. Will they welcome someone who, by all appearances, might have come from the moon? My heartbeat quickens and my pace slows.

In the encampment a dog is first to see me, and its barking quickly sets off others. Faces turn in my direction. I hesitate, uncertain what to do.

Suddenly three children run forward. '*Al-lo! Al-lo!*' They approach with outstretched hands and almost drag me into the village. To my relief, the faces which encircle me now are creased in smiles. There are perhaps thirty adults – ranging in age, I imagine, from twenty to seventy – and as many children again. The *yurts* are fifteen feet in diameter and perhaps ten feet tall. Outside three of their horses are tethered, and I notice they are saddled and sweating as if they have just been ridden in at some speed. Sheep and goats graze beyond. The dogs, their job done, are already asleep again, and my attention returns to the enquiring faces of my hosts.

I know from past experience that the questions on their minds will be: 'Where are you from?', 'Where are you going?' and 'Please can we see the wonderful things in your rucksack?' – not necessarily in that order. I decide to start by answering the simple ones.

'I come from England,' I venture, waving in approximately the right direction, 'and I'm going to Kashgar.'

'Ah, *Ang-lia!*' One man, at least, has heard of my country.

'Kashgar?' asks another, thumping his leg. I confess that I may not walk the whole way, but I expect I will be walking most of it.

Before the conversation can turn to what is really interesting them, I forestall matters by asking if I may look inside a *yurt*. There is some commotion as the elders decide which it will be. At length I am led to the furthest of the great tents.

The felt door is flung open and I step over the threshold. I am taken utterly by surprise. The tent is cool, spacious, airy and well-lit. A small stove is burning in the centre, its smoke led neatly via a metal pipe through a hole in the roof. The *yurt*'s floor is carpeted with richly patterned rugs; its walls and roof formed by a mesh of willow poles. Lashed on the outside are pieces of thick felt; inside, further insulation is provided by rolls of cotton and silk stacked high around the sides. The willow mesh also performs the functions of wardrobe, sideboard and mantelpiece.

Hung around it are ornaments, clothing, scissors, combs, a mirror and some faded snaps of family members long since passed away. One corner of the *yurt* has been partitioned off by a bamboo screen, and I take this to be the kitchen. My guess is confirmed when a woman slips behind the screen, to emerge with bowls of yoghurt and thick rounds of unleavened bread: the traditional Kirghiz gesture of hospitality. We sit on the rugs: five men, four women, a dozen children, and me. From the ages represented, I calculate that the *yurt* must be home to no fewer than four generations.

I break a piece of bread, dip it in the yoghurt, put it in my mouth and murmur my approval. The men motion me to take more, lifting their bowls to their lips to indicate that I should drink it straight from the bowl. I follow their suggestion gratefully, for the bread is rock-hard. However, the yoghurt, tart and slightly effervescent on the tongue, is quite delicious. I am sure that the dying desert traveller in Xinjiang dreams not of water but of yoghurt.

We talk in gestures about my clothes and boots, and I show one or two things from my pack. Then I play my trump card. 'I too have a *yurt*,' I announce.

There is some discussion among the men. Have they understood me correctly? What do I mean? How can I possibly be carrying a *yurt*?

'Of course, it's not quite as grand as yours,' I admit. 'But it suits me well enough.'

'Come on, then,' they challenge. 'Let's see this *yurt* of yours.'

For this trip the tentmakers Vango have given me one of their Hurricanes, the very latest in hoop tent design. I take it outside the *yurt*, spread it on the ground and slip in the two self-shaping hoops. A peg in each corner, and it is up. Dwarfed by the Kirghiz *yurt*, it nevertheless draws admiring looks. The men examine it closely, pointing to the heavy-duty groundsheet and the strengthening at key points. They are certainly well aware of tent technology. Then the children fall upon it, and for the next half-hour the air is filled with shrieks of delight as they tumble in and out in a Kirghiz-style game of house. I, too, am delighted that the Hurricane has met with the approval of the Kirghiz, who have devoted several centuries to considering the problems of tent design. As I settle in, I am pleased to find that it has even withstood the battering of thirty excited children.

At dusk I return to the *yurt* and am greeted by an unexpected sight. A paraffin lamp has been lit, a commotion is going on within, and through the open door I can smell the distinctive aroma of roast mutton. A glance confirms my suspicion. To honour their unexpected guest, the family has slaughtered a sheep!

It is not a sight for the squeamish. The animal has been butchered and the red meat cut into kebabs, which are now roasting gently on skewers over the open stove. After a communal washing of hands in a terracotta bowl, a melon is cut open and I am invited to take the first slice. It has been brought by someone from one of the Taklamakan oases. Then follows the main course, and the mutton is accompanied by sorghum and small bowls of an extremely hot sauce. I am offered more and ever more, and only when I refuse most insistently is the family satisfied that I have eaten my fill. The meal is concluded with bowls of green tea spiced with cinnamon and cardamom, and when at last these are cleared away I lie back, satiated and content.

The men ask if I smoke. I don't, but am compelled to join them anyway. The hashish is mild, and its effect merely to increase the fatigue which is already welling over me. I relax; for although there is now little conversation, I am confident that I will continue to be well looked after. Through the hole in the roof a bright star shines. Venus? The Pole Star? In my drowsiness I am unable to decide which.

From a recess, one of the men takes a stringed instrument. It is a *rawap*: sitar-shaped, but with a bulbous soundbox made from a single piece of rosewood. The fretboard is inlaid with ivory and cowhorn, and terminates in a dramatic curl containing the tuning pegs. After tuning the five strings, the player breaks into a melody which begins very slowly (like *Zorba's Dance*), then rises to a frenzy which has the whole *yurt* pulsating. I am reminded of the Appalachian banjo music which was used to such devastating effect in the film *Deliverance*. The comparison is thought-provoking – but by now my thoughts are beyond provocation, and I am ready for bed. After a further couple of numbers I make my excuses, retire to my 'yurt', and within seconds am asleep.

These generous Kirghiz people are part of a community of

100,000 in China and more than two million in the USSR. Their lives have not always been as peaceful as they are today. In 1919, after half a century of hounding by Russian settlers who coveted their rich Naryn River grazing grounds, the Kirghiz encampments erupted in spontaneous rebellion against the Tsarist regime. The uprising was ruthlessly quelled, and nearly a third of the population fled to China, conducting from there a guerrilla campaign to which, as nomads, they were well suited. For two summers the Tien-Shan ranges echoed to the sound of bullets, and only after the Tsar himself was ousted from Moscow did the exiles make peace. Since then they have worked with new settlers to build a semi-autonomous Kirghiz Soviet Socialist Republic, and have taken jobs in factories, down mines and on the settlers' mechanized farms. Only in China have they been true to the lifestyle of their forefathers.

I am up at first light. A bitter wind is blowing from the pass and I lose no time in dismantling my 'yurt'. My hosts are still sound asleep – even the dogs – so in lieu of thanks I leave a small memento of my visit under a stone by the door. It is a picture postcard: an old, creased view of Piccadilly Circus which I showed them last night in an attempt to explain where I was from. I wince at the thought of my country being represented in this way; but the Kirghiz found it enchanting.

There follows a day of horrors: fifteen river crossings, or, to be exact, the same river fifteen times. I am heading downstream, so each crossing is wider and deeper than the last. I pass the little grazing ground of Tarbashi, where in 1940 Shipton made his first acquaintance with the Kirghiz in a couple of *yurts*. Like me, he was hospitably received (no sacrificial sheep, though); but at this late season the pasture is deserted. I enter the twisting defile of Tangitar, the 'Black Gorge' which forced another British consul, Clarmont Skrine, to make a two-day detour when he passed here on his way to Kashgar in 1922. The path bucks and twists, alternating between clifftop and riverbank in its attempt to find a way among the buttresses and boulders.

I have an apprehensive moment when two men emerge from a hut and demand to see my 'papers', shouting officiously in my ear. One is wearing a faded People's Liberation Army uniform; but after a good deal of animated discussion I conclude that neither has any official capacity. Perhaps they are merely copying Chinese officials who have come this way? In any event my passport more than satisfies their curiosity, with its multi-coloured visas and photograph of a much smarter Pilkington than the one before their eyes. Before I leave, they absolve themselves by offering me a bowl of warming, revitalizing, milky porridge.

Towards the end of this day of descent I discover the first major error on my 1925 map, and luckily it is in my favour. A great side valley shown coming in from the north turns out not to exist. I am still watching for it when the main valley opens out and I find myself entering a village.

'Where are you going?' cry the villagers as I trudge wearily into the patch of dirt which serves as a square.

'I'm going to Toylepoulin,' I reply, quoting the next name on the map.

'Look no further,' they laugh in unison. 'You've arrived.'

It is an exquisite moment. I heave my pack against a mud wall and slump down beside it. Tea is brought, with a bowl of hot buttered rice. In spite of the decline in traffic, these people have not forgotten what a tired traveller needs. As usual, the centre of attention is not me but my belongings – rucksack, camera, tape recorder and clothing. Five years ago, in Nepal, my boots used to steal the show; but the years have taken their toll on them, and nowadays they get hardly a second glance. My cheap digital wristwatch arouses an undeserved interest, and I smile as I recall Clarmont Skrine's experience here, recounted in *Chinese Central Asia*:

I had given Ibrahim Beg [the headman of a nearby village] an official present in the shape of a watch. Just before leaving I discovered that he had already disposed of it to Hafiz for five taels (about 15s.). As it was only worth about four taels, and as I wanted to impress upon the Kirghiz the enormity of this insult to the British Empire, I publicly reproved Ibrahim, took back the watch, made him repay the five taels to Hafiz, and then gave him a cash present of four taels instead of the watch. Then, supposing that Hafiz really wanted a watch to tell the time by, I sold him the Government watch for four taels. The following day one of the other orderlies told me that Ibrahim had bought back the watch from Hafiz for four and a half taels, evidently thinking that as there was such a to-do about the article, it must be a good investment. It was not till after we reached Kashgar, however, that I heard the sequel from Harding, who passed Yambulak two days after us. This was that Ibrahim had changed his mind once more about the watch and sold it to Harding's orderly for three and a half taels.

I retrieve my watch – not to protect the dignity of the Empire, but because I seem to be the only one in the company who can tell the time.

The people of this village have longer faces – less Mongoloid, more European – than the Tajiks and Kirghiz among whom I have been travelling so far. They are Uyghurs, people of the desert. I am glad that my first acquaintance has been such an agreeable one because I will be meeting many more of them when I reach the Taklamakan. Unlike the Tajiks and Kirghiz, these villagers speak a little Chinese – about as much as I do – and we laugh at each other's efforts.

I hand round some Pakistani cigarettes: 'Princeton' brand, filter tipped, American-looking, and, from the villagers' reaction, quite unlike any they have seen before. A man puts one of them to his mouth the wrong way round and tries to light the filter.

From Toylepoulin my route lies north, over the 15,000-foot Buramsal Pass into the valley of the Karatash. As I gain height I find myself once again walking into a bitter wind, this time gusting down from the pass. By late afternoon I have had more than enough, and my thoughts drift towards visions of a sheltered campsite, a simple meal and a good night's sleep.

A shepherd's hut beckons invitingly from a grassy meadow overlooking the river. It is empty and derelict, its door padlocked, but the outer yard offers a place to pitch my tent out of the wind. I lose no time in establishing myself in this haven, and am soon settling down to sleep.

An hour after nightfall I hear voices. Am I dreaming? There are the unmistakable sounds of animals being unloaded. Snortings. Gruntings. I am out of sight in the enclosure, but blocking the door to the hut. I hold my breath as I wait for the inevitable.

After what seems like an eternity, the enclosure gate swings open and the glare of a lantern engulfs the tent. Amid gasps of Kirghiz astonishment I unzip the flap and put out my head, a most sheepish of expressions filling my tired face. 'Hello,' I say as brightly as possible. 'I'm afraid you've got a visitor.'

Six men look enquiringly at me. I explain in pidgin Turkish that

I had thought their hut wasn't being used. Given that they are probably as tired as I am, the men are ridiculously understanding. We move the tent bodily round to the side of the hut, and they laugh at the more bizarre of my belongings, like the water filter and compass. After making sure I am comfortable they say goodnight in turn, leaving me in the company of the four camels, which I heard being unloaded earlier. As I zip up the tentflap, I see the camels staring at me under the moonlight with an air of infinite disdain.

The next morning, as we share a breakfast of yak-butter tea and home-baked *roti* complete with gritty bits from the grindstone, the Kirghiz tell me that they are on their way to Buramsal, a small village just before the pass, with a cargo of sweet pears for the villagers there. They will barter them for sheep's, goat's and yak's wool – a bargain for the people of this upland hamlet who rarely have the chance to eat fruit, and good business for the camel-men who will sell the wool for a handsome profit in the desert bazaars.

As we are going the same way, I fall in behind their caravan, but it isn't long before my pack has been strapped on top of a sack of pears. Shortly a horseman joins us, and invites me to ride his animal for a few miles. When, eventually, he takes off up a side valley, it is only a matter of minutes before the leading camel-man offers me his camel.

Riding a camel is like riding an outsize horse. On the level its loping gait is relaxing, but going downhill you have to hang on tightly to its front hump to avoid being pitched forward. Another hazard is the camel's habit of twisting its head round, with a throaty roar, to bite you as you get on. Parts of my route from Tashkurghan have been too narrow for a beast of this size to follow, and it may be that my predecessors were limited to using donkeys on these sections. But for covering long distances on broad paths the camel is ideal. Thanks to coincidence and Kirghiz generosity, my feet can luxuriate for a few hours in the queer sensation of having nothing to do.

By the end of the day, however, I am on my own again, and gaining height quickly as I approach the pass. To avoid being caught by darkness on the pass itself I camp early at 14,000 feet, though there is no water to accompany my supper of gritty *roti*, the last of my supply from the generous camel-men. The starlit night is bitter, and even in my down bag I am too cold to sleep. I listen miserably to the silence of the night, waiting for dawn.

The Buramsal Pass, though fractionally lower than the Chichilik, is steeper on both sides. After my uncomfortable night I begin the climb sluggishly, but am soon in company again. A shepherd's keen eyes have spotted me from a good half mile away, and together we scramble the last few hundred feet to the summit. On the north-eastern horizon, Mount Kongur's south face glowers. Breathless, the Kirghiz and I scoff my last piece of chocolate, a treat long savoured; then, after some initial scree-running, we find ourselves descending through gently sloping meadows. I sing with joy at the easy going. Some 3,000 feet below the pass I begin to feel warm at last, and my mood rallies further as we follow a widening and deepening River Karatash to my companion's family *yurt*.

As we approach the Kirghiz gives a shout. '*Hoo-laaah!*' First one, then a second, and finally five small faces appear at the great felt door. 'My daughters,' he says with a smile.

His wife and daughters greet us with bowls of *sut* – mare's milk – still hot from the fire where his wife has been making yoghurt. Supper is soon being prepared, and it is a lavish one: noodles, mutton and parsnips, washed down with milk and yak-butter tea. Afterwards my host gives me a thoughtful look. 'Would you like a wash?' he asks.

The thought of the icy river outside makes me shake my head, and he smiles. 'Have a look in this mirror,' he suggests mildly.

The dirt-encrusted apparition is frightful. 'All right,' I say at once. 'You've persuaded me.'

Next morning, after a breakfast identical to the previous night's supper I am helped on my way by the family camel, led from a horse by my kind friend, his eldest three children skipping alongside. After a couple of hours he signals me down and they turn back towards their home. Perhaps this quiet-spoken Kirghiz family has treated me just a little too generously; for I find it difficult to say farewell, and it is with the heaviest of hearts that I continue along the Karatash.

But the way is downhill, and my spirits revive as I reach the wider and warmer lower reaches. The mountains around me are as gaunt as before, but the valley bottoms are well cultivated, and the people have a prosperous air. It is haymaking time, and everywhere grass is being scythed for winter fodder. The fields ring with laughter, and I am reminded of a similar season during my visit to Nepal. Then, as now, donkeys were being used to thresh the grain with their hooves, tramping endlessly round a pole while a boy harried them from behind.

Gentian, columbine and asphodel underfoot, sand lizards sunbathing on rocks, and orange-tailed dippers in the gurgling river by my side, confirm that I have arrived in a land of plenty; and for the first time I allow myself to believe that I really will reach Kashgar. On my second day in the Karatash valley I stop for lunch with an amiable Chinese geologist, prospecting for jade. The oases of the southern Taklamakan have been noted for centuries for their fine jade, but I have never heard of it in the Pamirs before. I ask if I may see some, but he shakes his head. '*Méi-yŏu*' ('There isn't any'), he explains sadly.

Over noodles the geologist looks disparagingly at my map. I show him my intended route down the valley, and point out the words *Yangi-hissār, 9 m.* where it disappears off the edge of the sheet. '*Bo! Bo!*' cries the geologist. ('No! No!') He goes on to explain that this is not the best way to reach Yanghissar. What my map has failed to tell me is that the Karatash downstream from here is too deep and wide to be crossed on foot. The geologist makes a gesture to indicate that the water would come up to my neck. Nobody goes that way, he says.

It seems that my alternative strikes east from here, climbing to the 13,200-foot Gadjik Pass, then descending east to the desert before turning north to Yanghissar. I groan at the thought of another pass. 'Don't despair,' says my friend. 'The last twenty miles is a jeep track. You may get a lift.'

I have no choice but to reset my sights. The geologist wishes me luck, and as I step outside it looks as if I shall need it, for the weather has taken a turn for the worse. Within half an hour – soaked, frozen and battered by quarter-inch hailstones – I am reflecting ruefully on yesterday's cocky plans. How difficult it is to abandon cherished ideas!

'*Hoo-laaaaaah!*'

The shout comes from somewhere to my right. I squint through the downpour to see a black-coated figure waving from across the valley. At first I consider ignoring the call; I am not feeling sociable just now. But in these conditions, why should I hurry? I am not likely to reach the pass before tomorrow. I hesitate, then hobble through muddy meadows towards the distant man.

He eyes me coldly from a buff. 'Who are you?' he demands in Chinese. 'Where are you going?'

I explain that I am English and am heading for the Gadjik Pass.

The man points at the darkening sky. 'That's not very sensible,' he says (stating the obvious). 'The pass is steep and high.'

For a moment we stand looking at each other as I wait for his next move. He is a tall character, a Uyghur perhaps, his features thick-set and face contorted into what seems to be a snarl. He sizes me up. The hail has turned to snow, and is beginning to settle on the ground and on us.

Finally, with an authority that makes it hard to refuse, the fellow gestures that I am to follow him up the valley. We walk over to where a camel and a horse are tethered to a gnarled tree. Although they are unladen the man offers me no help with my now sodden rucksack, so as our little procession sets out I silently take up the rear. Who is he? As dusk falls and the snow begins to accumulate in earnest, I am torn between curiosity and the unsettling fear that I may be walking into a trap.

After perhaps a mile the weather has become truly appalling, and my companion has quickened his pace. The camel bellows as he yanks again and again on the rope attached to its nosepeg. The effort of keeping up has warmed me sufficiently to look more closely at the animals in front of me, and suddenly I realize the identity of the man ahead. Draped over the horse's back is a grey blanket bearing a large red star. A similar one is folded between the camel's humps. The man's greatcoat, whose silhouette I can just make out through the swirling snow, has epaulettes. There can be no question about it. I am in the company of a Chinese soldier.

My mind is racing. I have been walking for a week now, on a route which is not only off-limits to foreigners but at some points just a score of miles from the Soviet frontier. I have known all along that the consequences of discovery would be serious. At best, I would be arrested and fined; at worst, I could face deportation. Over the past few days I have been lulled by the friendly and hospitable Kirghiz into a false sense of security, and now I have been caught off guard. But as we trudge steadily through the thickening blizzard, I notice that the soldier is keeping his eyes firmly on the path ahead. Inadvertently – or perhaps deliberately – he is offering me a chance to escape.

I slacken my pace, and as we pass a rocky outcrop I grab my opportunity. Climbing quickly, I have soon gained a hundred feet, and stop breathlessly at the foot of a higher cliff, listening for the inevitable shout which will come from my companion when he discovers he is alone. Everything depends on the next few minutes. Any longer, and my footprints will have been covered by the now heavily falling snow.

Five minutes pass. Ten minutes. I jump up and down to keep warm. It looks, for the moment, as if I am safe from discovery. I cast about for some level ground on which to pitch my tent.

The knack of camping in a blizzard is to avoid places where the snow will be driven against the tent, and if possible to find a spot where the wind will act as a natural vacuum cleaner, sucking it away from the tentflaps and keeping the entrance clear. Failing this, if the snow continues to fall, one has no choice but to make shovelling sorties through the night.

My luck is in. Near the foot of the cliff is a level patch, and after a couple of hours I put my nose out of the tent to find that the storm has eased. Safe here from both Army and weather, I relax and am quickly asleep.

I awake at dawn to the sound of snorting. The soldier? No, it is a yak. The creature seems to be trying to tell me something, but after a few minutes listening to its grunting and coughing I decide that these are simply yak-grazing sounds. The sky is clear and the snow firm, and I make quick work of packing the tent and getting under way.

Though marked on my map as lower than the Chichilik and Buramsal, the Gadjik Pass seems higher, probably a reflection of my lack of mental preparation and the other things on my mind. But today there is no sign of the soldier, or of the barracks towards which he was presumably leading me. I am cajoled upwards by Kirghiz muleteers, who share lumps of rock-hard sheep's milk cheese as together we make for the pass.

At last we reach the crest, and I have the joy of looking over ever-lower horizons until, in the distant haze, the foothills finally give out in the Taklamakan Desert.

From behind me comes a shout. One of the mules has lost its footing on the summit ramp, and is teetering on the brink of a cliff. Three of us dash down to help the struggling animal, but as we approach it panics, and for a dreadful second seems doomed to fall. Miraculously, it manages to regain its footing, and we wrench away its load of grain sacks and drag it back onto the path. The mule seems none the worse for its close shave, but I am gasping for breath.

I descend quickly, to the surprise of the muleteers who have had to suffer my groaning on the way up. To my relief there is still no sign of the soldier, and I camp in a meadow at 10,000 feet.

Although I am now at a lower altitude than at any time since entering China, this north-facing valley is cold – much colder, for instance, than the high plains around Tashkurghan. Huddling in my tent, I long for the warmth of Kashgar, and wonder if I will be there in time for my birthday, now just a few days away. I hope so, because today I have run out of food. Tashkurghan's bazaar, busy though it was, could supply little that was both edible and portable, and I left the town with nothing more than bread, chocolate, tea, powdered milk and a bag of boiled sweets. Kirghiz, Tajiks and Uyghurs have shared their larders willingly, urging me to fill my bowl again and again, or passing generous scoops of the dish of the day on their quaintly lop-sided wooden spoons. But in a land where food is scarce, I have sometimes hesitated before taking advantage of their kindness. And on a more practical note, the fare itself has become so monotonous that for the first time in my life I am beginning to lose interest in mealtimes.

Despite my empty stomach, I am sleeping soundly when the voices of early morning visitors bellow outside the tent.

'Good morning, get up!'

Snug in my sleeping bag, I decide to ignore the rude intrusion on my dreams.

'Get up, get up!'

I am wide awake now, but have no intention of obeying the instruction. It is cold outside.

Bang!

The tentpole receives a thwack which knocks it askew.

I unzip the flap a few inches, to see three boyish faces grinning at me. They must have noticed the irritation on my face, for two back away, leaving the third to hold out some rough-baked bread. '*Kahvaltı, efendim,*' he says sheepishly. ('We thought you'd like some breakfast.')

During the morning I walk off the edge of the 1925 Survey of India map which has served me since Tashkurghan. I am now at the very limit of the region covered by the pioneer surveyors, and to the north and east the terrain is marked simply 'unsurveyed' or 'unexplored'. Just sixty years ago the ranges around me were blank on the map. If it were not for satellites, some would still be so, for few human beings have ventured to the heights above these valleys.

As I descend it becomes blessedly warmer, and by mid-afternoon I am in shirtsleeves. I encounter greenery: at first scrubby bushes, then fully grown chenar trees, their leaves looking a ridiculously vivid green to my colour-starved eyes.

Suddenly an unfamiliar sound reaches my ears. It is a clanking, spluttering, wheezing noise – so completely out of place that I stand stock-still to listen. Eventually, infinitely slowly, out of a side valley appears an ancient lorry. It is carrying, of all things, coal.

The thing lurches to a halt. A Uyghur face grins down at me from under a battered Mao cap.

'*Yanghissar ma?*' I venture.

'*Yanghissar,*' he nods. 'Hop in!'

I cannot believe my luck. As we bounce and bucket down the valley towards the Taklamakan Desert, I reflect that I really will celebrate my birthday in Kashgar. And I do – in spite of four burst tyres which the driver and I repair, one by one, with a home-made vulcanizing kit. Each operation involves on hour by the roadside, struggling with greasy wheel hubs and hot rubber, and this adds a layer of grime to the coal dust which has already permeated every seam of my clothing and every pore of my skin. The soot in turn conceals the accumulated deposits of ten days' walking. And so, in the best tradition of desert travellers, I enter the city under a veil of filth. Passers-by stare briefly at me, smile at the obvious newcomer, and continue on their way.

The hotel receptionist bursts out laughing. 'Put your things in the dormitory,' she says. 'The hot showers are across the way.'

8
'Go In, and You Won't Come Out'

'Borsh! Borsh!'

The donkey-boy is manoeuvring his animal and cart through a lane crowded with stallholders and shoppers. The cart is four feet wide; the lane, five feet. Rough-hewn beams of timber project from the cart on either side.

'Borsh!'

Shoppers flatten themselves against stalls, and the human wave is parted for a moment. The boy sees his chance and quickly drags his cart and donkey through.

For two thousand years, Kashgar has assailed the senses. Sheltering behind mud walls between the Tümen and Kizil rivers, its bazaars have attracted traders of as many as twenty nationalities, and still do. The fruits of nearby oases are displayed cheek by jowl with goods from as far afield as Shanghai and Samarkand.

It was 1272 when Marco Polo came through Kashgar, but if he had strolled through its bazaars today he would have found them very similar. Outside the mosque, carpenters saw and leather-workers chisel at hides as if the Industrial Revolution were just a dream. Across the lane, a blacksmith fashions water containers with deafening blows on the anvil; his smithy is lined with buckets, bathtubs, and flues for Kashgar's distinctive stoves. A Tajik offers a dozen kinds of herbal medicine, and alongside him a Kazakh tobacconist squats amongst bulging sacks – the openly displayed ones piled high with tobacco, the discreetly hidden ones containing marijuana, or possibly hashish. Further down the same alley, you can buy a bridle for your camel or a pair of sandals for yourself: both will be made to measure. In another quarter, modern demands have led to the emergence of shops where electrical appliances, factory-made clothing and the ubiquitous Chinese vacuum flasks can be bought. There is even a lane devoted to audio cassettes. But as a reminder that this is Kashgar, the same alley is also the sheep exchange; so Kirghiz tribesmen can be seen most mornings, squeezing the rumps of fat-tailed sheep to the thump of disco music.

Yet if some of the sounds are new, Polo would surely have recognized the smells. Aromas of freshly baked bread, roasting kebabs, sawdust, charcoal and leather give way to the unmistakable whiff of an open drain, from which, if the day is hot, will come the merry shrieks and splashes of naked youngsters.

The fruit market is in full session. It is late September, and the grapes, figs and peaches are at their best, but pride of place on everyone's stall goes to the melon. Kashgar's scarlet-fleshed watermelons and cigar-shaped cantaloups grow to three feet in diameter, and are so popular at this time of year that the gutters run with melon juice and pedestrians wade ankle-deep in rind.

A barber has set up shop on a street corner. 'Mister, Mister!' he cries, flourishing an evil-looking razor at me; but I shake my head firmly and hurry on, leaving him to assail a more local clientele. The fashion amongst Uyghur men is to keep the head shaved, covering it in winter with a fur busby and in summer with an exquisitely embroidered velvet skullcap. The hatters' bazaar has both, and they are stacked almost as abundantly as the melons.

Although Kashgar's population includes no fewer than a quarter of a million Chinese, they rarely visit the bazaars, and the people brushing past me are Uyghurs, Tajiks and Kazakhs. They have an eastern European appearance, for their origins lie far to the west: the Uyghurs and Tajiks in the upper basin of the Oxus, Kazakhs on the shores of the Caspian and Black seas. Neither would look out of place on the boulevards of Trebizond.

On this sunny September day, the ice-cream maker whirling his centrifuge has no difficulty tempting customers with his piercing cry. The mixture tastes similar to the ices I enjoyed in Venice, and it may be that Polo had something to do with this. He could hardly have failed to note the Uyghurs' technique – in those days yet to reach Europe – of mixing milk, butter and sugar in a copper bowl embedded in ice. (In Polo's day the ice would have been hacked from lakes in winter and stored underground; today it comes from factory freezers.) Vanilla and other essences were added according to a well-tried recipe, and the solidified result served in terracotta jugs, precursors of the glass tumblers used today. Sicilians and Neapolitans use an almost identical recipe to produce their celebrated *gelati*, although historians maintain that these delicious concoctions have their origin in Chinese sorbets rather than the ices of Xinjiang. Either way, we probably have Polo to thank for them.

As I scoop the last mouthful from my second tumbler, my eye is drawn to a deep crimson carpet hung between translucent saffron silks, caught together in a shaft of sunlight from the roof of the covered market. How similar it looks to those of Erdoğan in Istanbul! I examine the carpet and wonder how this could be, but am distracted by an irritable Chinese merchant next door, clicking his abacus in sullen contrast to his jovial Uyghur neighbours. A jangle of bells heralds the approach of more donkeys, and the shouts of their drivers warn shoppers to get out of their way or be trampled upon. '*Borsh*, Mister. *Borsh!*' As I leap aside, a bouquet of freshly trodden donkey dung reaches my nostrils, and I look down to find my boot decorated with a generous helping.

Polo, arriving after an arduous journey through Afghanistan, was much taken by Kashgar's rich loess soils, its fine orchards and vineyards, and its flourishing smallholdings; but he gave the inhabitants short shrift. 'They are a wretched and mean people who eat and drink badly,' he observed. It is strange that Polo did not enlarge on this, for at the time of his visit Kashgar was in the grip of an avaricious line of despots, hated throughout Turkestan, who were no doubt the cause of the people's malaise.

Later chroniclers provide conflicting reports about the Kashgaris' lot. Doris Skrine, in a letter home in 1923, wrote:

In the autumn the bazaars, always well supplied, positively overflow with things to eat. Millers sit in their shops behind mountains of flour, next door to them grain-merchants squat surrounded by huge sacks of golden corn-cobs, rice, wheat and millet. The vegetable stalls are weighed down with enormous onions, lettuces, cabbages, bundles of spinach and strange local vegetables which are new to us. Even the tinsmiths, the cloth-merchants and the cap-sellers have fruit and vegetables to sell, and at every corner sits some one with baskets of peaches, melons, pomegranates and grapes. Luscious nectarines fall off the stalls and the street-boys do not even trouble to pick them up. Horses and donkeys snatch at bundles of hay or dried lucerne as they pass, and nobody minds, for the loss of one or two bundles matters little among so many. In this country everybody seems to be eating all the time. Not only in the town but for miles along the roads leading to it there are wayside food-pedlars every hundred yards. . . . The grander ones have booths or large barrows shaded by umbrella-like canopies of matting and piled up with sloppy white sweetmeats and 'mantas' – minced meat enclosed in thin cases of dough. . . . No wonder the Kashgaris are a fat and cheerful race.

By 1934, however, the ruthless General Ma Chung-yin ('Big Horse') had proclaimed himself King of Turkestan. The Swedish explorer Sven Hedin tells how Ma's army rampaged across Xinjiang, destroying farms and whole villages in an effort to fend off pursuit. Hedin quotes Ma's Uyghur subjects as saying: 'He has made Sinkiang a desert. We used to have everything in abundance, but now there is nothing. We are all hungry and poor.' In truth, the rot had set in nearly twenty years previously with the appointment of the general's equally brutal namesake Ma Fu-sin, who for eight years terrorized the populace by torturing and killing people, until he himself was assassinated in 1924.

In spite of the region's misfortunes, Peter Fleming, arriving in 1935 with Ella Maillart, found some long-forgotten comforts:

To most people Kashgar, which is five or six weeks' journey over 15,000 foot passes from the nearest railhead in India, must seem a place barbarously remote; but for us its outlandish name spelt civilization. The raptures of arrival were unqualified. . . . One night we slept on the floor, drank tea in mugs, ate doughy bread, argued with officials, were stared at, dreaded the next day's heat. Twenty-four hours later we were sitting in comfortable armchairs with long drinks and illustrated papers and a gramophone playing, all cares and privations banished. . . . Discovery is a delightful process, but rediscovery is better; few people can ever have enjoyed a bath more than we did, who had not had one for five and a half months.

In this respect, at least, little but the music has changed.

By common consent, the place to stay in Kashgar is the *Bīnguǎn*. The word means simply 'the Guest House' – indicating, I suppose, that there is no other worth considering. On arrival at the airport, tour groups are hurried away in minibuses to this shady enclave on the far bank of the Tümen River, to be greeted charmingly by English-speaking guides and entertained each evening with dancing and opera. The accommodation is outstanding, with proper showers and working toilets. The hotel staff are carefully chosen from among the minorities of the region, trained in the idiosyncrasies of visitors' demands, and dressed up in costume to remind guests that they are in Xinjiang. The bazaar is twenty minutes distant by donkey-cart, but the journey is rarely necessary because the hotel shop sells everything the visitor might need. A foreigner who asks about accommodation in Kashgar will be firmly directed here.

I observe all this luxury in an excursion one evening from my room in the town. I have fetched up at the former Russian Consulate, a hotchpotch of old and new buildings which make up Kashgar's second hotel. The Swede Jan Myrdal, who stayed here in 1976, claimed that in the dead of night the corridors echoed to the ghost of the villainous consul Petrovsky, rising on his toes, bending his knees, his shiny black boots creaking as he waited for the Russian cavalry to invade.

Certainly this would not have been out of character, either for the man or for the place which from 1882 to 1903 was his home. By the turn of the century the 'Great Game' between Britain and Russia was at its height. For ten years the Russians had been consolidating their diplomatic position in Xinjiang, and Petrovsky had the local Chinese officials virtually at his beck and call. By contrast, the British Agent, George Macartney, would have to wait until 1908 to be even given the status of Consul. Rivalries were intense, and when in 1905 Macartney discovered that the Russians were secretly building a road to connect Kashgar with their frontier, he lost no time in spreading the news. Rumours flew. The Chinese strengthened their garrison, and Macartney himself was soon presiding over the construction of a British consulate to rival the Russian one, just half a mile away at the 'Chinese Garden' or *Chini Bagh*.

Completed in 1913, the new consulate was placed under the guard of crack Indian Army regiments – initially Sikhs, later Hunzakuts – and George V's coat of arms was nailed over its imposing gates. It was to be the home of successive consuls for thirty-five years. Surprisingly the building still stands, easily recognizable from old photographs, its spacious reception rooms converted into dormitories for visiting Pakistanis.

The Russians never invaded. The Great War and the Revolution were to occupy their attention for the next decade, by which time the control of Xinjiang had passed to the Chinese. But the consuls continued to enjoy considerable status in Kashgar society, and were often called upon to join local dignitaries at civic occasions. By all accounts these junkets could be nerve-racking. To quote Peter Fleming again:

You never know what may happen at a banquet in Kashgar, and each of our official hosts had prudently brought his own bodyguard. Turkic and Chinese soldiers lounged everywhere; automatic rifles and executioner's swords were much in evidence, and the Mauser pistols of the waiters knocked ominously against the back of your chair as they leant over you with the dishes.

Sadly, Kashgar banquets are not what they were. But it is my birthday at last, and to celebrate I sit down in a noodle house and look on expectantly as the Uyghur at the dough-board practises his craft.

The skill of noodle making requires an apprenticeship of years. It is such an entertainment that eating the meal afterwards is something of an anticlimax. The tools are a dough-board not less than six feet long, and a ceiling not less than six feet high. Other than these, all you need are flour and water, and just enough oil to make the dough elastic.

Having rolled the dough into a thin sausage, and left it coiled beneath muslin for an hour or two to absorb the oil, the noodle-maker takes one end in each hand, and slowly, rhythmically, swings it to and fro. Almost imperceptibly the dough begins to stretch. It becomes longer and longer, and the noodle-maker's swings become wilder and more violent, until, just as it seems certain to hit the floor, he slaps the ends together and twists. Left and right halves of the dough sausage immediately join in a spiral, forming a new sausage half the length of the original, but containing two strands. The process is repeated a dozen times or more – swing, swing and twist; swing, swing and twist – and each time the sausage contains twice as many strands as before. When the strands are sufficiently fine – that is, no more than a couple of millimetres in diameter – they are thrown bodily into a vat of boiling water, and within a minute are ready to serve. A topping of vegetables or meat in a chili sauce completes the dish. The Chinese call it *fěn-sī*, the Uyghurs *laghman*, and with a bowl of tea or an eggcupful of the firewater *máo-tái* (although nobody ever allows you to drink only one eggcupful) it is to be my main source of nutrition for the next couple of months.

Five Uyghurs are seated at my table, and while our meal is being prepared a man opposite asks if I have any dollars. I reply noncommittally; my natural Western prudery about money becomes even stronger in the company of people many times poorer than myself. But the fellow is insistent. He gestures that he doesn't want to steal my dollars; merely to feast his eyes on them for a moment. Eventually, against my better judgement, I fish out of my moneybelt a single dollar bill. George Washington's benign features become steadily grubbier as they are passed around the restaurant, fingered, held to the light, chewed (to check the taste?) and finally returned to me.

Someone asks how much the note is worth. A little under four yuan, I reply. A whistle circulates round the table – and this strikes me as strange, since five and ten yuan notes are commonplace in the bazaar. But the man explains that just two years ago a dollar was worth only two yuan. Any nation which is getting richer at such speed must be a fine place, he says. Frustratingly, I lack the words and gestures to develop this conversation, which is a pity because it has great potential. Coming from a country whose own currency has fluctuated wildly against the dollar in recent years, I want to sympathize, but also to give my companions some reassurance. Fluctuations can go both ways – and, more importantly, the United States is still a few steps short of Paradise.

As if to make my point for me, the restaurateur chooses this moment to retune his radio, which has been playing Uyghur music, and suddenly I hear a deep voice speaking English. The accent is indefinable, but the voice announces that I am listening to Radio Tashkent and am about to hear the One O'clock News. There follows a short jingle, then I am subjected to five minutes of the most blatant propaganda I have heard for some time. The whole bulletin is devoted to the United States's various misdemeanours around the world. I have few quibbles with individual items, but as a summary of world affairs the bulletin is preposterous. Afterwards it is repeated in Chinese. Considering that for two decades the USSR and China have only just tolerated each other, it seems odd that the Soviets should continue to try to influence the Chinese in this way – particularly when the effort is so transparent.

I empty my bowl of noodles, and reflect that despite the improvement in communications, Asian diplomacy seems to have lost some of its refinement since Polo's time. But although credited as the world's first diplomat, Polo's greatest contribution to posterity, to my mind, was in a more practical field. As Kublai Khan's envoy in Burma and central Asia he must have eaten countless meals of noodles, and observed, as I have, how they were made. Back in Venice he is said to have astonished the citizens with the fabulous craft. Sadly no description survives of how he tossed the dough, but his performance must have been impressive, for the food has become Italy's most popular dish. It is of course spaghetti.

Kashgar today is going through a transformation which is probably the quickest, if not the most dramatic, in its long history. The ancient city walls have already all but gone, thanks to Mao Zedong's assertion that historical awareness was threatening the Cultural Revolution. In their place are boulevards – straight, wide and characterless. At present they carry few motor vehicles, and the traffic lights at the junctions flash their signals to no one. At the city's single roundabout, vehicles circulate in whichever direction they please.

This state of affairs is unlikely to last. The horse-drawn *tongas* with their gay canopies will soon give way to buses brought in from Beijing. The donkey-carts with their raucous drivers will be replaced by tractors, or by those two-stroke 'walking tractors' which assault the ears and nose throughout urban Asia. Lining the avenues, more of the old buildings will be torn down and replaced by Chinese blockhouses (earlier examples of which, after a mere thirty years, are already crumbling back into their sandy foundations). Outside the city, the irrigated fields which once fed Kashgar's people will be engulfed by development to house and employ the hordes of Han Chinese shipped in from the east.

Mass tourism is also just around the corner. Unlike Lhasa in Tibet, Kashgar has no great history of civil unrest; its population of Uyghurs, Kirghiz, Tajiks and Kazakhs are, for the most part, content to ply their trades and be photographed doing so. Located romantically at the historic crossroads of Asia, the city will be as popular a destination in the 1990s as Kathmandu and Cuzco are today. The more resourceful entrepreneurs will provide for the tourists' strange tastes and needs; and the Government will put up hotels to accommodate them.

Kashgar people are used to being overrun: in the last two thousand years they have been conquered five times by the Chinese alone. Generation after generation have quietly raised their crops whilst wars have raged around them. Their experience in this matter will, I suspect, be severely tested over the next ten years.

One of the saddest aspects of Kashgar's 'great leap forward' is that camels are now a rare sight in the city. Like the horses and donkeys, they are giving way to motor transport. The Shuli Transport Company has been recommended to me as a business that still employs them, but when I track down its premises in the city's north-eastern suburbs I find only lorries in varying stages of decomposition. Yes, an official says, the company used to run camel caravans, but they were too slow and unreliable to compete with motor vehicles. The last one left in 1983.

Looking at the heaps of mangled machinery around the depot, I find this curt dismissal of the Ship of the Desert hard to accept. Did any other companies use the poor beast? No, says the man; the Shuli was the last. With a final look at the contraptions which have replaced it, I turn my attention to the journey ahead.

Throughout history, wise travellers have avoided the Taklamakan Desert. Those venturing far from the roads along its northern and southern fringes have rarely lived to tell of their adventures. Indeed, in the Uyghur language, the very name means 'Go in, and you won't come out'. Modern traffic favours the northern route, and indeed a passable road connects Kashgar with the regional capital of Ürümqi, three or four days' journey to the north-east. But previously the southern route was more popular, and almost all the early travellers seem to have gone this way. To my disappointment, the southern route is now closed to foreigners.

Clutching at straws, I apply at Kashgar's Public Security Bureau for an Aliens' Travel Permit, a small cardboard document which allows you to visit a limited number of areas otherwise closed. To my surprise, after some discussion amongst the officers on duty, I am given one for Yarkand and Khotan, the first two oases along the southern route. Although the permit is valid for less than a fifth of the distance I want to go, it is a start. I will show it at every opportunity and see how far I can get. (It is to be two months before I notice, in Beijing, that it has been made out for the previous year.)

Despite their unprepossessing appearance, Aliens' Travel Permits have a distinguished pedigree. In Polo's time, couriers working for the Mongol Court could claim its protection if they carried the Khan's travel permit or *paizah*. Unlike today's permits, the *paizah* was a bar of silver or gold, engraved with instructions that the bearer should be given safe conduct. Anyone who failed to help the fortunate carrier of such a permit was deemed to have offended the Khan himself, and punished accordingly. Polo had a *paizah* for at least one of his journeys, though he does not record whether it did him any good – or, indeed, if it was made out for the right year.

A weak autumn sun hangs over the desert as I walk towards the Tümen bridge and the road south-east. Kashgar is already preparing for winter. The summer drinks and melon stalls have disappeared, and on each house's flat roof a woodpile is growing, ready to feed the winter fires. By the bridge I find a clutch of Uyghurs hitch-hiking, but within minutes a lorry driver has invited us all to clamber aboard, and we are bowling across the scrubby desert fringe. At Yanghissar we are joined by more hitch-hikers, so it is a merry throng which in early afternoon dismounts at Yarkand.

Most of the Taklamakan oases have two names: an ancient Uyghur one and a modern Chinese one. The accounts of the early traders refer to Yarkand, Kargilik, Keriya, Charchan and Charkilik, but today's traveller must learn to think of them additionally as Sache, Yecheng, Yutien, Qiemo and Ruoqiang.

The original Yarkand, described by earlier visitors as a place of alleyways so narrow that two loaded donkeys could not pass, is nowhere to be found. As in Kashgar, the Chinese have imposed their own ideas about town planning, but here the transformation is complete: the old town has simply been swept away. After wandering disconsolately along avenues lined with the familiar concrete monoliths, I come across a lorry heading onwards to Kargilik, and go with it.

Here the road to Lhasa departs from the Silk Road, and the transport depot is crowded with lorries preparing for the 1,500-mile, two-week journey, said to be the most arduous in Asia. I arrive at dusk to find the town in the grip of a power failure, a circumstance apparently not uncommon, for every stall in the small bazaar is well equipped with paraffin lamps. I dump my pack in the depot's dormitory and set out to find some food.

The bazaar has several eating houses, and their speciality is dumplings. Many of Xinjiang's bazaars seem to specialize in one dish or another – or maybe it is simply the *plat du jour*. Today I have a choice of mutton dumplings for the equivalent of 4p, vegetable dumplings for 2p, or 'dumpling dumplings' (dough right through) for 1p. The last seem to be the most popular: in every eating house, customers are munching their way through mounds of them. But it has been a long day, and I treat myself to the more sophisticated vegetable version. As I wait for the charcoal steamer to do its work, I bask in the pleasure of being back on the road. In Kashgar an enterprising Russian has opened a café-bar serving quiche, pizza, cheesecake, apple pie and – horror of horrors – 'Kashburgers'. Although I confess to having enjoyed his fare, I am appreciating even more my twopenny dumplings under the hissing paraffin lamps.

I sleep with a group of surly Tibetans, who spend much of the night arguing and drinking butter tea. A transistor radio blares from a corner, and they listen intently to each news bulletin before resuming their wrangling. (In Beijing, I was later to hear that Lhasa's uprising against the Chinese regime had taken place a few days later. This may have been why they are listening so avidly to the news)

A daily bus service links Kargilik with Khotan, the last oasis on my travel permit. The bus is billed to leave at 8.00 a.m., Beijing time – well before sunrise in this westernmost part of China. At 9.30 dawn breaks over the transport depot to reveal a growing knot of passengers beside the still deserted and locked bus. At 10.00 the driver emerges from a dormitory, rubbing his eyes. At 10.15 a scrum suggestive of Twickenham rather than the

Taklamakan develops, as driver and conductor walk over from the tea-house where they have been breakfasting on dumplings. At 10.30 we are on our way.

Anyone who approaches the Taklamakan Desert expecting a sea of sand is due for a surprise. Sand there is in plenty, and some of the dunes reach 140 feet or more in height. But in many areas the dunes have been colonized by marram grass: the same, I believe, as that found on the seashores of Europe. In other parts the desert consists of stones or rubble, either pancake-flat or furrowed by dried-up river beds. Yet other patches are grassland, grazed by herds of goats which seem to wander at will. Even in the true desert, clumps of thorn manage to cling to life, their roots tapping water supplies deep beneath the sand. And in some places, full-grown trees give the terrain the appearance of savannah, where giraffes and zebras would not seem out of place.

In the course of journeying across these landscapes, the traveller will sooner or later come to an oasis which may be ten miles or more across. You see them from a distance, a line of green which becomes steadily more distinct as you approach. Their edges are abrupt. One moment you are shielding your eyes against the glare of the desert sun; the next you have plunged into a world of cool paths shaded by poplar, mulberry and ash trees. Irrigation channels are everywhere, carrying water from the Tien-Shan or Kunlun mountains into fields which at most seasons are dotted with people. Resolutely they bend to their tasks of sowing, hoeing, reaping or simply talking to their precious crops.

Silk Road travellers before 1948 reported these oases to be primitive in the extreme. The bazaars were filthy and poorly stocked; schooling was non-existent; and many of the inhabitants suffered from goitres or other diseases. But recently the Taklamakan has seen much progress – for better or for worse. A road is slowly being built. All the oases now have schools and electricity, and some even enjoy the dubious benefit of satellite television. Most have a hospital or clinic. Nowhere do I see a goitre. Only in Khotan am I to find that in health matters, at least, the Taklamakan oases still have some way to go.

Khotan, like Kashgar, was once a kingdom. Polo reported that it took him eight days to cross, but was amply stocked with the means of life: 'having vineyards, orchards and cottonfields in plenty'. Unlike the degenerates of Kashgar, Khotan's citizens impressed Polo with their hardworking and peaceable disposition, and I look forward to seeing if these characteristics still persist.

My arrival in Khotan, however, is ill-timed. The city is in the grip of a hepatitis epidemic, and the news on the streets is that a hundred people have already died, with more cases being reported daily. The authorities have issued a list of do's and don'ts, and large-character posters are plastered everywhere, their warnings set out in stern scarlet ink. I decide that this is not the moment to explore Khotan, and within hours of arriving I am preparing to leave.

Beyond Khotan the road deteriorates. Tyre tracks are quickly obliterated by the shifting sands, and drivers' skills are tested as they search for the next patch of solid ground. I am in the company of a dozen passengers – Uyghur, Tibetan, Russian and Chinese – on a lorry bound for Charchan.

Unlike my companions, I am worried not about getting lost or stuck, but about getting caught. So my heart sinks when we approach a barrier and turn in to a police compound alongside. For the moment luck is on my side. The police show no interest in my permit, which is just as well, for I am some way beyond the limit of its validity. Instead they make a tour of the other passengers, inspecting small pieces of paper which turn out to be certificates showing that they have been inoculated against hepatitis. One of the Uyghurs fails to produce one, and is marched off into a mud building. I don't have one either, but being a foreigner I seem to be regarded as inhuman and therefore immune. The police wave me aside, and turn their attention to decontaminating the vehicle. First, everyone is ordered to remove their luggage, which consists mainly of large quantities of fruit and vegetables (the most likely source of infection). Then a police cadet appears with a basin of disinfectant, which he sprinkles daintily and randomly around the cab and wheels. After this baptism, the passengers pile back on board and continue munching their fruit and veg as before.

Through the afternoon and well into the night, the lorry bounces and lunges towards Charchan. With every jolt, its passengers settle more deeply against the sides and tailboard, sheltering as best they can from the dust-laden slipstream. I share my corner with a family of Russian *émigrés*, and spend much of the journey trying to make out what has brought them so far from home. They are from Kazakhstan. Could they, I wonder, be of similar stock to the unfortunate Borodishin, the one-time Cossack commander whom Peter Fleming and Ella Maillart found in 1935, eking out his dying days in a Qaidam *yurt*? Certainly the father of the family matches Borodishin's description: small and squat, with a black, square-cut beard and shining brown eyes. Speaking in deeply accented Russian, he maintains a continuous monologue towards his wife, two daughters and me. He seems quite unperturbed by my incomprehension. Recognizing my plight, however, his wife and daughters speak in monosyllables, their main contribution being to serve from beneath their voluminous greatcoats an endless supply of rock-hard buns.

Opposite, a villainous-looking Tibetan journeys in silence beneath the most immense fur hat I have ever seen. At the rear, a shiny-faced Chinese introduces himself as Zhang Jun Hui, a physical education teacher, and as if to prove his point launches into brief but furious jogging at every stop. I notice that the Uyghur driver and co-driver keep firmly aloof from their free-loading passengers. None of us is invited to share their cab, and when we stop for meals at wayside transport depots they take separate tables, glowering at us with such obvious contempt that I wonder if they are plotting to dump us in the desert.

It is after dark on the second day when the lorry pulls in to Charchan. I have shared the lives of its crew and passengers for thirty-six hours, and watch a little sadly as one by one they go off to their homes. The Charchan depot has no dormitory, so I am to stay at the 'guest house'. I am escorted through darkened streets to a concrete building behind high gates, to be given a room with a couple of taciturn Uyghurs. An enamel basin is brought in, and a jug of cold water, and I set about washing away some of the grime of the road. I have barely finished when the door opens to reveal a young Chinese face. 'How do you do?' exclaims a voice in perfect English. 'My name's Pin.'

Chui Cho Pin is a geologist with the Xinjiang Geological and Mineral Resource Bureau, working with a brigade of twenty looking for oil. For several days he has been waiting for transport to Khotan, and is as pleased to have company as I am. We spend the evening in the guest house yard, eating our fill of Charchan's superb peaches, which fall off the trees around us with every whisper of the breeze.

Oilfields are already being exploited on the northern fringes of the Taklamakan, and Pin tells me that the signs are favourable around Charchan too. Twenty-five years old, intelligent and keenly ambitious, he is already deputy leader of his brigade, and tells me he is earning 300 yuan per month. Although twice the average Chinese wage, this is less than £32, so I ask him what his living expenses are.

'Well, first of all there's the rent of my government flat in Kashgar,' replies Pin. 'That's 3 yuan per month. Then, groceries for myself and my wife usually come to just under 100 yuan. That leaves 200 yuan per month for us to spend on ourselves.' Pin smiles. 'I know that doesn't sound much, but actually we're very well off. We have a cassette player, and we're saving up to buy a television.'

Pin is an example of a new breed of Chinese which has emerged since the downfall of the Gang of Four. He is too young to recall more than dimly the horrors of the Cultural Revolution, though his father, a university lecturer, was sent away to work in a mine. He talks mostly of his own career, which he sees as a Westerner would. His immediate goal is to be a brigade leader, and he freely admits that his sights are on the status and money which the job will confer, rather than the opportunity to serve the brigade or the bureau. His motives may be lowly but his honesty is refreshing, and I am almost disappointed when news comes that the weekly lorry to Charkilik will be leaving in the morning.

Pin is confident that Charchan's police will pay no attention to me whilst I am in his company, and urges me to come and see the bazaar. 'I'll show you where they make *yù-zhū-bǎo*, the jade jewellery,' he promises, hurrying me down a side street towards some shacks.

Polo was not the first to observe that the riverbeds around Charchan were rich in jasper and chalcedony, the stone we call jade. A thousand years before his visit, a brisk trade had been established between Charchan and the cities of eastern China, and it continues to this day. The Chinese have always treasured the green-veined stone, considering it to represent the *yang* elements of the universe. Pin leads me to a dimly lit workshop where a Uyghur woman is carving bracelets and pendants by hand. The jewellery is elegant, but the chiselling and filing look desperately laborious. Today, she says, most of Charchan's jade is taken to be machine-tooled in Beijing, Suzhou and Guangzhou, and she is Charchan's only jadesmith: the last of a two-thousand-year line.

I arrive at the depot at the appointed hour of 5.00 a.m. local time, to find the Charkilik lorry already gone. I stare at the empty space in disbelief. Have I misunderstood the arrangement? Was the departure to have been at 5.00 a.m. Beijing time? But this would have been 3.00 a.m. by the local clock, which is plainly ridiculous. Or is it? Has the driver simply woken early and decided to make a move? The depot is in darkness; and with no one around to explain the mystery, I sit shivering and dejected by the gate. Only one lorry, they say, makes this run each week, so it looks as if I may be in for a long wait.

Staring into the darkness, I hear a distant sound. A vehicle! Half a mile away, headlights appear from a side road and turn towards me. Gradually they grow brighter, the sound grows louder, and at last they transform themselves into the missing lorry.

The driver, seeing my relief, grins down at me from the cab. 'You're nice and early. I've just filled up with diesel. Shall we go?'

A cold dawn creeps over the desert. Watching from the cramped cab of the 'Liberation' lorry (a model designed in 1950 and hardly changed since), I hug the heating pipe and peer at the ruts and boulders dancing in the flickering headlights. To the south, the jagged outline of the Kunlun Mountains is already beginning to catch the first rays of morning. But on the desert floor the night persists, and as we turn south alongside the Charchan River I strain vainly to see whether its bed carries water. The road makes a great loop here, and it is another hour before my question is answered. I have taken off my sweater and am already shading my eyes from a blinding sun by the time we cross the bridge, its dozen arches spanning nothing but rubble and sand.

The road teeters on the brink of existence. Some stretches are graded and firm; others difficult to identify as a road at all. On one of the latter we become hopelessly bogged down in soft sand, and it takes an hour of shovelling before we are able to move again. On some of these soft stretches attempts have been made to 'fix' the desert, using marram seedlings and netting. The resultant dunes, perhaps fifty feet high, look like thinning scalps under hairnets. Although they relieve the monotony of the desert, their practical value may be limited, for many have already been engulfed by the ever-shifting sands.

The European explorers Sven Hedin and Aurel Stein reported evidence of whole cities buried not far from here. Not only does the desert itself pose a constant threat, but river courses have been known to shift without warning, taking with them vital irrigation supplies. No oasis could survive for more than a season if its water were taken away. Communities relying on the Tarim River have been particularly at risk, because for no apparent reason it has changed its course twice in historic times. Several of today's abandoned cities used to receive their water from this fickle source.

During the afternoon a sandstorm appears on the horizon, and the driver pulls up, waiting for it to pass. The sky grows dark; then the lorry begins to rock on its suspension as gusts batter it on all sides. In the past, travellers less fortunate than myself would simply have lain on the ground and covered their heads during such storms, but I am thankful to be protected by the cab. The driver is nonchalant, and when after fifteen minutes the wind abates he starts the engine and continues without a word. The setting sun throws rays of deep orange over the roadside dunes, and I reflect that at last I am beginning to feel at home in the desert, as we approach Charkilik, the ancient city of Lop.

Pride, as they say, comes before a fall. Within an hour of arriving, I have been betrayed to Charkilik's police. Without warning, two uniformed constables burst into my dormitory at the transport depot, and march to where I am relaxing on the horsehair mattress which passes for a bed. '*Hù-zhào!*' ('Passport!'), they shout. I hand it over, and after a cursory glance the senior officer pockets it. He motions for me to pick up my rucksack. Then they grasp my elbows, and under the impassive gaze of the other guests I am frogmarched away.

To my surprise, our destination is not the police station, but a *bīnguǎn* in the middle of the town. After supervising the paying of my second bill for lodgings this evening, the officers gesture that I am to go and sleep. I will be dealt with in the morning. My room, a cubicle lit by a twenty-watt bulb, is filthy, expensive and, worst of all, directly opposite the police station.

One reason why I particularly didn't want to be picked up here is that Charkilik is a mere 130 miles from China's nuclear testing ground at Lop Nur – very close, by the standards of the Taklamakan. In 1986 a British journalist was deported for being found in this area, and I pray that this will not be my fate too. My sleep at the *bīnguǎn* is interrupted by nightmares of other possible punishments which might await me – like Chinese water torture.

There are occasions in foreign countries when it pays to know as little of the language as possible, and I decide that this is just such a moment. Facing the police sergeant and his two constables next morning over a wide polished desk, I explain what I am doing in Charkilik, and – as I hoped – succeed in thoroughly muddling them. After an hour or so an 'English teacher' is brought in to interpret, but, speaking no more than a few words of English, he only aggravates the confusion.

By the end of two hours the sergeant has reached a decision. I am to be fined 100 yuan (just under £20) and sent back to Kashgar forthwith. I wince – not at the fine, but at the thought of that loathsome road. For the second time in ten days, I find myself clutching at straws.

This time, however, I have a trump card, and in desperation I play it now. The ace up my sleeve is the hepatitis epidemic at Khotan. Its success will depend on the police having heard of the outbreak, and on no vaccine being available – and I am lucky on both counts. After some debate, the sergeant and his constables agree that it would be unwise to dispatch an unvaccinated foreigner on the road to Kashgar. But neither can they allow me to continue east. I watch anxiously as the sergeant points on a wall map to the nearest town open to foreigners, 300 miles to the north. The place is Korla – one of the Taklamakan's northern oases, on the Kashgar–Ürümqi road. A track has been built across the desert, and it happens that a jeep will be leaving for Korla tomorrow. One of the constables will have a word with the driver to make sure I am given a place on board. They have also been reconsidering the other part of my sentence, and rather than fine me they have come down in favour of a more original and beneficial punishment. I am to write a self-criticism.

I can hardly believe my luck. No fine; no return to Kashgar. I launch myself into the self-criticism and write like a man possessed. Never have I composed anything so incisive, so cutting. The pen flies across the paper, and what emerges is a character assassination – liberally sprinkled with words like 'sorry'.

I am on the tenth page, and just getting into my stride, when the sergeant stops me. It is 2.00 p.m. and he wants his lunch. Feeling like an examination candidate who has run out of time, I finish off the piece and exchange it for my passport. The passport goes back into my moneybelt, and I am comforted by its presence against my stomach. The self-criticism, I suspect, goes straight in the bin.

I cannot help smiling. My punishment has been decided with the decorum of three dowager ladies arguing about whether to go to the park or the pump room. Now, having followed two-thirds of the Silk Road's forbidden southern branch, I will soon be free to explore its northern course.

In spite of a lousy night, I cannot deny that I have been treated kindly, and for my remaining few hours in Charchan I am allowed to roam on trust. I take full advantage of the opportunity, but find the oasis much like the others, its wide streets lined by the now-familiar concrete buildings of the Chinese. In contrast to Yarkand, however, the reconstruction here is still going on, and it occurs to me that this may be why the southern oases are closed to foreigners. Could it be that Xinjiang's Chinese administrators, embarrassed by their relentless decimation of the minority cultures, are keeping outsiders at bay until the purge is complete?

Next morning, promptly at 9.00, a Toyota Land Cruiser screams up to the *bīnguǎn* and brakes in a cloud of dust. Music emerges, followed by cheers and whoops, and as the dust clears I find eight Uyghur faces grinning at me. They seem to have been to an all-night party. If this hadn't been obvious from a glance at their faces, it would have been evident from the body on the parcel shelf, snoring gently, unaware of anything but the dreams of drunken sleep.

It is usually not a good idea to take lifts from drunks, especially when nine of them are packed into a vehicle designed for six. I establish that this is indeed the lift that has been arranged for me, and keep the Uyghurs talking while I size them up. The group are homeward bound from a wedding. Three of them are very far gone, and are relying on one another's support to stay upright in their seats. However, the rest (discounting the one on the parcel shelf) appear to be merry rather than tight, and I notice that the driver seems quite sober. In any case, I argue to myself, I have little choice but to throw in my lot with this happy bunch. I join the four already occupying the front seats, and within minutes we are away.

My judgement of the driver was quite correct. He manoeuvres deftly around the potholes, of which there are many, and around oncoming vehicles, of which there are mercifully few. Those of us in the front seats engage in a hilarious though limited attempt at conversation, in between fending off the spirited efforts of those in the back to climb over and join us.

After an hour or so, our amiable bantering is interrupted by a loud bang. The Toyota lurches to one side and slews to a halt. All pile out to pinpoint the problem, which is not difficult: we have burst a front tyre, and it seems to have all but shredded itself in the process of stopping. There is silence while this sinks in, then someone remembers the spare wheel behind the back seat. A frenzy of activity breaks out; the stiff is removed from his position on the parcel shelf, and we open up the back of the vehicle. One by one the smiles disappear. There is no spare wheel; it has been left in Korla.

The driver takes command of the situation. We will flag down another Toyota, he says, and exchange wheels. The five capable passengers are deployed to lift the vehicle on one side while he places stones beneath the chassis, then he removes the stricken wheel and props it in readiness against a boulder. As we have hardly seen another vehicle since leaving Charchan, I cannot help feeling that the chances of a Toyota happening along, with similar tyre specifications, carrying a spare wheel and willing to part with it, are a bit remote. But then, in the desert one has to be an optimist.

Minutes turn to hours. A lorry passes by, and a couple of army jeeps. One of the jeeps stops and we compare wheels, but they are not the same. Then, suddenly, from the north, we see approaching the unmistakable shape of a Toyota. Wild gesticulations from nine excited figures succeed in bringing it to a halt, and we explain our predicament.

The vehicle is carrying a spare wheel, but the Uyghur driver is reluctant to part with it for less than its full value, which is considerable. We bargain with gusto, offering all sorts of non-essential parts from our own vehicle in an attempt to beat him down. But our efforts are in vain. The man is about to drive off, and I have resigned myself to more waiting, when the conversation takes a surprising turn. His attitude visibly changes as it emerges that one of our passengers is engaged to his cousin. Kinship has been established! Instantly all monetary considerations are swept aside, and the man quickly hands over the precious wheel. Within minutes it has been fitted, hands have been shaken, and once more we are on our way.

To celebrate our good fortune it is decided to open a crate of beer. I wince at the thought of the effect this will have on my still too-jolly companions, but am powerless to intervene. The wait by the roadside has been a thirsty one, and the crate is soon gone. For the next twenty miles I am treated to a discordant medley of Uyghur drinking songs.

Without warning, the Toyota begins to splutter and cough. It misfires, fires again, then dies completely and we glide to a halt. The symptoms are unmistakable – we are out of fuel. A moment's silence follows before it is remembered that there is a spare fuel can in the back. Out we tumble, the stiff is once more removed from his perch, and the back is opened up. Nine hopeful faces peer in; but alas, there is no fuel can. Like the spare wheel, it has been left behind.

The sun has become hot, and sitting in the vehicle's shade we are soon overcome by sleep. As a result we miss the approach of the first two vehicles, which pass in close convoy whilst we are still struggling to our feet. The third and fourth vehicles fail to respond to our waves and shouts, and it is more than three hours before we finally flag down a good Samaritan, secure a few gallons of fuel and continue on our way.

We are now extremely hot, tired, hungry and thirsty, and I notice that the driver is struggling to keep the Toyota on the road. I wriggle alongside him and help with the steering, directing a hefty thwack towards his ribs each time he seems to be dropping off to sleep. My other companions are drowsy too, which at least relieves me of their singing. After another half-hour I am doing all the steering, the driver having slumped to a position where he can no longer see through the windscreen. Somehow, this unorthodox and nerve-racking method of dual control keeps us on the road until the oasis of Tikanlik, where, with some difficulty, I steer up to a roadside rest house and persuade the driver to apply the brakes.

Staggering from the vehicle, I savour the peacefulness of this smallest and remotest of the Taklamakan oases. Beneath twin rows of poplar trees, chickens scratch in the roadside ditch. Beyond, sunflowers quiver in the breeze. A donkey-cart rumbles by. Only the chatter of my still tipsy companions, enlivened by an occasional belch, reminds me of my ordeal.

I don't often abandon a lift halfway through, but on this occasion I feel I have done my bit. Some Kazakhs from a truck which passed us earlier are sitting in front of the rest house, tucking into plates of noodles. They wave me over to join them, and, observing the state of the Uyghurs, quickly offer to take me on to Korla. I accept without hesitation. Before they fully realize what is happening, I have taken up a 'shotgun' position on the back of the lorry and left my happy-go-lucky friends to their fate.

My new mount is already piled high with an assortment of merchandise: tomatoes, aubergines, watermelons, a large quantity of timber, a diesel generator, three cracked mirrors and a galvanized tub. I find a niche amongst the watermelons and settle down to enjoy the ride. The first thirty miles are fast and smooth, but then we come to a section where the road is still being built, and the pace and smoothness deteriorate. Several dozen Chinese labourers stand back to watch us pass.

After a time we reach a point where a new embankment has just been completed; in the absence of a steamroller, passing vehicles are being directed along it to compact the surface. We seem to be the first to have this honour, and sink to our axles. It takes much revving by the driver and shoving by the road crew before we reach solid ground again, and I turn back proudly to see the two troughs we have made.

It is a critical moment. Nobody has noticed the telephone cables stretched across the new road, too low for a loaded lorry to pass beneath. A splintering of wood and a screeching of strained metal give a split-second's warning, then the world crashes about me. I dive for cover and pound desperately on the cab roof, but it is too late. The cables snap and recoil, whipping around me. A baulk of timber splits and falls across my back. By the time the lorry has come to a halt, all eight cables have been severed and are decorating it like tinsel on a Christmas tree.

I clamber down and examine myself cautiously. My back is bruised a little, but no bones are broken, and after disentangling ourselves from Charchan's only link with the outside world we continue on our way.

Korla reveals its presence whilst we are still some way off. For centuries a Silk Road staging post, it is today more famous for its factories; even from a distance, smokestacks dwarf the poplar and chenar trees. The city marks the western terminus of China's railway system, though this distinction will soon be taken by the long-awaited line from Ürümqi into Soviet Kazakhstan.

I have not seen such an unashamedly industrial landscape since Karachi on the far-off shores of the Arabian Sea. Only one of the factories gives any clue to its purpose – 'KORLA N° 1 CRACKING PLANT' (whatever that may be). I stroll among the great buildings, and indulge in the freedom to do so without the fear of a heavy hand upon my shoulder; for Korla is open to foreigners. Not for the first time, I wonder at the rationale behind a policy which encourages us to visit such hideous places, whilst keeping so much beauty out of bounds. Over the next few weeks I am to become familiar with this grim side of China, for belching mills deface almost every city from Xinjiang to the South China Sea. Many of them date from the 1950s, when heavy industry was seen as the key to modernization, and battalions of Soviet 'experts' were invited to help establish the black goliaths. It is true that they enabled China to ride the economic storms of those crucial early years: that every railway locomotive, tractor or goodness-knows-what coming out of the factories meant one less to be imported. But the programme has devastated much of the country's urban landscape, and placed millions of people in working conditions that would have made Charles Dickens wince.

I move on quickly, through the Turfan Desert to Ürümqi, hoping for better things. Ürümqi's gaily coloured tourist brochure describes it as 'a beautiful city nestling at the foot of the

Tianshan Mountains, at its best in the warmer season when all kinds of flowers are in full bloom'. Others, less kindly but more accurately, have described it as one of the ugliest cities on earth. The missionaries Mildred Cable and Francesca French, who lived here during the interwar years, wrote: 'No one enjoys life in Ürümqi, no one leaves the town with regret, and it is full of people who are only there because they cannot get permission to leave.' When they did finally make their escape – ignominiously, it seems, on a horse-cart – the ladies recorded ruefully that they had to leave behind their cameras and their organ. (I cherish a fond fantasy that the organ may still reside in an Ürümqi back parlour.) Eric Shipton added that a bazaar of unspeakable squalor surrounded the walled city, which was begrimed by soot from nearby mines.

Ürümqi is Korla on an altogether grander scale. The obscure village of earlier times has swelled into a regional capital of over a million people – helped by a considerable forced migration of Han Chinese, who now make up three-quarters of its population. If it were not for a rich natural setting of mountains and plains, the city would be quite unbearable.

In Ürümqi's sulphurous atmosphere I sniff the familiar smog of my childhood. Under similar rain-laden, smog-hung skies, one's only escape from Sheffield in the early postwar years was to the moors and cloughs of the Pennines. In Ürümqi, too, the urban gloom is tempered by a frame of mountains set enticingly on the northern horizon, surmounted by the peak known as Bogda Feng. I gaze at their outlines. Serrated ridges piercing a sky of pale blue, they represent all that I have hungered for during my days in the Taklamakan. When I entered the desert I hardly dared hope that I would emerge successfully on its opposite side. After all, doesn't its very name warn against such expectations? Now, having completed the crossing, I feel I have earned some time in more Elysian surroundings.

With a last look back towards the distant sands, I set off for the jewel at the heart of the Bogda Feng range, perhaps the most celebrated lake in China. Acclaimed by Chinese and Western writers alike, my destination is of course Tianchi – 'The Heavenly Pool'.

9
Through the Jade Gate

Ice-white and forest-green, the slopes of Bogda Feng tumble into a lake now cobalt, now almost indigo under a blustery autumn sky. My perch on the rocky shore is buffeted by a bitter wind from the icefields, and I find myself alternately bathed in sunshine and squinting through squalls of rain. It is late afternoon. The few day-trippers are clambering aboard their minibuses and will soon be speeding back towards Ürümqi, hot baths and soft beds.

My home tonight will be simpler but infinitely more fitting. Some Kazakhs have pitched their *yurt* near the foot of the lake, and the father of the family has invited me to stay the night. Like the Kirghiz of the Pamirs, Kazakhs are nomads and migrate seasonally between upland pastures and lowland plains. They are most numerous on the Russian side of the border, where they occupy the Soviet Socialist Republic of Kazakhstan. But here in northern Xinjiang a sizeable community of Kazakhs herd their sheep and goats among the forests and pastures of Bogda Feng. Kazakh tents are taller and more capacious than those of their Kirghiz cousins to the south-west – and necessarily so, for Kazakhs favour large families, and it is not uncommon to find a dozen sharing a single *yurt*.

Under the gaze of my hosts, I have washed the desert sand out of my ears and from between my toes, and soaked my travel-stained clothes in the frigid waters of the lake. Now, as the sun sinks towards the distant plains, I amble among pines and cypresses, absorbing the unfamiliar colours and enjoying this nugget of beauty in the wilderness of the Steppe. By world standards, it has to be said that the lake called Tianchi is neither large nor particularly breathtaking. The Alps, Andes and Rockies can boast many grander and more 'heavenly' pools. Those splendours, however, are thousands of miles away. For travellers in Xinjiang, the delight of Tianchi, hardly five miles from end to end and nowhere more than a few hundred yards wide, lies in the simple fact that it is here.

But I must make haste. Already winter is sweeping across central China. In Ürümqi the birches lining the avenues will still be glistening gold, but here on the shores of Tianchi their leaves are shrivelling and falling. Evening is accompanied by the onset of mist and driving rain. At home, in such conditions, I might turn up my jacket collar and head for the nearest pub; but here I can do neither. My thoughts cannot compete with such elements, and as the wind freshens to gale force I abandon my contemplation and make a dash for the *yurt*. Half an hour later my toes are thawing in front of a wrought-iron stove, hands warmed by a bowl of hot noodles, and ears assailed by a static-laden Radio Moscow, trumpeting from a radio at the back of the tent.

The Kazakhs of this valley are the most prosperous of the nomadic people I have met so far. Apart from the radio (a Bakelite monster from the 1950s) their *yurt* is bedecked with some fine pieces of furniture: a dresser, a kitchen cabinet, and even a bed. It is a single bed, and I wonder to whom in the family it belongs. I might have guessed. Within minutes of my arrival the father taps me on the shoulder. Melodramatically, he points to the pillow, thumps it, and puts it in my arms.

As the fire is stoked and we settle down for the evening, I try to count the number to whom this *yurt* is home. It isn't easy. Children skip in and out, oblivious to the storm outside, under the great felt flap which serves as a door. Just as I think I have a rough tally, yet another newcomer appears. Finally I decide that eleven people – children, parents, grandparents and great-grandparents – live in this sixteen-foot diameter circle.

Tianchi has for long attracted visitors from throughout China, and these days they come from all over the world. Over the years, its people have grown used to strangers. The parents no longer bombard them with questions; the children do not gaze wide-eyed. Unlike my hosts in the Pamirs, this family receives me into its midst with a casual ease, and when I broach the question of paying for their hospitality I am given a scrap of paper indicating the going rate. At first I am relieved to be no longer the centre of attention, for I can relax and observe my surroundings in peace.

But it foreshadows the intrusion of a wider world: a more sophisticated society, which as I continue eastwards will make itself ever more keenly felt.

Tonight's meal will be a simple one. From behind a partition, the mother of the family takes a jug and pours bowls of *kumis* (mare's milk), in which we all dunk slices of fried sour-dough bread. The sound of slurping fills the tent. Back in Ürümqi, the day-trippers will be disgorging from their minibuses at the Kunlun Hotel. Soon they will be filing into the dining room, to be served 'specialities of the region' by Kazakh women turned out in exquisite traditional costume. As I drink my fill of *kumis* and eat the sour-dough bread, I envy them not a jot.

Dawn breaks to reveal blue skies and a valley washed clean by the night's storm. Over the lake, a shallow mist hovers. Today the remaining birch leaves seem truly to be made of gold, and the morning breeze brings crystal droplets showering down from them. I am witnessing the very last throes of autumn, and I wander far up the valley absorbing the spectacle.

On the morning of my third day I awake to a sharp frost, a stiff wind and banked clouds to the north. Autumn is over; it is time to go. I book my seat on the daily minibus: the same one that on my first day here I watched so gleefully as it disappeared from view. Then I bid farewell to my Kazakh friends, who are making preparations for their own return to the plains. I join the day-trippers boarding the bus, and soon we are disembarking at the Kunlun Hotel. I take a room but shun the dinner. After my freedom of the last few days, I can't face the thought of sitting at a table making polite conversation with my fellow tourists about the joys of the Heavenly Pool.

Mid-October often brings Ürümqi's first snowfall, and this year is no exception. Pathetically ill-prepared, I trudge miserably through the sleet. I scour the department stores for a warm jacket like the ones worn by the Kazakhs – but they are sold out. I buy thick socks and woollen long johns, and over them I put all the clothes I possess. Still I am numb with cold. Realizing belatedly that my boots are leaking, I search in vain for a cobbler before returning to seek solace in the Kunlun's central heating. Alas, the radiators are cold. A breakdown? No, the maid assures me, the system is in perfect working order. It will be switched on in November, when winter begins.

I dive fully clothed into bed and shiver myself to sleep.

Two hundred and fifty miles south-east of Ürümqi, and 300 feet below sea level, lies the oasis of Turfan. In summer this dusty town records temperatures of up to 120 degrees Fahrenheit; and even in October the mercury is said to maintain a respectable presence in the thermometer. Galvanizing myself into action, I make for the bus station, and with a last impenitent glance at the chimneys of Ürümqi I head for the desert once more.

Turfan, or Turpan, or Turapan, is perhaps the strangest of the Taklamakan's many strange communities. The basin has been inhabited for at least 2,500 years: first by Uyghurs, later by Chinese of the Han Dynasty, and today once again by Uyghurs, who make up perhaps three-quarters of its sand-blown population. This settlement history is surprising when you consider the ways in which Turfan is hostile to human life. Its appalling extremes of temperature are compounded by an absence of surface water for miles in any direction. Worse still, at least thirty times a year, Turfan is engulfed by the *buran*: a sand-laden hurricane which rages with such ferocity that it has been known to overturn carts and jeeps.

The reason why people strive to inhabit such a place becomes clear when the bus deposits me in Turfan's bazaar. On all four sides, stalls groan beneath mountains of produce. Grapes, raisins, apricots, peanuts, walnuts and sunflower seeds occupy one side; bloody carcasses of sheep and cattle another. Turning again, I face sacks of flour and cereals; and when I try to leave, I find the exit blockaded by Turfan's *pièces de résistance* – the most majestic melons ever to grace a marketeer's barrow.

Of the nearby oasis of Hami, Marco Polo had this to say:

The inhabitants . . . live on the produce of the soil; for they have a superfluity of foodstuffs and beverages, which they sell to travellers who pass that way. They are a very gay folk, who give no thought to anything but making music, singing and dancing, . . . and taking great delight in the pleasures of the body. I give you my word that if a stranger comes to a house here to seek hospitality he receives a very warm welcome. The host bids his wife do everything that the guest wishes. Then he leaves the house and goes about his own business and stays away two or three days. Meanwhile the guest stays with her in one bed just as if she were his own wife; and they lead a gay life together. All the men of this city and province are thus cuckolded by their wives; but they are not the least ashamed of it. And the women are beautiful and vivacious and always ready to oblige.

Observing the potential, no doubt, for historical research, later explorers endured unspeakable discomforts in their eagerness to reach Turfan. The German Albert von Le Coq, arriving from Ürümqi in 1904, wrote of mosquitoes, fleas, sandflies, scorpions, poisonous jumping spiders and, worst of all, giant cockroaches. 'It was enough to make a man uncontrollably sick to wake in the morning with such a creature sitting on his nose, its big eyes staring down at him and its long feelers trying to attack its victim's eyes.' To add to his troubles, von Le Coq also suffered from prickly heat. In the same decade Aurel Stein almost lost his life on his way here through the notorious Desert of Lop. Even the redoubtable Misses Cable and French complained that it was one of those regions which surpassed all others in its power to horrify.

What drew these early explorers to Turfan? Did they go through all this on the strength of an 800-year-old report of loose women? It seems improbable (especially in the case of Cable and French). I dump my rucksack at the *bīnguǎn* and set off to find out.

My guidebook tells me that as well as being an important Silk Road staging post, Turfan was a centre of Buddhism for several hundred years before being converted to Islam in the eighth century. This comes as a surprise. I always thought the Chinese had adopted the faith direct from India, after the Emperor Ming Ti saw the Buddha in a dream. Further east, statues by the hundred stand in testimony to Buddhism's impact on a suppressed people seeking inspiration; and with his keen Catholic eye for idols, Polo was moved to write:

I can assure you that some are as much as ten paces in length. Some are of wood, some of earthenware, some of stone, and they are all covered with gold and of excellent workmanship. These huge idols are recumbent, and groups of lesser ones are set round about them and seem to be doing them humble obeisance.

But this is the first time I have seen it suggested that Buddhism had penetrated so far north-west. I am intrigued by the puzzle; so when a donkey-cart driver offers to take me to the ruined Han city of Jiaohe, I jump on board without even thinking to ask the fare.

The journey is no more than ten miles, but we jolt and bounce for an hour and a half before the crumbling towers come into view. A cobbled car park suggests summertime crowds, but today an old minibus is its sole occupant. A People's Liberation Army group waves from the top of a wall, but otherwise the donkey driver and I are alone.

Donkey and driver settle down to sleep while I wander through the dust-blown remains of what was once a bustling garrison town. It was Genghis Khan who finally drove the Hans out of Xinjiang, and one would be forgiven for thinking that the desecration of Jiaohe was his doing. Its disembowelled buildings have a ransacked air. Certainly the Khan's warriors would have helped themselves to any valuables left behind by the fleeing Hans, but it is more likely that the ruins owe their dereliction to twelve centuries of sandblasting.

I am about to return to the donkey-man when a niche in a tower catches my eye. Sitting inside, half eaten away but still recognizable, is an eighteen-inch-high Buddha. Hard-baked mud eyes return my inspection with a serene gaze. Flushed with my discovery, I assail the donkey-man about it for most of the return journey, and he listens, patiently but incomprehendingly, until we reach the *bīnguǎn*.

Surprising though the statue has been, I suspect that such things were not what attracted my learned predecessors. Aside from the women, what could it have been? After a night's sleep I set out to look at a likely candidate. Turfan receives its water through a remarkable system of underground channels which converge from the surrounding hills. These *karezes*, built to ancient designs from Persia, extend for several miles to where the water-bearing strata dive below the desert surface. Turfan's network of more than 500 *karezes* bears the stamp of impressive engineering skills, and also of a thorough grasp of hydrology. Having found their source, the builders sank shafts at intervals towards where the water was needed, and then connected the shafts with tunnels. To be watertight the *karezes* had to avoid loose sand; and to prevent silting up it was essential that they maintained a constant gradient – not an easy task using medieval technology. A Uyghur farmer leads me to a shaft on the edge of his plot, and I descend the channel for a few hundred yards until my torch gives out. Its headroom is sufficient for me to walk upright, but even at this low-water season the flow is powerful, and I emerge breathless and drenched.

Properly irrigated, the soils of the Taklamakan produce prodigious crops, as Polo observed. Hami melons are said to be the finest in China, and Turfan claims the tastiest grapes and raisins. Being Moslems, the Uyghur population is not supposed to indulge in the fermented juice of the grape, but Turfan wine is a popular item in the shops and I suspect that much of the crop goes this way. The *karezes* have also enabled trees to be planted, shading travellers from the summer sun. Early Chinese visitors so appreciated these that they called the route between Turfan and Hami 'The Road through the Willows'.

I cannot leave without attending to the last of the attractions which so impressed Polo. Turfan's days of prostitution have thankfully long since gone, but Uyghur women retain an assurance that I haven't seen since Europe. On my last night at the *bīnguǎn* an evening of Uyghur music and dancing is billed, and I make sure of a ringside seat.

For two and a half hours, ten dancers and six musicians entertain an audience of Westerners and Chinese to variations on the theme of 'boy meets girl'. Cameos which elsewhere would evoke tears of boredom here bring on tears of admiration and trigger off spontaneous applause. The performances are stunning. The singing is sensuous. And the evening convinces me once and for all that Polo was not exaggerating when he wrote of the temptresses of Turfan. On the contrary, he was probably understating what he had seen.

Turfan, like its mistresses, is seductive, and like previous visitors I find it difficult to drag myself away. The road from the town floats between a steel grey desert and a leaden sky. For once I am heading not east along the Silk Road, but north to a township called Daheyon, there to make an appointment with a mode of travelling I have not used since faraway Sind. China's railways – the westernmost terminus of which I have already encountered at Korla – are as central as the bicycle to the country's well-being. If I am to travel the way of the people, it is high time I took to the train.

I remember Karachi's railway station as being crowded; but it was like a sleepy wayside halt compared to Daheyon. Although the station stands alone in the desert, it is at a junction of lines and served by several trains a day. Passengers who have been refused tickets at the termini of Ürümqi or Korla sometimes take buses in the hope of catching the trains here.

The approach between goods yards and railway workers' cottages gives no hint of the mayhem at the station itself. From the booking hall a throng spills onto the concourse, presenting a harrowing prospect to ticketless passengers like me. Luckily I am not alone. A Hong Kong woman joined the little group of Westerners boarding the bus at Turfan, and now she takes charge. Not only does Sandra Kwok speak fluent Mandarin, but her Chinese features will enable her to buy tickets for all of us at the Chinese price.

Throughout China, it is the practice to double or treble prices when a foreign face appears at a booking office window. This happens not only at railway stations but at bus terminals, airline offices, hotels and the main tourist attractions. The policy is rooted in the idea that most foreigners are well able to afford a little more, and is simply a Chinese version of the worldwide ploy of charging what the market will bear. Budget travellers are understandably irritated by it, for although undeniably privileged by comparison with local people, they are anxious to make the most of their funds. It is bad enough when you are duped into accepting unwanted luxury, such as a five-star hotel room when a simple dormitory would do. It is even more infuriating when, after paying the extra money, you find yourself suffering the same discomforts as everybody else.

The foreigners' response has been to develop an array of tactics to outwit the receptionists and booking clerks. False student cards; People's Liberation Army uniforms: no ruse has been left untried, except possibly plastic surgery to narrow the eyes. But the simplest trick is to ask a Chinese to buy your ticket, and Sandra earns the everlasting affection of the group by securing tickets for us all.

An hour before the train is due, railway officials begin to marshal the several hundred passengers into queues: two for each carriage, lined up neatly at the point where the carriage will stop. We huddle together in the chilly night air. The train is late, and by the time the great steam locomotive hisses down the platform the crowd has burst from its orderly lines and is lunging forward in a wave of struggling humanity. The officials toil in vain to help those trying to alight. Fights break out. A Uyghur is frogmarched away. Only after twenty minutes does the *mêlée* subside sufficiently for the doors to be rammed shut and the train allowed to continue.

Inside, the scene is grim. A platoon of soldiers on home leave has swelled the train's complement, and as well as sitting two to each seat passengers are lying on tables, on luggage racks, on the floor, in the toilets and even in the unheated gangways over the couplings. I have resigned myself to spending the twelve-hour journey standing up, when Sandra comes once more to the rescue. Unbelievably, she has arranged sleeping compartments for all of us at the Chinese price. Dazed by our luck, we clamber over grunting bodies to the 'hard sleeper', and toast her again and again before falling into a deep and undeserved sleep.

Our destination, Liuyuan, seems to have even less to commend it than Daheyon. My ever-cheerful guidebook suggests that visitors should bring a costume and a song-and-dance act to comfort the inhabitants of this desolate place. Not a flower brightens its gardens; not a tree relieves the frontages of rotting concrete which line its single street. In fact, during the couple of hours I spend there, I scan the verges in vain for a single blade of grass.

But Liuyuan is the gateway to an oasis, the very name of which excites historians all over the world. Dunhuang is not only where north and south branches of the Silk Road come together after circumnavigating the Taklamakan; but the nearby caves of Magao once harboured some of Asia's most celebrated manuscripts – not to mention countless works of art. According to legend, the fourth century AD saw a Buddhist monk called Yue Zun passing through the area. Fifteen miles south-east of Dunhuang, in a valley flanked by sandstone cliffs, a thousand Buddhas came to him in a dream, and to commemorate the vision he dug caves in the cliffs, filling them with statues and frescos. For more than a millenium his successors continued the work, leaving some 2,000 statues and 45,000 murals in 500 separate caves. One cave contained a library of manuscripts chronicling desert life during the Han Dynasty. Surprisingly, Marco Polo seems to have been unaware of these 'Caves of the Thousand

Buddhas'. In the fourteenth century they were bricked up, and for the next 500 years their contents were preserved in the dry desert air.

In 1900, the hoard was rediscovered by a Taoist monk called Wang Yuan, and soon came to the attention of Aurel Stein. There followed one of the most contemptible lootings in the history of the Silk Road. Stein himself carted off twenty-nine packing cases of treasures to the British Museum, where they remain today. Other 'foreign devils' followed close on his heels, until the Empress Wu Cixi, outraged by news of the plunder, ordered the remaining manuscripts to be taken for safe keeping in Beijing. But few reached the capital, for during their journey yet more were pilfered, this time by local officials who had become wise to their value. Today you can see Dunhuang manuscripts in the museums of several Western countries – but none in China.

Dunhaung's modern visitors are taken through 'show caves', closely chaperoned in case they have ideas of carrying on where Stein left off. But little is left to see. The caves are poorly lit; the remaining statues and paintings impossible to examine closely; and my request to see Cave 17, where the library used to be, is met with a truculent '*Méi-yǒu*' ('No'). A sign opposite the bus park reads 'TO CHERISH CULTURAL RELICS IS EVERY-BODY'S DUTY', heralding a welcome change from the ortho-doxy of the Cultural Revolution, when anything carrying so much as a whiff of culture was torn down. But I can gain no understanding from this unhappy place, and after wandering for a while among the surrounding hills I catch the bus back to Dunhuang.

Whatever I may think of the Magao caves, they nevertheless attract a great many foreigners, and Dunhuang maintains a cosmopolitan air. The town's strategic position has made it a meeting place for centuries. Arriving after a month-long crossing of the Desert of Lop, Polo spent some time among its Buddhist population, observing their 'barbarous' religious practices. Sur-prisingly, he tells us that the people of Dunhuang were not traders, living mostly from the produce of their irrigated fields. Somehow this seems unlikely. Not only would the Silk Road itself have generated some passing trade, but the oasis marks the beginning of the great road south across the Qaidam Basin and the Tibetan Plateau to Lhasa. Tibetan traders were a familiar sight

in Dunhuang until the Golmud railway provided a more conveni-
ent outlet to the east.

By way of consolation, I hire a bicycle and set off to explore the
sand dunes a few miles to the south. Since the time of Christ,
travellers have reported supernatural goings-on in these dunes.
Let Polo explain:

The truth is this. When a man is riding by night through this desert and
something happens to make him loiter and lose touch with his
companions, by dropping asleep or for some other reason, and
afterwards he wants to rejoin them, then he hears spirits talking in such a
way that they seem to be his companions. Sometimes, indeed, they even
hail him by name. Often these voices make him stray from the path, so
that he never finds it again. And in this way many travellers have been
lost and have perished. And sometimes in the night they are conscious of
a noise like the chatter of a great cavalcade of riders away from the road;
and, believing that these are some of their own company, they go where
they hear the noise, and, when day breaks, find they are victims of an
illusion and in an awkward plight. And there are some who, in crossing
this desert, have seen a host of men coming towards them, and,
suspecting that they were robbers, have taken flight; so, having left the
beaten track and not knowing how to return to it, they have gone
hopelessly astray. Yes, and even by daylight men hear these spirit
voices, and often you fancy you are listening to the strains of many
instruments, especially drums, and the clash of arms. For this reason
bands of travellers make a point of keeping very close together. Before
they go to sleep they set up a sign pointing in the direction in which they
have to travel. And round the necks of all their beasts they fasten little
bells, so that by listening to the sound they may prevent them from
straying off the path.

Lest Polo's account seems fanciful, here is what the Swede Jan
Myrdal had to say after finding a lake among these dunes in 1976:

We slid along the high sand dune down to the lake, and the whole desert
started to sing beneath us. Mighty strings were struck and the tones rose
to the sky.

It used to be said that men dug the Caves of the Thousand
Buddhas, but gods fashioned the dunes of Dunhuang. The
modern explanation that the wailing is caused by the wind seems
feeble in comparison.

Some camel drivers are waiting where the road gives out, and I
rent one of the beasts for an hour. It is good to feel once more its

familiar gait. We head for Jan Myrdal's lake, and I strain my ears for the music of the sands. But the desert is silent. However hard I listen, and however diligently I stretch my imagination, the only sound I can make out is the gentle rumbling of the camel's stomach.

Back at the hotel, I mention to some Japanese tourists the failure of my quest. 'Oh, our guide took us there yesterday,' they say in unison. 'The dunes gave us a good song.' One of them takes out a cassette recorder. 'Listen.'

The machine is switched on, and I hear what sounds like a cross between a cow in distress and a hound baying to the moon.

'The dunes?'

'The dunes!'

No wonder Marco Polo thought the spirits had been talking to him.

I am on the brink of the Chinese heartland. Already I have passed earthen ruins attributed to a long-vanished extension of the Great Wall. Like countless desert travellers before me, I have scanned the horizon for evidence that the sea of sand is coming to an end. Soon my search will be rewarded.

The Chinese used to believe that central Asia was fit only for savages: a barbarous land in both senses of the word. In those days they had every reason to fear the 'savages', and it was to put an end to repeated invasions that Emperor Qin Shihuang conceived the idea of a single fortification linking China's western gateway, the Yü Pass, with the Yellow Sea. As trade developed with the Middle East and Europe, it became the custom for caravans to rest at the Wall in preparation for the dangers beyond. This was where civilization gave way to wilderness; and the portal by which they entered the wilderness was known as Jiayuguan, the Jade Gate.

For me, Jiayuguan will be as much a frontier as it was to earlier travellers. I have all but crossed the wasteland. What will the heartland hold? I set aside the disappointments of Dunhuang and turn my sights to the final stage of the journey.

'Mister! You like to change money? You like to buy souvenirs?'

The cry echoes through the great arch, carried on a biting wind, as the young tout spots me from beyond.

I have entered the land of the Chinese.

10
Beyond the Wall

I turn up the collar of my hopelessly inadequate jacket, brace myself against the wind, and set out to explore what may have been the world's first customs post. A relic of the Ming Dynasty, the present Jade Gate was begun in 1372, part of a fortress which the Chinese call 'the Impregnable Pass under Heaven'. Though traditionally seen as the westernmost outpost of the Han civilization, the fortress is in fact deep in the desert, and the view from its turrets confirms that I am still many miles from the true Chinese heartland. The wilderness stretches away in all directions, broken only to the south-west by the snow-dusted range known as the Qilian Shan. The Great Wall itself marches unswervingly to the horizon; but it is a pitiful structure, nowhere more than twelve feet high, a parody of the majestic sections near Beijing. Built to keep out the Mongol hordes, it is today breached by a dozen roads and tracks within sight of where I am standing. Looking north-east, I can make out a 200-yard length in good condition, but to the south-west the wall is literally crumbling into the desert. One push with a Mongol battering ram, and it would collapse to dust.

The fortress itself is in sounder shape, and as I tour its battlements I see that this is partly thanks to a battalion of blue-jacketed Chinese labouring with winches and pulleys on bamboo scaffolds. Four pavilions have already received their attention, and their eaves and pillars shimmer resplendently in lacquers of scarlet, black and gold. A fifth remains enshrouded in scaffolding. I peer at it and see to my surprise that it is being rebuilt from scratch. Of course! Mao Zedong would never have allowed such reminders of the days of Empire to sully his people's minds. No matter that the fortress of Jiayuguan reflected a foreign policy on the part of the Ming emperors identical to that which he himself was prescribing. Between 1966 and 1968, self-appointed gangs of wreckers were at his disposal in the form of the Red Guards. In later years they were to become uncontrollable, but not before Mao had succeeded in harnessing their destructive urges to eliminate systematically almost every major reminder of China's past.

The restoration is impressive. Early line drawings and wood-cuts show the Gate of Conciliation (the Western entrance to the fortress) looking very much like the version before me now. Only the new timbers and fresh paint betray the monument for the phoenix that it is.

Similar restoration programmes are, of course, taking place all over China. In Tibet, an added irony has been the appointment of Tibetan monks – sometimes the very ones who were tortured so cruelly by the Red Guards – to work on the rebuilding of some of their devastated monasteries. Whilst undeniably better than doing nothing at all, the programmes highlight an indifference to authenticity which I am to notice again and again as I become more familiar with the Chinese. I have already come across a variation of it in the hordes of individuals sporting People's Liberation Army uniforms. Many have no official status whatso-ever; the uniforms have simply been passed on by friends or relatives.

Wayfarers leaving China by the Jade Gate used to pause briefly outside the fortress to hurl a small pebble against its outer wall. Tradition held that if the pebble rebounded, the traveller who had thrown it would safely return. I am not sure what the custom signified for inbound travellers, but compulsively I pick up one of the pebbles lying outside the gate. It strikes the wall with a ping and rebounds.

At this late season the fort is all but deserted. Only the howl of the wind and the tap of the labourers' hammers breaks the silence of the plains. Even the moneychanger has slipped disconsolately away. I shelter behind the battlements and stare back, as thousands of travellers must have done before me, across the 'land of the barbarians'. For those heading east, the most fearful part of their journey – 2,000 miles of danger and discomfort – would be an ordeal quickly forgotten as they basked once more in the joys of civilization. As for those heading west, one can only wonder what went through their minds as they tossed their pebbles against the great stone bastions, before casting their fate to the desert which they still call 'Go in, and you won't come out'.

The next evening finds me back at the railway station, clutching a ticket onward to Lanzhou. It is almost a week now since I entered the Province of Gansu, but its capital, straddling the muddy Yellow River, is still 500 miles distant. Even the promise of an express train cannot reduce the journey to less than eighteen hours, reminding me that I have not yet quite left central Asia. A quarter the size of neighbouring Xinjiang, Gansu is nevertheless as big as Texas.

This time there has been no Sandra Kwok to smooth my way through the booking hall, and I have had to accept a foreigners' ticket. For the same fare that on my previous journey secured me a berth in a sleeping compartment, I am entitled only to a 'hard seat'. Even this is a hollow promise, for predictably the train is packed, and once more I find myself wedged in a capsule of sullenly dozing humanity as it thunders through the night. Opposite, his legs jammed against mine, a PLA cadet introduces himself as Chin Zhongjin and proffers a bag of buns. He is from Pingliang, 600 miles east of here but still in the same province. He will not reach home until the day after tomorrow. Chin laughs at my attempts to speak his language, and spends an hour or so teaching me the Chinese names of objects in the carriage. In return I show him the colour magazine I have been carrying since faraway Pakistan. At first he turns the pages with polite curiosity, but on reaching an illustrated feature about the plight of whales his eyes shine with pleasure.

'What are these? What is this here? What is this man doing?'

Dumbly I presume that he must have heard about the world's concern for the unfortunate creatures; but as Chin leafs excitedly through the article it dawns on me that his interest is a much more simple one. Like millions of his compatriots, Chin has never seen the sea.

Dawn breaks near Wuwei to find us ploughing through deep snow. The locomotive is lost in an eruption of steam and snowflakes as it struggles to haul its carriages out of the last of the desert basins. From this modest summit, the waters snaking alongside the track will be flowing not to the Taklamakan but to the Yellow Sea. At Lanzhou I present the magazine to Chin and tumble drowsily onto a snow-caked platform between a maze of interlacing tracks. The 'City of the Lotus' lies at over 5,000 feet and, as in Ürümqi, I find that winter has preceded me. I dump my luggage at the nearest hotel and set out grimly to look for warmer clothing. With over two million inhabitants, Lanzhou boasts several department stores, and it is not long before I have found what I want. As I try on the padded jacket, I become aware that I am being observed. First a dozen, then twenty, and finally perhaps a hundred shoppers gather to watch the developing drama. To me the transaction is simple, the jacket ridiculously cheap; but as I hand over the money I am aware that to my audience it must represent the wages of a month or more. I slink away – the rich, boorish foreigner – self-consciously clutching my prize.

For all its present-day importance, Lanzhou features little in the annals of the Silk Road. By the time they reached here, eastbound travellers had already set their sights on the fleshpots of Xi'an, while those heading west were no doubt preoccupied with the hazards beyond the Jade Gate. Polo commented briefly that the hills surrounding Lanzhou were a source of rhubarb – unknown in medieval Europe and perhaps one of the most surprising of the Silk Road's cargoes. But if the Yellow River, drowner of millions, 'China's Sorrow', will always have a place in history, few have reason to recall this colourless town upon its banks. Were it not for a young man called Yang Zhongming, neither would I.

'Mister John!'

The familiar call comes from over my shoulder as I leave the Post Office. I turn to find a bespectacled face smiling owlishly a foot from my own.

'I was behind you when you collected your mail,' explains the face's owner, a Han Chinese of perhaps twenty years of age. Without waiting for a reply, he falls in with my stride. A new sports jacket, white open-necked shirt, well-pressed trousers and slicked-back hair give an impression of careful grooming. I stroll on expectantly.

'You are American, yes?'

I shake my head. 'No, British.'

A trace of disappointment appears and is instantly gone. 'I am an English teacher. May we talk?'

Yang Zhongming is from Shanghai, one of hundreds of professionals dispatched to the north-west to help develop China's hinterland. Like many, he has a family back home; but his aspirations are already drifting towards more distant places and grander things.

'Do I speak good English?' he asks querulously.

'Very,' I reply – though I wouldn't have had the heart to say otherwise, whatever the truth had been.

'Would you be kind enough to help me practise?' he continues. 'You see, I need to speak more fluently so that I can apply for a job in America.'

'You have relations in America?' I ask.

'Oh no,' Yang blushes. 'I don't know anyone outside Shanghai or Lanzhou.' He smiles wistfully, naïvely. 'Here in Lanzhou my salary is 150 yuan per month. In America teachers are paid fifty times that. I know they are, because I read it in *Newsweek*. That's why I want to work in America. Wouldn't you?'

We emerge from our sheltered side street to face the full blast of a snowstorm funnelling down one of Lanzhou's wide boulevards. I wince simultaneously at the blizzard and at Yang.

'Do you think money would bring you happiness?' I ask him through the thickly falling flakes.

'Oh, yes! I've read about America. I know I'd be happy there.'

I remember Chin Zhongjin, the PLA cadet on the train, and for a moment regret having left my magazine with him. I am not in the mood for an argument. But already Yang's mind is racing and he is addressing me earnestly once more.

'You must come and meet my work unit! Come to my school! Come and speak English to us!' His voice rises to a squeal. 'We will entertain you, feast you, our honoured foreign guest!'

I stop walking, and look Yang hard in the eye. I want to persuade him that the happiness he is seeking can't be found this way; that it comes from putting effort into other things. But his calm, mad eyes tell me that he would not be receptive to such reasoning. And on this wintry avenue in Lanzhou I suddenly see what I am facing. The same single-mindedness which drove the Red Guards to such wanton destruction in the 1960s is at large once more. Its new ideology is money. The very affliction which for so long has characterized the capitalist world has at last infected China, and a billion people are on the brink of an epidemic. When Deng Xiaoping promised his people that by the year 2000 they would be a 'modern power', they understood him to mean they would be *rich*. Always impressionable, but especially so in the emotional vacuum which followed the Cultural Revolution, the Chinese have found the return of capitalism irresistibly tempting, and are grasping the new opportunities as if their lives depended on them.

Yang's eyes seem to say it all. After sharing tea in a nearby café, we exchange addresses and I wish him luck, but as I turn towards the railway station I weep for him. What can the future possibly hold for a generation with such clear and impossible ideals?

The eighth-century poet Li Bai tells us that the dilemma is not new:

Clear wine in golden goblets, ten thousand cash a cup,
And costly delicacies on jade platters.
Yet I spurn drinking and toss away my chopsticks,
Sword in hand, restless, I wonder what to do.
I want to cross the Yellow River, but it's ice-bound;
I want to climb the Taihang Mountains, but they're snow-covered . . .
Travelling is hard! Travelling is hard!
So many crossroads; which to choose?
One day I'll skim the waves, blown by the wind,
With sails hoisted high, across the vast ocean.

Across hillsides yellow with loess and green with cabbages, potatoes and swedes, the train carries me away from the Yellow River and east towards Xi'an. A burst of late October sunshine, the first for days, illuminates a frenzy of activity as villagers take advantage of the brief respite. While some are gathering the limp remains of this year's crop, others are already preparing for next year's – ploughing or hoeing with crude implements, many of them hand-drawn. The yellow dust which assaults one's eyes, nose and throat in Gansu Province shares its origins with the sands of the deserts to the west. Here, however, rainfall has transformed it into a fertile soil. The train twists round terraced hillsides, climbing steeply before diving into a long tunnel to emerge in the valley of the Wei. It was here that Polo first encountered the white mulberry on which the silkworm feeds, gorging its own weight daily in the nutritious spring leaves before settling down to spin its silk cocoon.

For the first time I am on a daytime train, and while I gaze at the farmland wheeling past, the carriage's 300 occupants gaze at me. Other travellers have warned me about these 'staring squads', and I have laughed them off, unable to imagine either that I could be a source of such intrigue or that the discomfort of the victim could be so gaily ignored. Now, as eyes crawl over every inch of my clothing and skin, I writhe in irritation and embarrassment. From the seats opposite, from across the aisle, from the spittle-covered floor and even from the luggage racks come the laser looks – expressionless, unblinking, like fish. I wriggle into a more comfortable position on the hard bench seat. Three hundred pairs of eyes follow me. *The foreigner is wriggling!* I rub my weary eyes. *The foreigner is rubbing his eyes!* In desperation I take out a book and start to read, but the crush of heads vying for a glimpse of the pages makes me abandon the effort and return my attention to the countryside speeding by.

The land which I have entered is so yellow that an early ruler of the region styled himself *Huáng Dì*, or 'Emperor of the Yellow Earth'. Trees and people are embalmed in this ochre talcum; walls and houses are embedded in it. It penetrates the sealed windows of the carriage, and works its way under my clothing and into my skin. Pinned down by my 300 unwitting tormentors, I have no hope of getting to the washroom, and even if I did the crush of passengers would make it impossible to wash. Taking my cue from others, I tie a handkerchief across my mouth and nostrils and sit patiently as the miles roll by. Sunset ignites the western horizon, turning the valley briefly blood-red. Rattling on now through the more densely populated Shaanxi Province, the train passes brightly lit stations and goods yards before finally, just before midnight, disgorging its 5,000 groggy passengers at Xi'an.

Xi'an, *alias* Ch'ang-an or Quengianfu, was the seat of eleven dynasties, the destination of a hundred thousand caravans, and (thanks to the Ming emperors) at one time the most heavily fortified community on earth. Two thousand years before Polo reached its massive western gate, it was already one of China's largest cities, rivalling Khanbalik (Beijing). By the time of his visit the population had swelled to no fewer than 2,500,000. Here, 6,000 miles from its origin on the coast of the Mediterranean, the Silk Road came to an end. From Xi'an, eastbound traders who had crossed Asia together would have ridden their separate ways: north to coastal Cathay, or south across the Yangtze to the South China Sea. So extensive were the city's markets that many visiting merchants sold their entire stock on the spot.

For me, as for them, Xi'an provides the first taste of China proper. I gaze in fascination at the bicycles making tidal waves down Bei Dajie; the monolithic department stores; the backstreet noodle shops where dumplings steam day and night in blackened bamboo trays. I can see how the city must have kindled Polo's business instincts. 'Quengianfu is a thriving centre of trade and industry. . . . There is ample provision for man's every bodily need, to ensure a life of plenty at low cost.' More recently, Colin Thubron has described it as a vast rectangle of Ming ramparts, bulging with crenellated towers, but enclosing almost no building older than themselves – like armour for a body which has gone.

Modern Xi'an is not much larger than at the time of the Tang Dynasty, thirteen centuries ago. It has retained an unashamedly commercial outlook and, like most Chinese cities, its horizon today is proudly punctuated by smokestacks and dimmed by a pall of smog. By a stroke of luck, its finest monuments – the Bell and Drum Towers, the Great Goose and Little Goose Pagodas, and the mosque which serves Xi'an's Hui community – escaped the demolition hammer of the Red Guards. They stand sentinel among hooting vehicles or float on the horizons of forgotten suburbs.

Today's visitors to Xi'an, however, come not for its towers, pagodas or mosques, but for the Terracotta Warriors. For two millennia an army 7,000 strong lay buried in the red earth of the Wei floodplain, in full battle array, guarding the remains of their emperor buried nearby. This exalted character was in fact a tyrant by the name of Qin Shihuangdi, whose megalomania rivalled that of Mao Zedong's final years. During his lifetime Qin Shihuangdi built no fewer than 270 palaces, each decorated in the style of one of his conquered races, and his sumptuously decorated tomb was under construction for thirty-six of the thirty-seven years of his reign. Some said the tomb's ceiling was inlaid with pearls to represent the heavenly bodies; others that mercury was pumped through channels to simulate rivers, lakes and a silver sea.

The Emperor's tomb lies beneath a 130-foot mound, its secrets still untold. But in 1974 some farmworkers digging a well nearby broke into the vault where the terracotta warriors had been standing to arms, undiscovered since the third century BC. An aircraft hangar now protects the site, and while excavations continue at one end the world's tourists surge across catwalks from the other. On some days there seem to be more visitors than warriors: and the glazed, abstracted expressions are the same on both.

I stopped long ago being angry at such scenes. After all, there is a Philistine in all of us, and tourism has opened up avenues of understanding which could yet save us from man's worst obduracies. But in large numbers tourists have a depraving effect on those who serve them, and in few places is this more crassly evident than outside the Tomb – or, rather, the Hangar – of the Terracotta Warriors. You approach the building by what must once have been a graceful promenade, but over the years it has become flanked by pedlars' stalls and hawkers' barrows. Some of the riff-raff are apparently sanctioned; others furtively await their marching orders from the PLA officials who strut bumptiously to and fro. The bus park has been extended on several occasions since the first acre of gravel was laid down in 1977, each time to overflow a year or two later. Now some passengers have to run (or hobble) a 300-yard gauntlet of trinket, junk food and soft drink sellers before reaching the sanctity of the entrance booths.

'Hey, Mister! You want fine sculpture? Postcard? Pepsi? Come here please!'

I fix my eyes firmly on the exit sign, and do not slacken my pace until I have passed it and am out on the road.

At 3.00 a.m. on the seventh floor of Xi'an's People's Hotel, I make an entry in my diary:

The enigma of the new mandarins:

They destroy most of their heritage; then invite people to come and see it.

They spend a third of the time trying to stop you visiting places which they say are boring; a third cajoling you to visit places that are even more boring; and a third scheming to prevent you going anywhere at all.

They regulate their heating according to the calendar, not the temperature.

They short-circuit the black market in foreign currencies by providing a special Chinese currency for foreigners – then turn a blind eye to black marketeering in the special currency.

They trample all over their 'minority people', yet wonder why the minority people hate them.

They lock up toilets on health grounds, so you have to urinate in the street.

And the enigma of the people:

They queue politely for buses, but when the buses arrive they batter down the doors and fight for seats.

They shout when they're trying to be friendly.

They eat monkeys, cats, armadillos, snakes, racoons, toads, tortoises, dogs, owls, birds' saliva, fishes' lips, ducks' feet and bears' paws.

And they think *foreigners* are odd!

As on other nights in other hotels, my sleep has been interrupted by Chinese guests yelling amiably down the echoing corridors, and by couples in nearby rooms hollering sweet nothings in each other's ears. I have been told that to be understood in Chinese you have to shout – it is the only language in the world that can't be whispered – but even as I begin to comprehend what is being said to me I grow weary of the clamour. It is all too easy to get ruffled, when for example a shopkeeper laughs uproariously in your face, or a street vendor grips your arm as if in a vice. But no rudeness is intended; these are simply their ways of soliciting your attention in the face of a billion others.

Predictably but sadly, after a few months in China many foreigners become irritated by the Chinese. Sometimes the antipathy is well deserved, but more often it is a reflection of our own characters and conditioning as much as theirs. Western patterns of logic, etiquette and body language play no part in Chinese life; indeed, most Chinese are oblivious to them. Looked at this way, it is hardly surprising that the Chinese seem rude and clumsy to the Western eye. The foreigners I hear complaining seem equally unaware of how their own behaviour is viewed by their Chinese hosts. Frustrated by the obstacles that arise from these cross purposes, they grapple with the obstacles while doing nothing about the cross purposes themselves. Allowances have to be made on both sides. The Chinese seem to make plenty, though I sometimes see them giggling in disbelief. Occasionally I meet a foreigner – more often a resident than a visitor – who has learned to make allowances too. But they are rare birds in a wilderness of misunderstanding.

One problem is that few foreigners can be bothered to learn Chinese. I can sympathize; it certainly isn't easy. But when you travel in China without speaking or reading the language, you are the equivalent of a deaf, mute illiterate. Direction signs turn out to be party slogans; party slogans turn out to be advertisements for toothpaste; and more than once I have spent the best part of an hour looking for something which was right under my nose. Whatever the tour operators may say, very few Chinese speak another language, and those who do rarely understand what you say in return. Why should they, when their own tongue is spoken by more people than any other on earth?

I put the diary aside and force myself to sleep. But I am reminded of the gulf next morning as I check out of the hotel. 'Xiè-xie,' I venture, summoning my best accent. 'Thank you.'

The clerks on the desk titter uncontrollably. 'Xiè-xie! Xiè-xie!' they chuckle. 'The foreigner speaks Chinese!'

One thing I can't blame on the People's Hotel is an ailment which has afflicted me in Xi'an. Travellers are easy prey to unfamiliar germs, and the city's suffocating atmosphere – product of a hundred thousand coal-fired stoves – affects its own people too. The queues at the chemists' shops are the longest I have ever seen. I have booked a sleeping berth on the afternoon express to Beijing, but wince at the thought of the twenty-four hour journey as I haul myself onto the train.

Three Japanese businessmen share my compartment. They look at me aghast. I apologize for my green face and demonstrate my problem by retiring to the washroom to be ill.

Returning to the compartment, I find my bunk made up and my rucksack stowed tidily in the luggage rack. The Japanese turn to me with concern. 'Fellow traveller!' declares the eldest. 'I am Okumura; this is Yamamoto; and over here is Ogino. You look terrible, so we have decided to give you traditional Japanese medicine. Please lie down!'

Rummaging in his briefcase, Okumura comes up with a herbal extract which he mixes with water to make a paste. To this he adds a dose of non-traditional multivitamin powder. The mess tastes revolting, but I wash it down with a mug of green tea, and after a few hours have recovered sufficiently to take an interest in the journey.

A curse of Chinese trains, yet to afflict those of other countries, is the on-board radio station. The railway authorities believe – quite without evidence, as far as I know – that passengers' appreciation of their journeys will be enhanced by programmes of 'muzak' combined with a merry commentary on items of interest along the way. In the 'hard seat' carriages the speakers are placed in the ceiling and the sound is swamped by the general hullabaloo. But in the sleeping cars they are positioned alongside the pillows in the upper berths. As I travel further into eastern China I am to become increasingly irritated by these contrivances. They can't be switched off, but each model presents a different exercise in disablement. On this occasion I find to my relief that by unscrewing the grills and packing them with toilet tissue, I can reduce their twittering to a strangled and scarcely audible croak.

The journey passes quickly. A late afternoon thunderstorm turns the Yellow River almost black as we clatter across it, and dawn breaks to find us speeding through the cottonfields of Hebei. At Shijiazhuang the trackside walls are plastered with slogans, blazing scarlet in the morning light. 'Long Live the People's Republic!' 'Long Live the Wise Thoughts of Marx, Lenin and Mao!' 'Careless Cycling Kills!'

For the next hundred miles the train passes through a sea of cabbages: acre upon acre of sprouting greens, some proud and fresh, others sagging with frost, yet others turning visibly yellow as peasants toil to harvest them before they rot. On the roads, convoys of lorries speed the vegetables to feed the multitudes of Beijing. But from Dingxing onwards, as we approach the capital, the cabbagefields give way steadily to factories, the rutted lanes to highways, the huddled shacks to rows of apartment blocks. At last the train slows to a crawl, swinging north and finally west, and the horizon which pivots round it is one of steel, concrete and tarmacadam. I have arrived in Beijing.

I assure you that the streets are so broad and straight that from the top of the wall above one gate you can see along the whole length of the road to the gate opposite. The city is full of fine mansions, inns and dwelling-houses. All the way down the sides of every main street there are booths and shops of every sort. All the building sites throughout the city are square and measured by the rule; . . . and in this way the whole interior of the city is laid out in squares like a chess-board with such masterly precision that no description can do justice to it.

The city which so impressed Polo has been razed and rebuilt several times in the intervening centuries: most recently in the 1950s and 1960s, when today's chessboard of eight-lane highways was carved from the hugger-mugger of *hútòngs* inherited from Imperial Peking. Unlike its medieval visitors, modern arrivals find little to commend China's capital. The urban desert created at such cost tends to provoke not admiration but dismay. 'Is this *it*?' In their eagerness to sweep away the ghosts of their predecessors, China's leaders have more than once thrown out their babies, so to speak, with the bathwater. Throughout history, observers have watched in horror as the nation has plunged headlong towards yet another catastrophe. In earlier times the means of destruction were limited; bare hands can only plunder so much. But today, in both the cities and the countryside, bulldozers and draglines have given the Chinese the power to rip their country apart, and each year brings new incentives to do so. The dilemma is, of course, not unique to China. In Nepal they chop down trees to cook for trekkers; in Brazil they lay bare the rainforest to plant crops; in Chile they stripmine the desert for nitrate. So, throughout the world, old problems are traded for new ones. China's only distinction is that her problems – and hence her solutions – are on a massive scale.

I deposit my rucksack at the Qiao Yuan Hotel and make for a quarter which the town planners have yet to destroy. South of the Forbidden City, where Qianmen Gate floats above a sea of swirling bicycles, a web of *hútòngs* spills its clientele onto the thoroughfare. Here the trading instincts of the Chinese, repressed by the Cultural Revolution, have burst out in a mishmash of barrows and stalls. On this raw November day, boots, jackets and other winter clothing occupy pride of place, but among these functional wares are finer goods. Some stalls display radios and cassette players; others carry rolls of printed silk. And where twenty years ago a hint of lipstick would have been sufficient to condemn a young girl to a labour camp, her contemporaries today are wearing skirts or trouser suits. Amongst the men, jeans are conspicuously *de rigueur*. Had I come in summer, both sexes would have been wearing teeshirts, and I smile at the thought of the messages which might have been emblazoned upon them.

It is difficult to believe that these are the children of the Cultural Revolution: the most devastating social experiment the world has ever known. Twenty years ago, Red Guards scarcely past puberty tortured their elders and pillaged historical monuments in an uncontrolled frenzy of paranoia. Now, their efforts are directed towards making money to buy ghetto-blasters. It is said that a revolution is often the best way for a beleaguered society to jettison a bungled past and sally forth in a new direction. If this is so, then Mao Zedong certainly offered this chance to China's long-suppressed masses, and they grasped it with a fervour which must have surprised even Mao himself. Now Mao's doctrine has made way for a new wisdom under Deng Xiaoping, which is being pursued with similar zeal. It is a more pragmatic line, seductively appealing to a people whose instinct for survival runs strong. 'Black cat, white cat – it's a good cat if it catches mice.' But watching the eager shoppers of Beijing, I cannot help wondering how long it will be before another reappraisal sweeps their barely established world the way of the previous ones.

Another part of Beijing was also spared during the Revolution years. Home of khans, emperors and finally Mao himself, the Forbidden City stands in symbolic defiance of China's turbulent past. It was Kublai Khan who first threw up a palace on this site, moving Polo to write:

It is the largest that was ever seen. . . . Inside, the walls of the halls and chambers are all covered with gold and silver and decorated with pictures of dragons and birds and horsemen and various breeds of beasts and scenes of battle. The ceiling is similarly adorned, so that there is nothing to be seen anywhere but gold and pictures. The hall is so vast and so wide that a meal might well be served there for more than 6,000 men. The number of chambers is quite bewildering. The whole building is at once so immense and so well constructed that no man in the world, even if he had the power to put it into effect, could imagine any improvement in design or execution. The roof is ablaze with scarlet and green and blue and yellow and all the colours that are, so brilliantly varnished that it glitters like crystal and the sparkle of it can be seen from far away.

Polo was one of the few people who had also visited Kublai Khan's private rooms:

In the rear part of the palace are extensive apartments, both chambers and halls, in which are kept the private possessions of the Khan. Here is stored his treasure: gold, silver, precious stones and pearls, and his gold and silver vessels. And here too are his ladies and concubines. In these apartments everything is arranged for his comfort and convenience, and outsiders are not admitted.

Later incumbents extended the prohibition to the whole exquisite two square miles, and protected their 'Forbidden City' by a system of moated ramparts guarded by eunuchs. It is said that competition for these prized positions was intense, though half of them died after the necessary operation, which was administered with a sharp knife (but no anaesthetic) in a special chair. Even if you could get past these devoted sentries, you entered the city on penalty of death. Today the fee has dropped to a few yuan.

As you leave the touts of Tiananmen Square and stride through Wumen, the Meridian Gate, the timelessness of the Forbidden City envelops you like a shroud. Mao still peers down, incongruously but benignly, from his great portrait overhead. The original pavilions were razed by fire, and those you see today are mostly eighteenth-century copies, but the site has nevertheless earned a place in legend alongside Peru's Machu Picchu and India's Taj Mahal. Here, over the five marble bridges which flank the Golden Stream, behind the Gate of Supreme Harmony, beyond the Hall of Middle Harmony and the Palace of Heavenly Purity, were pleasure-domes outranking even those of Xanadu. Nine thousand concubines and no fewer than 70,000 eunuchs served the court of the Ming emperors, not to mention a herd of elephants (whose purpose is unclear). When you consider the taxes necessary to pay for such extravagance, it's not surprising that the emperors hardly ever dared venture outside the city walls, and then only in cortèges so closely guarded that a spectator was once moved to comment: 'One would think he was making a journey through enemy country rather than through multitudes of his own subjects.'

After months in central Asia I have grown used to the hardships of the desert; now I have to face the comforts of the city. Winter has at last officially arrived, so my £1.50-per-night dormitory at the Qiao Yuan Hotel is sensuously warm. My bed is covered by a soft eider quilt. The food in the restaurants, free markets and shops is tastier than any I have encountered since Peshawar. And today the sun is even attempting to shine. Yet already I am beginning to reminisce about the hours spent shivering in my tent, or struggling to converse with Kirghiz nomads, or arguing with Turkish officials, or scouring the quaysides of Haifa and Eilat. From now on, whatever I do, I am doomed to be a tourist. I can revel for a while in the novelty of toast and coffee for breakfast, but I know from experience that the pleasure will fade. Since Xi'an the journey has gradually, imperceptibly, changed character: a warning, perhaps, that it will soon be over.

But from Beijing I still have several hundred miles to cover before I can turn west once more, and as the nights draw in over China's capital I set about organizing the next stage. As a child, my imagination sometimes used to take me to a town I had read about in the lower Yangtze Basin, where women in white spun the finest silks in canalside gardens. The place was called Soochow. One day in Beijing I call at the offices of the China National Textiles Corporation, and find to my astonishment that Bill Carr's importing agent back in Britain is one of their customers. Almost certainly, they say, the mill at Whitchurch, where six months ago my journey began, will receive its raw material from Suzhou Nº 1 Silk Mill. Suzhou, on the Grand Canal in Jiangsu Province, is none other than the Soochow of my childhood dreams.

Recovered now from sickness, I take a 'hard seat' on an express to the old Chinese capital of Nanjing, transferring there to a Shanghai-bound stopping train. The last of its several dozen stops is Suzhou. I walk out of the station into a light drizzle. It is odd to feel familiar with a town I have never visited before, and as I head across the Grand Canal I wonder if Suzhou will live up to my expectations.

I tell you quite truly that in this city there are fully 6,000 stone bridges, such that one or two galleys could readily pass beneath them. In the adjacent mountains rhubarb and ginger grow in great profusion, so that one Venetian groat would buy forty pounds of fresh ginger of excellent quality. The city . . . has so many inhabitants that no one could reckon their number. . . . They live by trade and industry, have silk in great quantity and make much silken cloth for their clothing. . . . I can assure you that they are capable merchants and skilled practitioners of every craft, and among them are wise philosophers and natural physicians, and many magicians and diviners.

With the Grand Canal's innumerable offshoots winding between its whitewashed houses and weeping willows, Suzhou must have seemed a home from home to the young Marco when he arrived here in 1276. Nor have the Chinese been immune to its qualities. 'In heaven there is Paradise, on earth Suzhou and Hangzhou,' said one of its early admirers. Under the Ming Dynasty the town began to attract artists, poets, scholars and retired civil servants, and over the years these newcomers supplemented its natural beauty with a series of exquisite walled gardens, many of which survive today. Each uses rocks (representing life's *yang* aspect) and water (representing the *yin*) in a different combination to reflect the condition of the world from different points of view. They were designed as places for contemplation, meditation and study: for what their originators would have called *wú-wéi*, or flowing with the tide. Amazingly they have survived, and for a few pence visitors can unwind for an hour or a day in the Humble Administrator's Garden, or the Garden for Lingering In, or the Garden of the Master of the Nets.

Like Xi'an, Suzhou escaped the worst ravages of the Cultural Revolution. Visiting the town in 1972, the Belgian Simon Leys thought that when Mao's activists saw how much work needed to be done they probably lost heart. As well as its gardens, Suzhou is blessed with avenues shaded by plane trees, a heritage once shared by many of China's cities. But it is the canals which remain in the mind: both the glassy backwaters picking their way around gardens and landing stages, and the oily arterial waterways with their belching, chugging barges, helmsmen standing proudly at the wheel, decks piled high with cement, bricks, tiles, or the inevitable mounds of cabbage. No wonder they call Suzhou the Venice of the East.

The Grand Canal, the greatest of them all, embraces the town in an arc from south-east to north-west. On its southern bank, near the People's Bridge, lies the dowdy red-brick building which is my goal. Suzhou N° 1 Silk Mill announces its presence to the ears well before it comes into sight behind the serried factories and warehouses which line the canal. From the gate it looks not unlike its Lancastrian cousins. I approach the main entrance gingerly, prepared speech in hand. 'I BRING YOU GREETINGS FROM BRITAIN'S WHITCHURCH SILK MILL. YOU SUPPLY

THEM WITH SILK. IS THERE ANYTHING YOU WOULD LIKE TO SAY IN RETURN?'

The reception area is deserted, so I grit my teeth, cup my hands against the roar, and enter the building. Silhouetted against windows set high in each wall, four lines of steeping and reeling machinery are attended by four lines of women, their hands deftly finding the end of each thread on a million cocoons. Although not allowed to leave their work, the women look up and smile. Encouraged by their complicity – an accredited trespasser now – I back out and continue my quest more assertively at another door. Here my luck is better. I have stumbled across the mill's showroom, an emporium of prints and cloth, and am soon being introduced to the manager. He listens to my speech, then frowns as I repeat it. 'I BRING YOU GREETINGS . . .' He shrugs his shoulders in perplexity. He is baffled.

The Chinese language has many dialects, but this is the first time I have completely failed to make myself understood. I curse for not having asked someone to write down the speech in Chinese. I mime my message in half a dozen different ways, but the manager only looks more confused than ever.

Suddenly the door opens and a crowd bursts in. I can hardly believe my eyes. They are elderly, they are Westerners and they are speaking French.

After some moments, I pinpoint their Chinese guide and cautiously tackle him. '*Excusez-moi, mais j'ai un petit problème.*'

'*Oui, monsieur?*' he replies in faultless French. '*Comment puis-je vous aider?*'

Within minutes my greetings are delivered. The manager beams and bows. A consultation ensues, and I am invited to join the French party which has already begun its tour of the mill. When we return, ears ringing, from the machine shed, the manager is waiting with a hurriedly scribbled note. Working together, the guide, the manager and I translate it first into French and then – with some difficulty – into English. The group is taking tea, and they call boisterously for me to join them. The manager bows and disappears. The guide, in turn, rolls his eyes in the international gesture of resignation, before disappearing to intervene in a wrangle between one of his charges and a showroom assistant. I make some polite conversation with the rest of the party, but can think of little to say. My mind is on the piece of paper in my pocket. At last I make my excuses, recover my rented bicycle from behind the shed, and start off back across the People's Bridge.

Digging deep into my pocket, I extract the crumpled note and read again the words I have helped translate: 'THE STAFF OF SUZHOU N° 1 SALUTE THEIR COMRADES AT WHIT-CHURCH, AND WISH THEM SUCCESS IN MEETING THEIR TARGETS FOR THE COMING YEAR.'

It is more than I could possibly have hoped for. As I stare at the note, the bus carrying the French party overtakes me, sounding its horn. Pedalling happily, I give them a cheery wave, and only just avoid tumbling into the Grand Canal.

11
Among the Revolutionaries

Marco Polo spent seventeen years in China, but I have been limited to just a few months. Autumn has long since turned to winter, and my time in the Middle Kingdom is running out. How, in so fleeting a visit, can anyone hope to understand this country of a thousand paradoxes? I have been privy to a period of rapid and profound change, both in the land and in the outlook of its people; but I find myself wondering, at heart, whether this latest revolution will be any more lasting than the others.

Before returning to Beijing, I sample a little more of the new revolution by visiting Shanghai. China's second city, which between the wars offered a choice of casinos, brothels and opium dens as sumptuous as any in the East, has been commended to me as the flagship of the new doctrine. Good, clean living, I'm assured, is now the order of the day. Shanghai is where I will find the finest shops and the latest fashions – the best of Paris, New York and Hong Kong rolled into one.

I stroll along the Bund, the city's Manhattan-like river frontage, absorbing the new spirit. Neon advertisements (the first I've seen in China) pulsate around me, vying for attention with the art deco monoliths of the hotels, consulates and banks. 'Seagull Shoes! Stylish and Cheap!' 'Radio Watches! Waterproof, Scratchproof!' On Nanjing Lu, the shoppers flow in tidal waves, conspiring to sweep me into department stores or wash me up in side streets where hawkers line the pavements three deep, peddling tee-shirts, cheap jewellery or combs. The shoppers finger the goods critically, quartering the ground for bargains. They elbow me relentlessly on. A beggar in a shabby mackintosh waylays me, and continues to gibber on my heels until I escape by boarding a trolleybus.

Disembarking by Suzhou Creek, I return to the Bund, hoping to find a link, however tenuous, with the city's rumbustious past. A brass plaque announces that I am at the entrance to Heping Fandian, a soaring Edwardian pile which, as the Cathay Hotel, once belonged to Victor Sassoon. In its heyday, the Cathay provided well-heeled travellers with the finest accommodation east of Suez. Noël Coward wrote *Private Lives* beneath its glittering chandeliers. The building is still one of Shanghai's smartest hotels, and wandering through its corridors I am surprised to see these most bourgeois of status symbols still intact, their low-wattage bulbs the only evidence of a new regime. But the hotel staff are firmly of the present mould. Tired and fractious, they treat their $100-per-night customers with a studied insolence. I withdraw in despair to the Friendship Store next door, but the reception is no better. Less than ten years into the new revolution, the seeds of resentment which gnaw so cancerously at our own 'enterprise' society are nowhere more visible than in the hotels and shops of Shanghai.

Disheartened by this rancorous atmosphere, my thoughts turn to Shanghai's near-namesake in China's distant north-east. At Shanhaiguan, a small town in Hebei Province, the Great Wall reaches the end of its 3,500-mile journey on the shores of the Yellow Sea. It will provide a fitting finale to my own trip. But first I return to Beijing to keep an appointment with Dagfinn, a Norwegian friend working for the United Nations, and we drive together to a newly opened stretch of Wall at Mutianyu north of the city. On soaring ridges flanked by wooded slopes now gold and russet under a November sun, we wander for miles along the ramparts as they loop from peak to peak. Unlike its more famous counterpart at Badaling, this section has yet to be restored, and in places we scramble like schoolboys. For our afternoon picnic we choose a crumbling watchtower with a view stretching almost to the Yellow Sea. I scour the horizon vainly for a glimpse of the place where, in a few days' time, my journey will end.

Polo, normally so thorough about recording the sights he saw, never mentioned this, the greatest of all China's wonders. Begun during the Qin Dynasty, the Ten Thousand Li Wall (as the Chinese call it) occupied 100,000 workers at a time, and legend has it that the less fortunate ones ended up contributing bodily to its foundations. In spite of the effort put into building it, the Great Wall never really achieved its purpose of keeping out the Mongol barbarians. As Genghis Khan put it, 'the strength of a wall depends on the courage of those who defend it.' Genghis' grandson Kublai extended his empire far into Mongol territory, so demonstrating another of the Wall's weaknesses: it couldn't be moved. Stripped of its defensive role, it fell into disrepair, and Polo may have considered the crumbling battlements not worth commenting upon.

Although restored and strengthened under the Ming emperors, the Great Wall never resumed its former importance, remaining as a symbolic frontier rather than a bulwark. Today, far from repelling the barbarians, it is attracting them in huge numbers – entrance, one yuan. From our crumbling watchtower Dagfinn and I gaze over an empty land, but forty miles away at Badaling visitors will be queuing by the hundred to be photographed, and the Wall will be creaking beneath their weight.

The day is brilliant but bitter, and snow lies in the shadow of the stonework at our feet. We drink coffee from a vacuum flask and devour the fresh bread and spiced sausage which Dagfinn has thoughtfully brought from the Friendship Store in Beijing. Such luxuries would have been unimaginable in Kashgar, or Ürümqi, or even Lanzhou. Savouring the almost forgotten tastes, I settle back against a tree which has impudently taken root in the watchtower, and think about the billion Chinese for whom such pleasures will always remain an impossible dream.

Or will they?

The Chinese often use the phrase '*dà-gǎo*'. Literally translated, it means 'to do something in a big way'. Within an average Chinese lifetime, the Government has demanded *dà-gǎo* of its people almost constantly: first to repel the Kuomintang, then to pursue the Great Leap Forward, and finally to implement the crazed notions of the Cultural Revolution. In each case the people have responded with an enthusiasm almost beyond belief. Now, a fourth revolution is on the way, and I see no reason to believe that the people will not embrace it as assiduously as before: more so, in fact, because the materialist revolution – as we all know – has a potency quite its own.

At the Thirteenth National Congress two weeks ago, Deng

Xiaoping defined the new revolution as 'socialism with Chinese characteristics'. 'Those who accuse us of taking the capitalist road simply don't understand,' he told reporters. The new ideology stresses the right of individuals to act for themselves rather than for the Party or the State: to trade, to pursue careers, to make money, and to spend it as they wish. The result, quite naturally, has been an explosion of consumerism, fettered only by the speed at which people can lay their hands on the necessary money. Yesterday's *China Daily*, in which our sausage is wrapped, boasted that by the end of 1986 the average Beijing family owned 1.93 bicycles, 1.20 television sets, 0.39 washing machines and 0.05 refrigerators. From what I have seen in the shops and free markets, these figures will soon double, and double again. Getting rich is not just condoned these days; it is extolled as an essential contribution to the national economy. It is also, as many are discovering, quite fun.

Whatever words China's leaders choose to define and defend the new wisdom, there can be no arguing that this time – literally –they have struck gold. The previous revolutions were rooted in blind faith; the present one is founded solidly on greed. Where the earlier revolutions were inherently precarious, the new materialism, though still in its infancy, appears to be in rude health. As Lao Tzu predicted, the *yin* is making way for the *yang*. The old school has nurtured the seeds of its opposite, which will replace it as surely as night follows day.

In China, as in other countries where initiative and incentive are encouraged, two consequences are apparent to anyone who glances behind the façade. First, the less fortunate members of society are being neglected. I would not have encountered beggars, in Shanghai or elsewhere, in the 1960s or 1970s. Second, the environment is suffering shamefully in the rush for riches. Urban China, already a monument to the mindless destruction of the Cultural Revolution, is being further bulldozed to prepare for the twenty-first century. State architects have given way to state engineers, and it is difficult to say which of the two tyrannies will do more harm.

Neither is the countryside safe. *Beijing Review*, a journal not normally given to criticizing the Government, reported recently that two pine forests in Sichuan Province, each downwind from a sulphur processing works, had been decimated by acid rain. In one of the forests half the trees had perished; in the other, nine out of ten. The airborne destruction had been compounded by pollution of the rivers, so that for a square kilometre around each works, not a blade of grass was to be seen.

Countries which have travelled further down the materialist road can afford to debate these issues, and are beginning to agree that something must be done. Governments in Europe and North America are belatedly taking action to reduce the pollution of the atmosphere, and there is a small but growing movement towards a more 'human' architecture. But as societies become better off, it seems that the trickiest questions – those relating directly to personal wealth – become ever more difficult to tackle. Success breeds success, and the high fliers will always aspire to further heights, arguing that it is for everybody's good. We are witnessing in China the creation, with full government approval, of a class of self-made men and women. Will we soon see the emergence of Chinese 'yuppies'?

The sun has set. Already a frost is beginning to form. Scattering the crumbs of our picnic, Dagfinn and I clamber over rocks through deepening twilight to the warmth of his car below. Two hours later we are back in Beijing.

How can a foreigner, so privileged at home, hope to gain an insight into the Chinese predicament merely by touring? Berated by green-uniformed officials; stared at by pair upon pair of almond eyes; shoved; jostled; insulted; overcharged; engaged day after day in identical conversations with earnest students of English – it isn't surprising that most independent visitors become preoccupied with survival. At Shanhaiguan, a summer resort for well-to-do Beijingers, I am briefly spared these torments as I walk on a deserted beach beneath the Great Wall's terminal ramparts. The Yellow Sea stretches to the eastern horizon – not yellow, but shades of grey, except where a discharge of detergent from a chemical works whitens it with patches of frothy scum. Can foreigners contribute anything to the new China, I wonder – apart from technical know-how, English grammar, and money?

The answer, I think, depends on us. If we expect the Chinese to meet us on our own terms, we will be disappointed. If we visit China without bothering to learn its basic codes of behaviour, or if we deliberately flout them, we will arouse resentment and belligerence in return. But visitors who have had the patience to learn the Chinese language, and to look at themselves – even briefly – from a Chinese point of view, point out that the differences are not all that great. Both sides have much to learn.

Paul Theroux, sailing down the Yangtze in 1980, was pessimistic about China's prospects for self-improvement:

Would it always be these people in cheap cotton clothes, walking through the streets, carting the steel rods that are used for these awful buildings, saying nothing? . . . It worried me that China might never be better than it is now, and that water might always be scarce, clothes always rationed, food never plentiful, houses always tiny, and the hard work never done.

Whether you call the new revolution 'capitalism' or 'socialism with Chinese characteristics', it is clear that the majority of Chinese have every intention of proving Theroux wrong. For better or for worse, they are about to share in the Western merry-go-round. It is up to Westerners, having pointed out the many pitfalls, to help them do so.

After their seventeen summers in the service of Kublai Khan, the Polos were rewarded with a fleet of seagoing junks for their return to Venice via the South China Sea. My homecoming will have to be rather more modest. As the Trans-Siberian Express heads out of a Beijing dawn, I settle with my back to the locomotive, drinking in the last sights and sounds of the city. Drab suburbs quickly give way to cabbagefields, then to the forested hills of Hebei, and finally to the grasslands of Inner Mongolia, devoid of habitation and glistening with fresh snow. Most of the passengers are from Europe or North America, but I fall into conversation with a Chinese woman, one of three people sharing my compartment. Zhang Yuzhi is bound for Vienna, where her husband is attending university. 'He has many friends; we will live well,' she assures me. It is Zhang Yuzhi's first time outside Beijing, let alone in Europe, and as yet she speaks no German. 'But I will learn,' she insists with a wide-eyed smile.

At Erlian, the last station in China, we are asked to disembark while the carriage bogies are changed to the broader Mongolian and Russian gauge. It is late evening and bitterly cold. I resign myself to an hour's wait on the icy platform, and am grumbling idly with the other passengers when a railway official comes hurrying across the tracks. 'Come,' he orders. 'You must come and join the disco!'

As he speaks, a generator is cranked up and the station building is flooded with light. Gaily coloured bulbs illuminate a sign which reads: 'EXCHANGE – BAR – DUTY-FREE SHOP'. Through the window, grinning Mongolian faces watch our approach. We dive gratefully into the smoky but warm interior, just as the disc jockey, also a Mongolian, is cranking up the hi-fi.

The arrival of the Express, with its complement of foreigners, is clearly the high point of Erlian's week. The youths in the bar buttonhole us one by one. For the next hour we will be prisoners, and they know it. 'From which country are you?' 'Do you speak English?' 'Please come and dance!'

The music bursts upon the room, and I join Americans, Canadians, Australians, Europeans, Mongolians, Russians and Chinese in a bizarre shuffle to a medley of crackly 1960s classics. Light shimmers across the ceiling from a revolving mirror ball. On the dance floor, my gaze wanders from the company, through the frosty window and out into the empty Mongolian night. Nothing, I remind myself, is as bad – or as good – as you expect it to be.

Glossary of words used in the text

TURKISH

Bedesten	Warehouse
Beyaz peynir	A soft white cheese, similar to Greek *feta*
Çay	Tea
Dolmak	To be full
Dolmuş	Shared taxi
Efendim	Sir
Ekmek	Bread
Ekşisu	Hot springs (literally, 'bitter water')
Gümüş	Silver
Güzel	Pretty
Han	A Turkish caravanserai, built around a court-yard
Hane	House
Kahvaltı	Breakfast
Kapısı	Door, gate
Kaplumbağa	Turtle
Maden	Mine, pit
Meydan	Village square
Oğul	Son
Raki	Turkish spirit
Suçlu	Criminal
Yumurta	Egg
Yumurtalık	Egg-cup, 'egg-town' (literally, 'the place of the egg')

URDU, PUSHTU AND OTHER PATHAN LANGUAGES

Burqqa	Pathan veil
Chai	Tea
Chowkidar	Caretaker, concierge
Dal	A thick lentil soup
Ghee	Clarified butter, usually made from buffalo's milk
Inshallah	With luck (literally, 'the will of Allah')
Jihad	Holy war
Kamiz or *kurta*	Tunic, long-tailed shirt
Lassi	Yoghurt drink
Mujaheddin	Afghan freedom fighter
Muzzaffar khan	Pathan inn
Paise	Money
Pilau	A rice dish, often strongly spiced
Powindah	A nomad of south-west Pakistan
Pugri	Turban
Qahwa	Green tea
Roti	Bread (usually unleavened)
Sahib	Sir
Salaam	Peace
Salaam alaikum	Peace be with you (literally, 'may Allah bring you peace')
Shalwar	Baggy trousers, worn by both sexes in Afghanistan and Pakistan

CHINESE (PINYIN)

Bīnguǎn	Guest house
Dà-gǎo	To do something in a big way
Fàndiàn	Tourist hotel
Fěn-sī	Noodles
Huáng	Yellow
Huáng Dì	'Emperor of the Yellow Earth'
Hútòng	Lane or alley of old Beijing
Hù-zhào	Passport
Ma	Word used to indicate a question
Máo-tái	Chinese spirit
Méi-yǒu	No; there isn't any
Nǐ-hǎo	Hello
Tael	A silver coin, worth about 15p, which circulated in China before 1949
Tiān	Heaven

Tiānchí	'Heavenly Pool'
Wú-wéi	To flow with the tide, to let Nature take its course
Xiè-xie	Thank you
Yáng and *yīn*	Elements of the Tao, representing male and female aspects of the human psyche (literally, *yáng* = bright or hot; *yīn* = dark or cool)
Yù	Jade
Zhū-bǎo	Jewellery

MIDDLE EASTERN AND CENTRAL ASIAN LANGUAGES (MOSTLY KIRGHIZ OR UYGHUR)

Buran (Turkish: *bora*)	Desert storm
Dawan	Pass; col
Dhow	Arab sailing craft
Karakoram	Literally, 'crumbling mountains'
Kareze (Persian: *qanat*)	Subterranean water channel, used in Iran, Afghanistan and Xinjiang to irrigate the desert
Khan	Mongol emperor
Kibbutz	Israeli communal farm
Kumis	Mare's milk
Kurghan	Tower
Laghman	Noodles
Muezzin	Islamic crier, caller to prayer
Nan	Persian-style unleavened bread
Paizah	Mongol travel permit, used by Marco Polo
Rawap	A stringed instrument of central Asia
Souk	Arab market-place
Sut (Turkish: *süt*)	Sheep's, goat's or cow's milk
Taklamakan	Literally, 'Go in, and you won't come out'
Tash (Turkish: *taş*)	Stone
Tashkurghan	Stone tower
Yurt	Circular felt tent used by central Asian nomads

EUROPEAN LANGUAGES

Autoput	Yugoslav motorway
Corte	Courtyard
'Divisament dou Monde'	'Description of the World' (the book of Polo's travels)
'Il Milione'	'Mister Million' (Polo's nickname)
Rio	Backwater
Sotoportego	Covered passageway

Bibliography

(Original editions are quoted first, followed by British
and/or paperback editions where different)

HISTORICAL ACCOUNTS OF THE SILK ROAD

Bellonci, Maria (trans. Teresa Waugh), *The Travels of Marco Polo* (Sidgwick and Jackson, 1984)

Boulnois, L. (trans. Dennis Chamberlin), *The Silk Road* (Allen & Unwin, 1966)

Franck, Irene M., and David M. Brownstone, *The Silk Road: A History* (New York and Oxford: Facts on File, 1986)

Hart, Henry H., *Marco Polo: Venetian Adventurer* (Norman, Oklahoma: University of Oklahoma Press, 1967)

Hedin, Sven (trans. F. H. Lyon), *The Silk Road* (Routledge, 1938)

Hopkirk, Peter, *Foreign Devils on the Silk Road* (John Murray, 1980; Oxford University Press, 1984)

Myrdal, Jan (trans. Ann Henning), *The Silk Road* (New York: Pantheon, 1979; London: Gollancz, 1980)

Polo, Marco (trans. Ronald Latham), *The Travels* (Penguin, 1958)

Severin, Timothy, *The Oriental Adventure: Explorers of the East* (Angus & Robertson, 1976)

OTHER TRAVELLERS' ACCOUNTS

Arlen, Michael, *Passage to Ararat* (Chatto & Windus, 1976)

Cable, Mildred, and Francesca French, *The Gobi Desert* (Hodder & Stoughton, 1942; Virago, 1984)

—— *Through Jade Gate and Central Asia* (Constable,1927)

Danziger, Nick, *Danziger's Travels* (Grafton, 1987; Paladin, 1988)

Dodwell, Christina, *A Traveller in China* (Hodder & Stoughton, 1985; Sceptre, 1987)

Fisher, Richard B., *The Marco Polo Expedition* (Hodder & Stoughton, 1988)

Fleming, Peter, *News from Tartary* (Jonathan Cape, 1936; Futura, 1980)

Lloyd, Sarah, *Chinese Characters* (Collins, 1987; Flamingo, 1988)

Maillart, Ella K. (trans. Thomas McGreevy), *Forbidden Journey* (Heinemann, 1937; Century/Cadogan, 1983)

Michaud, Roland and Sabrina, *Caravans to Tartary* (Thames & Hudson, 1978)

Moorhouse, Geoffrey, *To the Frontier* (Hodder & Stoughton, 1984; Coronet, 1986)

Seth, Vikram, *From Heaven Lake* (Chatto & Windus, 1983; Abacus, 1984)

Severin, Timothy, *Tracking Marco Polo* (Routledge & Kegan Paul, 1964; Zenith, 1984)

Shipton, Eric, *Blank on the Map* (Hodder & Stoughton, 1938; republished in *The Six Mountain-Travel Books*, Diadem, 1985)

—— *Mountains of Tartary* (Hodder & Stoughton, 1950; republished in *The Six Mountain-Travel Books*, Diadem, 1985)

Stein, Aurel, *On Ancient Central-Asian Tracks* (Macmillan, 1933)

Theroux, Paul, *Riding the Iron Rooster* (Hamish Hamilton, 1988)

—— *Sailing through China* (Michael Russell, 1983)

Thubron, Colin, *Behind the Wall* (Heinemann, 1987)

BACKGROUND ON ITALY AND TURKEY

Curzon, Robert, *Armenia* (John Murray, 1854)

Glazebrook, Philip, *Journey to Kars* (Viking, 1984; Penguin, 1985)

Lister, R. P., *Turkey Observed* (Eyre & Spottiswoode, 1967)

Michaud, Roland and Sabrina, *Turkey* (Thames & Hudson, 1986)

Morris, James, *Venice* (Faber & Faber, 1960 and 1983)

BACKGROUND ON AFGHANISTAN AND PAKISTAN

Goodwin, Jan, *Caught in the Crossfire* (New York: Dutton, 1987; London: Macdonald, 1987)

Keay, John, *The Gilgit Game* (John Murray, 1979)

—— *When Men and Mountains Meet* (John Murray, 1977; Century, 1983)

Lessing, Doris, *The Wind Blows Away Our Words* (Picador, 1987)

Miller, Keith, *Continents in Collision: The International Karakoram Project* (George Philip, 1982)

BACKGROUND ON CHINA

Le Coq, Albert von (trans. Anna Barwell), *Buried Treasures of Chinese Turkestan* (Allen & Unwin, 1928)

Leys, Simon, *Chinese Shadows* (Penguin, 1978)

Liang Heng and Judith Shapiro, *Son of the Revolution* (Chatto & Windus, 1983; Fontana, 1984)

Mosher, Steven W., *Broken Earth: The Rural Chinese* (New York: The Free Press, 1983; London: Robert Hale, 1984)

Schell, Orville, *To Get Rich is Glorious: China in the Eighties* (New York: Pantheon, 1984; London: Robin Clark, 1985)

Skrine, C. P., *Chinese Central Asia* (Methuen, 1926)

Skrine, C. P., and Pamela Nightingale, *Macartney at Kashgar* (Methuen, 1973)

Index